Nyifie Brothers Publishing

The Artisan Author

The Low-Stress, High-Quality, Fan-Focused Approach to Escaping the Publishing Rat Race

Johnny B. Truant

Copyright © 2025 by Johnny B. Truant and Nyfie Brothers Publishing. All rights reserved.

No part of this book may be reproduced in any form or by any electronic or mechanical means, including information storage and retrieval systems, without written permission from the author, except for the use of brief quotations in a book review.

Thank you for supporting my work.

For Robin, who thought she was marrying a scientist but got an artist instead.

I'm an artist and I'll do what I want.

— Bob Schneider

Contents

Foreword xiii
We Were Promised Unicorns. We Were Given TPS Reports xix
Double Down or Run Away Screaming xxv

Part One
This Is Not My Beautiful House

1. Previously, In Self Publishing 3
2. The Big Bait and Switch 19

Part Two
The Way of the Artisan Author

3. Make Publishing Non-Dumb Again 49
4. Change Your Paradigm, Change Your World 65
5. The Six Pillars of Artisandom 91

Part Three
Making Artisanship Work in the Real World

6. Producing Like An Artisan Author 111
7. Selling As An Artisan Author 129
8. Finding Readers and Creating True Fans 161

Part Four
Details, Details, Details

9. What If? 205
10. Tips and Tricks 223

Artist, Go Forth 247
Also by Johnny B. Truant 251
Untitled 257

The Artisan Author

Foreword

By Kevin J. Anderson

I tried to be an artisan author a long time ago, but Trad publishing wouldn't let me. They didn't understand the concept, and to be honest, most of us didn't. I was ahead of my time. (But I'm still here, thank you very much.)

I published my first novel in 1988, a completely different era. I was always a fast writer, two novels a year, three novels, sometimes more. It was nothing like the insane rapid-release writers you'll learn about in this book, but still it was enough that some snarks branded me a hack because "you can't possibly write that fast and produce anything good." But I loved writing, loved the stories I was telling, and I kept going.

Unfortunately, Trad publishing just wasn't designed for a writer who did more than one book a year, and so I had to go to different publishers to handle my output. One of my editors jokingly labeled me "Books R Us" and said I had no choice but to work with multiple publishers. (Is that called being "polywriterous"?) To this day, the publisher of a major line is still pissed off at me because I didn't immediately drop all other work and only concentrate on the big fantasy trilogy he had bought. Yes, they had paid me a pretty decent advance, but they didn't *own* me! I turned in the books on time and I gave them my absolute best work, but I had other stories to tell and I wasn't going to ignore them for four years.

I had different series, different types of novels, and I promoted them all, tried to get fans of one series to try another series. When I started writing for Star Wars, I got a ton of very enthusiastic fans who showed up at my signings in costume. Then I wrote for the X-Files (and yes, they showed up dressed as Mulder and Scully in FBI uniforms), then I wrote Batman and Superman novels, and then huge Dune novels with Brian Herbert. And I always wrote my own original series, too.

Hey, Star Wars fans—you might also like my Dune books.
Hey, Dune fans, you might also like my Saga of Seven Suns.

The publishers never facilitated that, of course. I did. In fact, in the front of a book, you would always find a list of "Other Bantam Books by..." or "Other Pocket Books by..." As a fan and a reader, I wanted to read *all* the books by my favorite author. I didn't care who published them. Nobody does. But they wouldn't list the competition, even if readers never saw it as the competition.

Early on, I realized that *I* was the brand—Kevin J. Anderson, the author of your favorite books—not [insert publisher here]. I built my fan base, and they came to my signings. Sure enough, the Dune and Star Wars fans did buy Saga of Seven Suns. Or they bought Terra Incognita, or Clockwork Angels. Or they would buy a book from their favorite series for themselves, then maybe pick up a signed copy of something else for their partner, or their dad.

I remember one stubborn publicist from HarperCollins giving me a stern lecture when I was about to go on tour for a new Batman/Superman novel. "Now remember, you are on tour for *us*, not for those other publishers. I don't want you signing or promoting any of your other books." I refused. I crossed my arms over my chest and challenged him, "So, next time I'm on tour for Dune or Star Wars, I should refuse to sign any Harper-Collins books?" He was indignant, and I didn't follow instructions.

If the Batman and Superman fans came, great. If the Star Wars fans came, I would serve them. If the Dune fans came, I would serve them. I wanted to earn the loyalty of the readers across the spectrum, not just specific flavors of readers.

If you make the connection, the fans will come to see *you*, not just the book.

In order to facilitate this, I started collecting names and addresses (yes, even before email). I went to science fiction conventions and comic cons. I hung out with fans, I had kaffeeklatsches. I would pass a clipboard around to ask people to sign up.

And I had a quarterly newsletter—a *printed* newsletter, produced by the local quick-print shop. I had a bulk-mailing permit and had parties with friends to spend hours sticking address labels onto the newsletters. Eventually I graduated to electronic newsletters, but I still miss that concrete, tangible connection of sending a real paper publication to my fans.

I connected with readers through social media. I would talk about my books, especially the works in progress, so the fans felt invested in a new story or novel long before it came out. But I also showed pictures of my cats, my hiking photos, shared recipes, made fanboy commentary on new movies or TV shows.

I built up a pretty massive following on MySpace—14,000 people. Man, I loved MySpace. You could post animated banners of new projects, but most importantly, you could easily target specific fans. With a click of a button, you could identify all fans within, say, a 50-mile radius of Seattle, and send them a specific email, "Hey, I'm doing a signing at University Books in Seattle. Please come and say hi, and you're welcome to go with me to the local craft brewery afterward to hang out." It was great. I miss MySpace.

But I made do with Facebook, or Twitter, and other platforms where I could share pictures, interact, get to know the people who liked my work enough to seek me out.

My Trad publishers never did that. It was organic on my part, to train the readers and entertain them, to make them vested in the works I was creating, to feel like participants in the gestation and birth of a new novel or comic or anthology. Sometimes I used their names as minor characters. Sometimes I asked them to come up with titles. I always let them know what I was doing, where I was going, where they could meet me in person.

I remember one incident that really proved how this was working. I had agreed to do a book signing at a Big Bookstore, but I knew they weren't likely to do much promotion for the event. So I sent the word out to my True Fans, said I would make an announcement about a cool new project (a new comic gig I had) that night and I asked them to show up. Eighteen people came to the event—not a blowout, but not bad. I passed the clipboard around and asked them to sign up for my newsletter. The clipboard zoomed from seat to seat, and nobody put their name down. Disappointed, I asked why no one was interested. "Freebies!" I said. "Cat photos!"

Turns out, 15 of the 18 people were already on the list. Of the entire crowd, *only three* had shown up because of the bookstore efforts. It would have been a pretty miserable evening if I had *not* sent out my call to action.

Cultivate your own fans and readers, be a person to them, give them love and attention, give them news, give them sneak previews. When I ran my first Kickstarter several years ago, these were the people who backed it in droves. When I launched my Patreon last year, these were the people who came aboard right away.

Two years ago I was at a writers conference, where everyone was agitated about how AI would churn out books so fast that all of us "real" authors would be lost in the noise. While I understood their concerns, I said, "I'm not all that worried because I've spent years building connections with my fans, giving them not

Foreword

just great stories but also time and attention, that extra secret sauce that makes me a person and a favorite author. Those fans will spend the money to buy *an artisanal KJA book* over an AI-written book any day."

That always stuck with me. And then Johnny B. Truant stole my term.

Seriously, when he told me about this book, I instantly asked to read the manuscript. Even though I hadn't codified it myself, the insights and advice he gives in *The Artisan Author* are exactly on point. I was nodding and grinning all the way through. Find your readers and treat them right.

Make them see you as a storyteller, a person (preferably an *interesting* person), an author...no, an *artisan* author. But you have to treat them as more than just page reads. They are people, too. They are readers. They might become fans, or even True Fans. A thousand True Fans—and then you've got it made.

Tell good stories. Pay attention to your readers. Be a good person. Become an artisan author.

This book will put you on the right path.

Kevin J. Anderson
Colorado Springs, CO
June 2025

We Were Promised Unicorns. We Were Given TPS Reports

I'll bet you remember the day you realized you wanted to be a writer.

Maybe it wasn't one specific day. Maybe it was a year, or a season of life, in which the idea of writing slowly grew within you. Maybe, like many authors, books saved you at a time when you needed them most, and a deep part of you decided you wanted to do the same for others. *You'd* build fantasies for strangers to lose themselves in. *You'd* plumb the depths of the mundane with your words, trying to make sense of it all. *You'd* build worlds like sanctuaries: a refuge from the everyday; a pause button for the frenzy — or the difficulty — of your future readers' lives.

Maybe you've always had stories within you. Maybe, like a seedling finding its way through hard earth, a fragile idea struggled for years inside your mind — shaping and reshaping itself until one day, it broke free and became words on a page. Maybe that process took decades. Maybe it happened in a snap. Either way, a feeling came with it: *You no longer had to accept the reality you were given. Now* you *were a creator, and could live in worlds of your own.*

You were free. And as soon as you figured out how to make some money selling your books, you'd be freer still.

Speaking for myself, the dream of writing full-time was all that kept me sane for a while. I was in a job I hated, and the prospect of advancing in that job (thereby earning the right to do it forever) felt like sailing headlong into a storm. But I couldn't see an alternative. I'd set my sails and was qualified for nothing else. Worse, it was 1999: a decade or so before the Kindle made digital self publishing possible. Back then, "becoming an author" meant submitting short stories to magazines that nobody read, then sending query letters to agents to trumpet those credits and hope they'd deign to represent you.

It was a one-in-a-million shot. My odds of escape were not promising.

Before ebooks and print-on-demand, there were only two paths to becoming a writer. One was to pay to publish thousands of copies of your book and sell them from the trunk of your car, and the other was to win the lottery by finding not just a good *agent*, but also a good *editor*. But it didn't stop there. You also had to luck into a publishing deal big enough to buy more than ramen noodles ... and even then, if your book didn't sell as many copies as the publisher wanted, they'd pass on publishing your next book and send you right back to zero.

My dream of writing for a living felt about as possible as being struck repeatedly by lightning, but I didn't care. It was my only way out. My only way to do what I truly wanted, and enjoy my life instead of hating so much of it.

If you've been at this a while, maybe you can relate. If you're brand new, be glad the world has changed. Because it *did* change. After ebooks and print-on-demand became a thing, the draconian trad scene was no longer the only way to get published. Technology had given us new formats, and the internet had given us a voice. Writers didn't need permission anymore. Now we could reach readers directly, and deliver our books through sites like Amazon.

The sun came out. Bunnies hopped through beautiful meadows. Unicorns blessed us all with the fertile magic of unlimited possibility, and writers' dreams came true the world over.

Maybe that's where you entered the picture, or maybe you're just entering the picture now. Whether you were a writer in the good ol' days or just became one recently, you're probably familiar with the dream that began in the late twenty-aughts and early teens. Suddenly, writers didn't need permission to write, nor to publish. We could reach readers everywhere without middlemen! *Unicorns rejoice!*

Well ... not so fast.

Let me ask a question. *Is that how the writing world feels to you right now?*

If this is the first book about indie publishing that you've read, maybe it *does* still feel that way. If, however, you've read other books — or attended writers' conferences, or lurked in author forums, or followed authors-talking-about-authoring on YouTube or elsewhere — you've probably gotten a very different picture.

Yes, you *used* to be able to write whatever you wanted, but now everyone knows you really need to write to market. Research a genre, study the recurring elements, then write a book with all that same stuff and be sure to commission a cover that looks like all the others.

Yes, you *used* to be able to put your book up for sale and people would buy it, but obviously you have to do more than that now. Have you chosen the right keywords? Picked all the right sub-genres? Is your description SEO-optimized? Oh, and what about social media promotion and advertising? You don't actually think you can sell books without learning to run ads, do you? Well, don't worry. Ad strategies change all the time, but if you join all the courses and spend a few hours a day staying current, your ad game might only be *slightly* behind the curve.

Yes, you *used* to be able to sell your book for a decent price, but now we're told readers won't pay more than about $2.99. You could make your book exclusive to Amazon with the hope of earning more through Kindle Unlimited, but KU is hit or miss. You might do great there ... or your books might earn almost nothing. Either way, you'll be attracting readers who don't actually like to pay for books because they're paying Amazon for an all-you-can-read subscription. That's cool, right?

Yes, you *used* to be able to publish a book occasionally and do okay. Can't do that now, though. You *do* have enough new releases lined up to publish at least one a month indefinitely, right? No? Well, then you'd better cancel your vacations and weekends and start writing yourself into burnout if you hope to survive. These days, "Rapid Release" is all the rage. If you can pump out books fast enough, you might outrun Amazon's extraordinarily short shelf life. If not, good luck. Books older than about a month might as well be invisible. *Nobody* sees them.

Yes, you *used* to be irreplaceable to your readers. Those were the good old days. Now, we're told that if you don't publish something new immediately, your readers will move on to someone else. They probably won't remember your name anyway, seeing as you were just one more snack in their neverending book buffet. Oh, and don't forget about AI. Some folks who've really dialed into writing with AI can produce a few new books a week. I guess you're pretty replaceable after all.

Doesn't feel like unicorns anymore, does it?

These days, with so many indie writers praying at the temple of so-called "Rapid Release publishing," it starts to feel like there are only two options for authors, be they established or newbies. Choice #1 is to join the rat race and publish commoditized, written-to-market, coloring-within-the-lines fiction at a rate of one book every two to four weeks if you want a chance of success. Choice #2 is to write whatever you want however you want ... but sell almost nothing.

I was one of the early voices in digital self publishing — one of those excited souls who, starting in 2011, publicly sang this industry's praises. When I returned in 2023 after three years away, though, the lose-lose dichotomy I've just described hit me like a hammer. I'm an art-first author, so Choice #1 felt worse than the most tedious office job. Choice #2, while creatively satisfying, wasn't any better. Yes, I love writing and would do it for free ... but how could I justify taking much time to write if I couldn't earn money doing it?

I stared out at those newly-foreign lands in 2023, wondering when someone had swapped my unicorns for a world of TPS reports and officiousness. When had writing become such a grind? All my old hopes fell away in a heap. I suddenly realized that the WOPR supercomputer from the movie *Wargames* was talking about authoring as much as global thermonuclear war when it said, *"The only winning move is not to play."*

More and more, what passes for "normal" among self-published authors is unpalatable to someone like me — someone who wants freedom in what I write, genuine connections with readers, to enjoy my work instead of burning out, and to actually make a living instead of selling my books for pennies. Maybe you're like me. Maybe you've done your research, looked out into the wide world of writing, and decided it sounds no better now than it ever did — even back in the *query-and-pray* days.

Maybe the "normal" way of doing things is unpalatable to you, too. Maybe once upon a time, you dreamed of being a writer. Maybe, against all odds, you actually became one. But maybe now you feel like I felt, and like the WOPR felt. Why bother writing if the only winning move is not to play?

Well, don't give up just yet. Don't declare it all a loss just yet. This book might contain the breath of fresh air you've been waiting for.

As it turns out, there *is* an alternative. There *is* another way to be a successful author — a way that almost nobody talks about in the faster-faster world we indies unwittingly find ourselves in. There *is* an alternative to the Rapid Release race to the bottom. There *is* a way to write what you want, charge what's fair, court loyal fans who love you, and build a writing life in which you can start every day with the rainbow-loving unicorn joy you were promised.

You don't have to obey the rules that everyone else follows.

You don't have to rush.

You don't have to sell your heartfelt stories for pennies on the dollar.

And you don't have to worry, if you dare to *live your life* instead of working 24/7, that you'll be left behind and forgotten.

If what you've just read strikes a chord, then it's time to buckle up, buttercup — because I'm about to share an evolutionary writing renaissance with you.

Come with me, dear writer, into the way of the Artisan Author.

You can't possibly imagine the creative joy you've been missing.

Double Down or Run Away Screaming

Let's get something out of the way: The Artisan approach is awesome for a lot of authors, but it's not for everyone.

Some writers genuinely enjoy pumping out books like machines under the aforementioned "Rapid Release" model, and do well selling them. For some, creative fulfillment isn't super important — or they find fulfillment in things that don't seem fulfilling to me at all. Some authors narrow their focus, write a billion words for a very specific audience, and absolutely *kill it* within their niche while enjoying the process. For some of them, forming long-term relationships with their readers isn't that important. They'd rather work at arm's length, keeping up with constantly-changing online tools and algorithms, selling at low prices and making up the difference with bulk, quantity, and speed.

If you're one of those authors, you should close this book now and pick up a different one. There are many to choose from. Information on how to do Rapid Release publishing is everywhere these days — enough that it's often seen as the default. So much so, in fact, that a lot of the authors I speak to are shocked to hear there's another option.

But Rapid Release is *not* the only way to be an indie writer. There *is* another way.

- **This book is for you if you don't want to have to publish a book every month in order to survive.** You *can* publish a book every month as an Artisan Author (just ask my friend Katie Cross), but it's not at all necessary. If you don't want the obligation (if the idea of slowing down is more appealing), then you're in the right place.

- **If you've been publishing fast but are now seeing diminishing returns and getting burned out, this book is for you.** A lot of authors were dragged into Rapid Release slowly, and never would have chosen the writing life they've ended up with if they'd known what the future held. Maybe you were okay with where you were two years ago, but now you're working twice as hard for half the reward. If that sounds familiar, read on.

- **If you have a high standard for your books — if quality really matters — this book is for you.** Rapid Release moves too fast to produce superlative, top-tier, human-touch books ... and, frankly, there's no point in doing so. All-you-can-read "whale" readers don't care about special touches. They churn through books super fast and just want the next story and the *next* story, usually in the cheapest form possible so they don't go broke.

- **If you want to find readers who like and are loyal to *you* rather than to a genre or bookstore, this book is for you.** Amazon readers — especially those who subscribe to Kindle Unlimited — aren't loyal to you. They're loyal to Amazon. Readers who will buy any cozy mystery probably aren't loyal to you, either. They're loyal to cozy mysteries. A key aspect of being an Artisan Author is finding and nurturing fans who *think of you first* when they're ready for a new book. It's the difference between worrying about competition (because you're just another author) and never worrying about competition again (because only *you* can be *you*, and your loyal readers know it).

- **If you don't like rushing your stories and would write better ones if the market didn't punish you for taking your time, this book is for you.**

- **If you don't want to worry about losing half your income because you dared to go on vacation and broke your usual publishing schedule, this is for you.**

- **If your books are closer to art than commodities, you might be an Artisan Author.** You don't need to write books worthy of hanging in the Louvre to be an Artisan, but you shouldn't think of them as all-the-same and disposable like razor blades, either.

- **If you write unique, unusual, or eccentric books — or if you simply refuse to stick to one genre — the Artisan Author life is probably for you.** Rapid Release only works if the algorithms can push all of your books to the exact same group of readers, and *that* only works if your books are very similar to one another: same genre, ideally the same series. Artisan Authors *can* write that way if they want, but they don't have to. Personally, I have books in almost every genre there is. The single thread that unites them is simply *the fact that I wrote them.*

- **If you want to make beautiful books, you're likely an Artisan Author.** Looking to make that leather-bound, foil-stamped, slipcase-enclosed, die-cut-and-embossed special edition of your best series? KU readers won't buy it. Only readers who appreciate the artistry of books will.

- **If you don't like following rules or doing what you're told, if writing is a passion for you as much a business, or if you like the idea of creating a passionate cult following, you're *definitely* an Artisan Author.** Nonconformists unite! As my favorite Artisan musician Bob Schneider (more on him later) says, "I'm an artist and I'll do what I want."

You and I are also artists, and we should *write* what we want.
The good news is that if you follow what's in this book, you'll actually be able to *sell* your books, too.

Plus, There's No Downside!

Well ... actually .... the subhead above is slightly untrue.
Okay, it's *a lot* untrue.
Come to think of it, there's nothing true about it.
In reality, every approach to writing and publishing you'll run into has *significant* downsides. Taking an Artisan approach is no different. Anyone who says otherwise is either an idiot or trying to sell you something.
Traditional publishing is not THE WAY.
Writing to market is not THE WAY.
Rapid Release is not THE WAY.

Running Kickstarter campaigns, selling direct, doing pay-per-click advertising, and any other hot topic being discussed in the Facebook groups and subreddits and conferences? Those things are also not THE WAY.

Similarly, Artisan Authordom is not THE WAY. It absolutely won't work for everyone. Even for those it suits, it's not a clear path full of sunshine and roses. I'm glad you bought this book, but if you expect nothing but smooth sailing and big, fast profits after reading it, you should leave now and get your money back. There's too much self-serving bullshit in the self-pub world as it is, and I'd rather not add to it.

We're all adults, right? Deep down, we understand there's no magic Easy Button that will get us everything we want without hassle or risk, don't we?

In truth, everything is a balance. Every strategy, tactic, approach, and philosophy in self publishing is an attempt to maximize pros while minimizing cons, given a specific author in a certain set of conditions. I'm not going to lie; Rapid Release is perfect for some authors and *their* unique conditions. I'm just not interested in those conditions for myself and career — and if you're reading this book, you probably aren't, either.

If you're willing to write and release very quickly, make books that look and feel similar to each other, and trade creative freedom for a chance at cash, Rapid Release honestly has some real advantages. You might (but also might not) get more readers faster that way, because algorithms can be powerful things. Your chances for quick, breakout success are higher — *if* you get lucky. It's *also* possible, however, that you'll contort yourself into Rapid Release, trade self-expression for a transactional business model, burn yourself out trying to keep up, feel like a sellout ... and then fail entirely.

Similarly, it's possible that you'll try this Artisan thing, put your heart and soul into the best books you can make, and flop. It could happen.

Did you hear what I just said? It's important that you do. *This is not* THE WAY. *It's* A *way, but not* THE *way*.

You'll need to work hard and hands-on to build an Artisan career. You'll sometimes have more on your to-do list than you can handle. You will, at times, be disappointed, frustrated, hurt, and angry. You'll also have to forge your own path, because I can't give you a blueprint. (That's all true of all approaches, though. The difference is, I'm being honest about it.)

Being an Artisan Author isn't easy. It's *simple*, but not *easy*. It's fulfilling and fun and feels like you're making a difference for readers ... but it's definitely not easy.

Things won't always go smoothly. You'll have to pay more attention to your readers and spend time interacting with them, even when they don't buy. You'll have to watch with jealousy whenever a Rapid Release book explodes onto the charts while yours languishes, and in those moments you'll wonder if you made the wrong choice. *Art sucks,* you might think. *I want cash instead.*

In those moments, I'll ask you to remember a few points:

First of all, I'll ask you to remember that in all things, we only notice the outliers. We notice when someone gets rich in this business, but we don't usually see the thousands of others who fail doing the exact same thing. The internet acts like a magnifying glass, making outliers look like the majority. New authors start to think that breakout profits are normal ... and if *they* don't make the same breakout profits, *they're* the weirdoes.

The truth is exactly the opposite. Many authors who earn well from their books feel like failures because they compare themselves to the top one-tenth of one percent. Don't do that. In this book, we won't chase millions or superstardom, though it's technically possible. Mid-list success is a far more sensible and normal goal ... and the good news is that the Artisan approach (which is based on creating True Fans while ignoring flashy get-rich-quick schemes) makes mid-list success very achievable indeed.

Second, I'll ask you to remember that some of the authors

who trumpet their success aren't actually having as much success as they claim. Some, rather, are lying or delusional. I've known "six-figure authors" who've extrapolated one month at a six-figure pace into an annual income, when in fact their true annual income was much lower. I've known "seven-figure authors" who do, indeed, earn seven figures .... but spend that much or more on expenses and advertising. Some big-profit claims are legit. Plenty, though, are lies based on ego.

And lastly, I'll ask you to remember why you picked up this book in the first place. Remember the downsides of the *other* ways of doing things. Does the high-stress, low-profit, impersonal and career-insecure "normal" approach still sound bad to you? Do you really want to leap into it now that you've hit a roadblock, ignoring all the reasons the Artisan approach sounded so much better — like such a relief, and a way to write like you used to dream of writing?

Yes, there *are* downsides to being an Artisan Author. Of course there are.

But I'll remind you that good things take time. That you're strong and smart enough to understand that. I'll remind you that when something seems too good to be true, it probably is. I'll remind you of all the reasons "the usual way" didn't appeal to your artist's soul. And lastly, I'll remind you that there's a tradeoff between a tortoise and hare approach, especially where other human beings are concerned.

If you take the time now to form real, lasting, time-tested relationships with your best fans, you'll be building an asset that the *profit right now* crowd will never have ... and in all likelihood, you'll be around long after the impatient trend-chasers who only care about money fail.

Soon, we'll dive into what makes the Artisan Author approach fundamentally different from the way most authors currently do things — why it's the opposite, really, and how essential it is to understand its oppositeness if you want it to work. After that, I'll show you how to use the Artisan approach in the real world, including everything I've seen and learned from 13 years in the trenches as a leader in the self-publishing space, and as a prolific author myself.

Before that, though, we need to talk about how we got here: why and how the indie publishing world evolved the way it did. Pay attention, because what follows isn't just some boring history lesson. It's a necessary deprogramming you'll need before you get started ... just like they do after people are brainwashed by cults.

The self-publishing dream sounded so wonderful and reasonable at the beginning.

Where did it all go wrong?

Part One

This Is Not My Beautiful House

Chapter 1

Previously, In Self Publishing

A lot of people don't know this about me, but I'm an expert at song analysis.

In M.C. Hammer's song "U Can't Touch This," for instance, Hammer at one point rings the bell (because school's in, sucka), then later says, "Ring the bell; school's back in!" *without actually dismissing school in between.* What about all the scholars who'd never realized school was out, and they could have been taking a break the whole time? It's not like they can rest *now* — not once school's back in. Why is nobody thinking about Hammer's poor students?

Bringing this same expert analysis to "Once in a Lifetime" by Talking Heads, it seems to me to be about the vertigo of life and the way things just sort of happen when you're not paying attention. I mean, there you are one day, living in a shotgun shack or in another part of the world, or maybe you're behind the wheel of a large automobile. Or, hell — you may find yourself in a beautiful house, with a beautiful wife. And you may ask yourself, "Well, how did I get here?"

We understand that, right? Especially as storytellers, we understand most people's obliviousness to the forces that shape their lives. Our characters are pawns in our fingers, going where the plot takes them and reacting to each new set of circumstances — sometimes with delight, sometimes with alarm — without understanding how they truly got there. Good characters operate from an emotional wound at the beginning of a story, then heal and move past that wound by the end. When they're in wounded mode, though, they don't see the forces that led them where they ended up. Their internal programming makes them blind.

And then, confused, they may wake up one day and suddenly tell themselves, "This is not my beautiful wife." And they may tell themselves, "This is not my beautiful house."

That was me a few years ago. I'd found myself in a beautiful house called self-publishing, but one day I realized in a sudden gestalt leap that it was a *different* house than the one I'd moved into a decade earlier.

The furniture had been rearranged. The paint colors had changed and the walls had moved. There were now weird stairways to nowhere and strangers living in the basement. While I wasn't looking, someone had renovated my house with help from the mad architect behind the Winchester mansion. I *swore* my beautiful house had been sane and sensible back in the day — back when I'd fallen in love with it and moved in. I didn't think I would have moved into a madhouse on purpose, but who could say for sure?

And I may ask myself, "Am I right, am I wrong?"

And I may say to myself, "My God, what have I done?"

So I looked back in time, to the days when publishing had been different, to figure out how exactly I'd ended up living inside a monstrosity. The retrospective was enlightening. It showed me a clear path to follow: a path that led me away from crazytown with all the justification in the world.

If you're a new author — if the self-publishing "house" you see around you feels like it was *always* this way — you might not care about the past.

You should, though. A quick trip down our industry's memory lane will give you the grounding you need for the Artisan

Author approach ... and all the reasons why, given what happened in the past, what we'll talk about in this book is a hell of a lot more sensible than the alternatives.

The Ask-For-Permission Era

Back in ancient times — and by that, I mean prior to about 2008 — authors needed the help of a gatekeeper to publish their work. If they really wanted to DIY it, they could technically pay tens of thousands of dollars to a vanity press and fill their garage with books to hand-sell one at a time, but the self-publishers back then were a different breed: sometimes clever souls with outside-the-box ambitions, but usually deluded suckers who'd fallen for a con.

Mostly, you needed the help of a gatekeeper. Mostly, it was the era of asking for permission.

To be clear, this "asking for permission" thing still happens for a segment of the writing population, but back then it was the only sensible option. It went like this:

The first step was to write short stories, then contact literary magazines to try and get them published. Sometimes these magazines would pay you a little bit, but when you were new, you had to start on the ground floor. That usually meant you'd be paid only with a few free copies of the magazine.

After you'd had a few things published in small literary magazines, you could parlay your so-far writing credits into publishing in bigger ones. Maybe you'd earn a few hundred bucks, if you were lucky, from those second-tier magazines.

After accumulating a few decent pub credits, it was time to start contacting literary agents. You'd tell each agent which outlets had already published your stories, then try to interest them in your novel. This was done via a one-page letter back in the day, then moved to email later on. You'd look up agents in a huge book (now online) called *The Writer's Market*, shooting almost blindly at agents who seemed to represent the sort of book you'd written. Maybe you'd go to a convention and meet a specific agent in the flesh, but more often than not it was scattershot at best.

At that point, most writers would enter a phase of constant and unrelenting rejection and discouragement. It was awesome.

In 1999, when I was pitching my first book, I tried to take back the power by pretending my rejections by literary agents were actually achievements. I put a sign reading WALL O' REJECTION in my office, then covered that wall with all the *thanks-but-no-thanks* letters those agents sent back to me. It was supposed to allow me to laugh at all that silly rejection so I could still feel worthwhile as a writer instead of feeling like a talentless loser. It didn't work.

In theory, if you kept at this game long enough, you were supposed to eventually find an agent who wanted to represent you. I never did. A few agents requested the first three chapters of my book (the next step after querying), but that was just false hope. It simply delayed my rejection, which always came later.

Cue more certainty that I was, indeed, a talentless loser.

Most writers give up at this point. I certainly did. I completely shelved my ambitions to write for a living because it seemed downright impossible. I went back to work at my crappy job — which, by the way, was in a genetics lab, looking at fruit flies under a microscope all day.

But if you were one of the lucky ones, an agent would finally say yes. Yay! You'd gotten your letter past the angry, failed writer interning at the agent's office, and you'd gotten past the agent. They'd liked your first three chapters, then your complete novel. They might tear it apart at that point and have you rewrite it to suit their preferences, or they might try to shop it as-is.

Either way, you'd then enter the next phase: your agent attempting to sell your book to an acquisitions editor at a publishing house.

If an editor bought your book, they might tear it apart again, having you rewrite it to suit *their* preferences. You'd get an advance if the deal went through — probably a small one. Then, after a year or two of painfully slow administrative time, the publisher would order a print run, ship finished books to bookstores, and possibly send you out into the world to do all of their marketing and publicity work for them.

Sometimes that first run would be successful and you'd stay with the publisher, earning an embarrassingly small percentage in royalties. If you were very lucky, it might even be the beginning of a fruitful author career. Other times, though, your book wouldn't sell as well as the publisher wanted. If this happened, they'd fire you for future books. You'd have to start again ... but this time, you'd be branded as an author that someone had taken a gamble on and lost.

The Ask-For-Permission era created a few superstars, a lot of middling mid-list authors, and a ton of failures. It was more like a lottery than a career path, because you didn't just have to write good books; you also had to catch exactly the right people in exactly the right moods at exactly the right times.

Fortunately, digital self publishing came along soon after to save us.

The Kindle Gold Rush Era

In November of 2007, Amazon released the first Kindle e-reader. Ebooks, which had previously been limited to downloadable PDF files, suddenly became legitimate.

It took readers a long time to warm up to Amazon-style ebooks, but there were enough early adopters in the late aughts to give reading a whole new life. There was only one problem: The world didn't yet have enough ebooks to fill all those shiny new Kindles.

Fortunately, Amazon had anticipated the problem. Following the Kindle, they launched Kindle Digital Publishing (KDP), which allowed authors to create and sell their own ebooks. Stuffy traditional publishers weren't willing to sell anything digital ... but the unwashed masses of self-published authors didn't have the same hubris.

And just like that, the great Kindle gold rush began.

The late aughts and early teens were exciting times for authors, but it was a *good news / bad news* situation. The good news was that we could finally sell our books on a major platform without asking editors and agents for permission, but the bad news was that self-publishing had the stink of all stinks. Ebooks by independent authors were seen mostly as trash at the start: the unedited, incoherent ramblings of all the losers who couldn't cut it in "real" publishing. And honestly? A lot of early ebooks were exactly that.

Nobody knew how to do their own editing.

Nobody knew how to make their own book covers, and it's not like there were a lot of freelance cover designers around yet.

And although the good news was that there were no gatekeepers, the bad news was there were no gatekeepers. The good news was that anyone could publish a book, but the bad news was that anyone could publish a book ... even if their book was terrible, and they were completely delusional.

This era birthed some real juggernauts. Amanda Hocking and John Locke (not the philosopher or the character on *LOST*, regrettably) come to mind, along with Hugh Howey, who's still prominent today. The big thing back then was to price ebooks at 99 cents because readers during the dearth of ebooks would buy anything for a buck, just so they'd have something to read. John Locke had a great zinger about that, actually. He said that he no longer had to compete with traditional publishing, because even trad's first ebooks were $10 or more. Instead of proving that he was as good as established authors, those established authors now had to prove that they were ten times as good as he was.

It was solid logic, and in those first years, 99 cent ebooks sold quickly enough to make millionaires. They were the new pulp, hated and looked-down-upon by "legitimate" authors and publishers ... but they were bestsellers just the same.

The Maturing Era

By the time I entered self-publishing in 2012, I felt like I'd missed the boat. 99 cent success stories were still happening, but they were declining in number. The industry was beginning to mature, demanding more than just cheapness from its authors.

Some of the early heroes had already burned out, or couldn't adapt from their earlier pulp and went out of business. John Locke torpedoed his success by being one of the first to break the heady joy of the gold rush by gaming the system, thus proving that if there's a way to use tactics rather than talent to succeed, someone is going to exploit it and ruin things for everyone.

As ebooks became more mainstream, readers became more savvy and discerning. They started to discriminate against books with bad covers, badly-written descriptions, and bad reviews. You suddenly had to be a bit more pro to get by.

My own early books had to meet higher standards than those early gold rush books, so I couldn't phone it in and expect to sell well. I had to have decent (though not amazing) covers made, and I had to write my descriptions carefully if I wanted to lure readers. Ebooks were still mud on the shoe of trad publishing, but plenty of readers now saw them as legitimate, lower-cost alternatives to pricey traditional titles.

Looking back, the Maturing Era was the sweet spot of early self-publishing. We weren't entirely legit in the eyes of the world, but we were legit to enough people to make it work. Those days felt like the 1980s in the punk rock movement: a grassroots, DIY creative ethos that appealed in part because it wasn't part of The System. Our books were still cheaper than those being sold by the big boys, and readers were starting to respect them. The thrill and joy of the gold rush was still in full swing, but now our books were more professional, too.

This era was also when, looking back, I first realized I was destined to become an Artisan Author. You *could* sell books with so-so covers, but I wanted good ones that looked like they belonged on a shelf at Barnes & Noble. Print-on-demand was finally feasible, so I uploaded my first books as paperbacks despite the fact that they never sell in paperback ... just so I could hold them in my hands like pieces of art, and feel them as real.

As we excitedly hacked our way through the opportunities and turbulence of the early teens, Sean Platt, David Wright, and I decided to launch a podcast to share our author journeys with others.

We called it *The Self Publishing Podcast*.

We had no agenda other than to talk with others like us, and to learn. Self publishing was still the Wild West, and our hope was that we and other authors could find ways to navigate it together.

The Self Publishing Podcast and Write Publish Repeat Era

In truth, Joanna Penn's *The Creative Penn* podcast predated ours by four years. We weren't the first, and we weren't the biggest. But we were still a quiet cult phenomenon, full of something Joanna (who's British) once affectionately called "blokish" appeal. I think it was our unpolished, irreverent style that attracted a lot of writers at the time, while of course completely alienating others. The mid to late teens wasn't "The Self Publishing Podcast Era" for everyone by any stretch ... but hey, I'm writing this book, and it certainly was for me.

(I'm an artist and I'll say what I want, remember?)

Sean, Dave, and I entered the podcasting world just as millions upon millions of authors were discovering that YES, they *could* actually write, publish, and sell their own books! To authors, the (somewhat) legitimization of ebooks and self-publishing was like the crumbling of the Berlin wall. Everyone was *so excited*. But that excitement came with a lot of questions and confusion, too, because we were in uncharted waters. Nobody was sure how to maximize their literary chances in those days, but it sure was thrilling to try and solve the puzzle together.

As *The Self Publishing Podcast* grew into a major voice in the indie publishing movement, Sean, Dave, and I decided to publish a book about what we'd learned. The podcast was charming but all over the place — far from the orderly, professional, and informative *Creative Penn*. We were wiseass American philistines, and we couldn't manage to stay on topic or avoid crass jokes. Our book was meant to change that: to deliver the podcast's core knowledge in orderly form.

The book was called *Write. Publish. Repeat: The No-Luck Required Guide to Self-Publishing Success.* It took off like a rocket in late 2013, and despite being kind of out-of-date, remains an industry cornerstone today.

The More and Faster Era

I won't claim that we changed the course of self-publishing. I do, however, think we contributed to its poison.

We didn't do it on purpose. We were just three idiot yahoos, remember: three blokish fools with fun-over-professionalism manners and plenty of unadvisable dick jokes. In our minds, all we did was share what we were doing. We didn't see any downside to it.

In truth, there were many downsides. For one, readers of *WPR* and listeners of *SPP* saw what we were doing in our own author careers, saw that it was working, and understandably copied it.

Sean and Dave wrote serials instead of novels? Okay, then *everyone* should write serials. It even became prescriptive: readers emailing constantly to ask how long serials should be, and how many parts should be in them.

Johnny wrote fast? Well, then obviously that was advice for *everyone* to write fast. How fast does Johnny write? How many words a day, how many hours, and does he take breaks? It was important to know, if others were to follow our single, only-path-possible methods to success. Right?

We shared, and people took our sharing as advice. Some of what we said was meant that way, but a whole lot of it wasn't. The fact that nobody could tell which was which was our fault, because we never made it clear. Although honestly, I don't think it would've mattered if we had. Everyone is looking for THE WAY, remember ... and back then, in the minds of a lot of our listeners and readers, our way *was* THE WAY.

It hurt our own efforts when everyone started doing the same things we were doing, but it also hurt the ethos and expectations of the industry. We were just one force in the mid-teens, but just like Billy Joel, we didn't start the fire. Human nature started the fire. Authors had been bottled up before self-publishing became legit — and now that it was, all they wanted was to succeed through any means possible.

The message of *Write. Publish. Repeat.* was that consistency and persistence were important. You shouldn't just write and publish; you also needed to repeat the process. Do it again and again, we said, until you'd racked up enough books and readers to reach your goals.

But the world took things further. If *repeating* was good, authors decided that *repeating faster* was better. *Repeating willy-nilly*, without regard to the art and creativity of it all, was just fine if it meant releasing books faster.

And faster.

And faster.

The Rapid Release Era

By the late teens, a lot of tactical thinking had entered the self-publishing mindset. This wasn't a bad thing. Unlike traditional authors, indie authors were solopreneurs. We weren't just making stories; we also had to market and sell them. We needed to be savvy and clever and cunning in ways traditionally published authors didn't.

No wonder trad hated us. We must have looked like industrious rodents to them, peddling what they saw as trash in any way we could.

People started advertising. That made sense, right? You'd buy a spot for an email list promotion (BookBub being the granddaddy), a bunch of people would learn about your book, and they'd take a chance to read it because it was cheap or free. Then Facebook ads became a thing. Also sensible, right? Anything to get your books out there.

People started playing with pricing — something trad books almost never did. We didn't have the big distribution networks they had, but we could make up the difference by being wily. We could run discount deals. We could price-pulse, moving prices up and down to put them in front of bargain hunters. The "first book free" epiphany arrived, and suddenly that, too, became THE WAY.

People began experimenting with bundling. Because hey, if one book for 99 cents or free was good, a big box set at the same price was obviously better. The only problem was that in order to sell a box set cheap and still make money, you needed more books. But that was cool, right? The SPP guys had written a book all about that. What was it called? *Write, Publish, and Repeat as Fast as You Humanly Can Even If It Crushes Your Art and Kills Your Soul?* Yeah, that was it.

If fast was good, faster was better.

If cheap was good, cheaper was better.

If using some ninja tactics was good, using all of the ninja tactics was better. Writing good books — or putting all of yourself into them — was optional if you had enough ninja tactics.

Day by day, more new authors came into the mix and looked at the mounting pile of "conventional wisdom" about how to make it as a self-published author. The Wild West adventure of it all was gone, replaced by dogma. Then, as now, questions in author forums stopped being answered with popcorned ideas in a spirit of discovery. Instead, they were instead answered definitively, with authority. Because by then, everyone knew THE WAY. You'd be stupid not to follow THE WAY.

What do you mean, you don't have an email list offering a free "reader magnet" story as a bribe? You'll never succeed that way.

What do you mean, you aren't on social media and don't buy Facebook ads? That's the right way to do it, so enjoy your failure without it.

What do you mean, you're writing in different genres instead of only one?

Wait — you write stand-alone books instead of series? How's that supposed to work?

Hang on. Let me get this straight: Your cover looks different than others in your genre? Your story doesn't have the expected tropes? You're pricing how *high? You're making paperbacks? Special editions? Why the hell would anyone buy a special edition? Ebooks are where the money is; everyone knows that.*

You aren't in Kindle Unlimited? Don't you know that's where the voracious readers are? It doesn't matter if you don't want to be there, if you don't like the expectations inside, if you don't like how much your books sell for, or if you'd honestly rather publish at your own pace. Oh, you're "going wide" instead, and not even bothering to play to to Amazon's algorithms? Enjoy your artistic pride and poverty, sucker!

I don't remember when I first heard the term "Rapid Release," but I do know it was tied presumptively to *Write. Publish. Repeat.* Of course it was the natural next step: First repeat, then repeat rapidly. Makes sense, right? I mean: Johnny writes fast. The SPP guys have a lot of books for sale. So what if we all did that ... but improved it all by going *faster*?

"Rapid" was indeed how Sean and I worked as a co-authoring team, but it was an attribute, not a core ideal. I'm most comfortable when I write fast. It's how my best stuff comes out. But from the start, the idea of Rapid Release — which put speed at the forefront, rather than an optional secondary — bothered me. Going fast was something you *could* do, not something you *had* to do.

But it was out of control. There was no stopping the train by then.

Faster. Faster. *Faster.*

And now, as I write this book in 2025, AI has entered the mix. I'm not anti-AI, and although I'd never use it for writing my books (that's the fun part!), I don't begrudge people who do. Still, right, wrong, or indifferent, AI lit booster rockets under Rapid Release. It turned "fast" into "much, much faster."

People used to think I was crazy in 2015, when I said I wrote 1.5 million words (about the full Harry Potter series and a half) every year. Nowadays, though, enough authors have become word machines that I'm considered slow. If they use AI, some produce 1.5 million words a *month* ... and believe me, kids: That bullet train is only getting started. There are folks out there aiming to produce multiple books a *day* — and even then I'm understating.

In a "Rapid Release" world like *that*, how can a single human with a story in their soul possibly compete?

There's an answer to that question in the way of the Artisan Author. It's a good one, too: one that will restore your hope, reignite your passion, and reawaken the creative joy that brought you to writing to begin with.

Before we dive into Artisandom, though, we need to go a bit deeper into the past.

Because ... it *was* good for a while there, wasn't it? In the mid 20-teens, there were nothing but blue skies for independent authors. Everything was looking up. We'd finally won the freedom we wanted, and there were no longer gatekeepers to stop us. Self-expression and self-determination had, in their own ways, defeated the soul-crushing force of big business. Authors with stories trapped inside for their entire lives could now share those stories, and many of them began making side-hustle (if not full-time) incomes from their art.

But then, somewhere along the line, things changed.

It happened so slowly that just like the proverbial boiling frog, we fell into the Brave New World of Rapid Release without even realizing. Without ever consenting. Without awareness enough to look around at the beautiful house we'd built as it reshaped itself — never noticing its metamorphosis into a house of horrors.

Or worse: *its metamorphosis into an office full of cubicles.* Into a workday spent ground down by stress and long hours, told what to do by rules even dumber and more restrictive than the ones we'd broken to become indies in the first place.

We were promised green pastures of possibility ... but in the end we got days spent doing the literary equivalent of filing interdepartmental memos.

The truism says: *Those who don't understand the lessons of history are doomed to repeat them.* So with that in mind, let's see if we can spot the moment when the dream turned sour for art-first authors like us. Let's see if we can find the place where the fun train went off the rails — when our glorious escape from Walmart culture became a quest to create our own new Walmart.

In what's left of this section, we'll explore the pivot point of self publishing: the place where tactical thinking overtook art rather than both riding side-by-side like they were supposed to. Once we understand what led us astray and why, we'll know what to double-down on in the future versus what to avoid.

I promise to keep it short. We don't want to dwell too long on the past, when there's such a bright future ahead of us as Artisan Authors.

And make no mistake: The future *is* bright for us, if we learn our lessons.

In truth, we're not far from the freedom and creative success we wanted from the start. This change in our industry? It hasn't destroyed opportunity for slower, more artistic, more deliberate creators. It hasn't sabotaged authors who want no part of a commoditized race to the bottom, but instead seek lasting and loyal connections with readers who will stay with us forever.

Those opportunities are very much still alive ... buried beneath layers upon layers of capitalism run amok.

In fact, as we'll talk about shortly, the extremity of Rapid Release actually did us a favor. It made our chances of thriving as Artisans *better*. It turned our future True Fans into *truer* fans. It made the readers who were willing to pay for quality *even more* willing to pay for quality. It made connection and humanity *more* important to the right readers, not less.

In fact: *Thank you*, Rapid Release. Your absurdity made the Artisan Author life *more possible and powerful now than it could have been otherwise.*

But that's only true if we avoid the traps. If we learn from history. If we see the reasons that good times turned bad for so many authors — and how, rather than letting fate carry us along like bad characters without agency, we could have made our own damn choices and been thriving as Artisans all along.

If, like Talking Heads, we'd stopped for a second and wondered, "Well, how did we get here?", things might have turned out differently.

This is not my beautiful wife. This is not my beautiful house.

Am I right?

Or am I wrong?

Chapter 2

The Big Bait and Switch

How did we indie authors — a smart and attractive group of people if ever there was one — earn our freedom from the trad world only to turn around and build a whole new prison? We'd broken away. We'd removed the barriers between us and what we wanted. Within a few short years, all the tools necessary to create our own fortunes had dropped right into our laps. But ... well ... you know what they say: *Meet the new boss, same as the old boss.*

Only this time, the new boss was us.

So how did it happen? It happened because we confused *means* and *ends*.

From the start, we knew the goal: the "end" we called *being writers*. We also realized, sensibly enough, that earning income was a pretty reasonable way (or "means") to get there. It made all the sense in the world. If you can earn money from writing, you can buy time away from other work to write even more.

But then "earning income" became the new *end*: a subtle replacement for the first *end* of "being writers." Instead of asking "How can we be writers?" we began asking, "How can we earn income?" What *means* would get us income — ideally a lot of it?

And the answer was: *Why, selling a lot of books, of course.*

We shuffled on down the line. "Selling a lot of books" had

begun as one possible *means* to earn a lot of income (so we could justify being writers), but now it was an *end* in itself. "Selling a lot of books," in other words, had elbowed its way into our minds and become the goal. Instead of trying to figure how to be writers like we'd originally planned, we began trying to figure out how to make a lot of sales instead.

Maybe you're starting to see the problem. "Selling a lot of books" isn't the same as "being a writer." It's not even the same as "earning income." In truth, selling books isn't the only way for writers to earn money. You could use your book as a credential to get paid speaking gigs. You could ghostwrite for someone else. You could be a freelancer. There are plenty ways to earn money beyond just selling books ... and there are other ways to be a writer that don't involve money at all.

In other words, there were always plenty of different *means* to reach each of our *ends*, but we ignored them. It wasn't wrong choose the options we did (after all, selling books is the lowest hanging fruit and the most likely to pay off), but it *was* wrong to equate each new *means* with the *end* it was meant to achieve. Selling books is a good way to earn income, and earning income is a good way to justify time spent writing ... but I think we can all agree that nobody should put an equals sign between them and call it a day.

I hate to break it to you, but "selling books" isn't identical to "being a writer." The people working the cash registers at Barnes & Noble are not "being writers" when they ring up a sale, and you're not "selling books" when you sit down to write a scene.

But, hey: forget the semantics. We certainly forgot them as an industry. We were far too excited and impatient during the rise of self-publishing to consider any paths that didn't feel like home runs. We'd decided that selling a lot of books was the way to go, so we wouldn't allow alternatives to enter the picture and ruin our fun. Instead, we wiped our minds free of everything that wasn't *making a lot of sales.*

And so we asked: How *do* you make a lot of sales? How do you reach *that* end?

Here's one option: *Write. Publish. Repeat.*

I liked that one enough to write a whole book about it. I even still agree with *WPR*'s original message: persist, keep at it, and publish again and again. My co-authors and I argued in one of *WPR*'s many verbose prologues that if an author could just write more books, each book in their catalog would need to earn less on its own. If you put those books in a series, the effect was magnified. You could compel people to buy the second book and beyond because they'd want to know what happened after the first. And in the beginning, it made sense. We just never knew our point would be taken to the extremes it eventually was.

But whatever. In order to *sell* a lot of books, we'd decided we needed to *write* a lot of books. It made sense ... until *writing more books* became the end — the *only* end — that we were willing to consider..

And so we wrote more. And faster. And more. And faster. "Fast" wasn't fast enough. What began as consistency and persistence became the fever-pitch machine that so many authors bow to today.

It happened brick by brick. Day by day, we built our own walls out of impatience and narrow-minded thinking, closing off options and alternatives to create dogma instead. Soon enough, we'd decided there was one and only one decent way to succeed as a writer, and it was very specific. You *could* try different ways to run your author business ... but let's be real; the hive mind thought you were dumb or naive if you did.

How do you become an author? Simple. Just follow this formula: Write as many books as quickly as you can, turn them into ebooks, and sell those ebooks exclusively to the mostly-American readers who buy from Amazon. Run your email list in exactly this way using exactly this kind of reader magnet, run these kinds of ads in the ways everyone says you should, write what's hot right now, and price the way everyone else prices even if it contradicts common sense.

Don't deviate. Don't trust your gut or the logic of human interaction. Instead, conform and obey.

There was — and still is — a whole world of other ways to succeed as writers beyond the "official formula" that so many preach as gospel. The problem was, we were too focused on *writing more books* to see them. We stopped being able to see anything at all after we'd built the last wall of the faster-faster cage.

If you fell for it — if you ended up in that cage without meaning to, just because you'd followed the crowd — don't feel bad. You're in good company, and I for one don't blame you. Each step we took as a community seemed to make sense at the time. It's only with hindsight that the absurdity of it all is obvious.

This is how we all came to believe something that makes no logical sense. This is why so many new and established authors think there's only one option: Rapid Release's way, or the highway.

When I first started talking about Artisan Authoring, I heard all sorts of objections to Rapid Release from my fellow authors. They knew it came with too much pressure, too little longevity, too much razzmatazz and not enough common sense; they just couldn't see a way out of it. They all felt like they were riding a bubble even if releasing rapid-fire books was currently working for them — as if they *knew* the system was a house of cards, and were just waiting for the absurdity of it all to collapse.

Before we dive into the "other way" offered by the Artisan Author, let's take one last gander through the absurdities of the "current-best" system.

I want you convinced before we begin in earnest. I want you to see Rapid Release in all its dysfunctional glory, so it never tempts you again.

But First: Rapid Release Isn't the Same as Kindle Unlimited

Before we go any deeper, I'd like clarify that Rapid Release and Kindle Unlimited aren't the same thing — not in reality, and not in the context of this book. I don't want anyone thinking I'm shit-talking KU when I'm actually shit-talking Rapid Release.

It's true that I don't like KU for myself. It's true that I'd rather smash my face between the iron plates of a George Foreman grill than put my ebooks into KU. It's true that if I had to make a default recommendation for Artisan Authors (one to be followed unless there's a specific reason not to), it'd be to skip KU and go wide. I don't like exclusivity, even if it's only for ebooks. Without a plan to leverage that exclusivity into some larger benefit, it strikes me as bad business.

But some authors — not many, but a few — *have* that larger plan, and hence use Kindle Unlimited as a tool rather than letting KU use them. Because KU only requires exclusivity for ebooks, those authors often sell physical copies beyond Amazon in ways I describe in this book, or have other strategies to turn KU to their advantage. Romance authors in particular can fit this mold — especially the scrappy ones. They'll write for a passionate audience in Kindle Unlimited, then parlay that audience into fans who will support them beyond KU's borders — fans drooling to buy extremely fancy, extremely *Artisan* versions of those same books from direct stores and Kickstarter campaigns. Their ebooks are basic ... but their sprayed-edge, foil-stamped, leather-bound limited edition hardbacks are anything but.

Unless you're already splitting your time between KU and off-Amazon special editions (or know that such a split can work for you), I suggest ignoring this section's nitpicking and avoiding Kindle Unlimited entirely. People accidentally conflate the two for a reason, making Artisan objections true of both. In order to succeed in KU, you almost always need to release books rapidly — and for Rapid Releasers, KU is an ideal (and often *the only*) tool to supercharge that rapidity. If KU is the only tool in a Rapid Releaser's toolbox, then the two *are* the same.

As you read this book, keep that caveat in mind because I won't keep mentioning it. I'd bog things down by constantly pointing out the differences, especially since for most Rapid Release authors (and most KU authors) there *are* no differences. Artisans who make KU work are the minority, not the norm. Feel free to try KU if you must ... but have a plan to use KU to your long-term advantage if you do, okay?

And so, to my friends who intelligently use Kindle Unlimited as part of their Artisan business, I say this: *Forgive me if I imply that KU sucks for everyone. It sucks pretty hard for me, but I know it's a great tool for some of you.*

With that said, let's get back to explaining how Rapid Release crushes authors' souls like a drunk Santa ruins children's dreams.

The Four Horsemen of Rapid Release

There are four main ways that Rapid Release publishing, when taken to its extreme, is untenable. Four main ways that it's the emperor's new clothes ... and if you'll just look closely at the ridiculous machine of it all for a moment, you'll see there's very little substance — just a lot of smoke and mirrors.

Horseman #1: Joy Became Stress

As Dennis Hopper said in *Speed*, "Pop quiz, hotshot."

Let's say you take a bunch of people who want to tell their stories to the world. They're largely sensitive types who got into writing because of the magic they felt while creating, or because books once upon a time offered them a more enjoyable world than the real world.

Now, pretend you take those people and make them spin their magic as quickly as possible. Glue that wand to their hand

and force them to perform their spells over and over and over again ... forever.

What happens? Suddenly, the magic isn't fun anymore. Suddenly, writing becomes stressful. Oh, it might take a while to get there. And oh, those storytellers might tell themselves tales for a while about it: *It's fine; I'm doing what I love; I'm glad my readers like me enough to want more; some people never get to truly express themselves, so I should consider myself lucky.* But how long can they believe those things? Does it wear thin after a year of writing? Or does the delusion last for two years? Maybe three, if you're a machine?

I know so many people who lived the indie dream for about six months. Then, the dream became a job. Then, they burned out and quit.

You might be able to work on an assembly line your entire life and still gut through it, telling yourself it's something you need to do to feed your family and survive, but things are different with writing. Writing requires delving deep. It requires putting yourself out there. It requires taking your innermost thoughts and making them real. It requires creation. It requires, again, *magic*.

Maybe Rapid Release die-hards get a kick out of the grind, but people like us can't work for long without loving it. Our stories are good because we put our hearts into them. We make what we make because it comes from something deeper than obligation. Cutting that cord — asking someone who works art-first to speed up their art lest they lose everything they've built — is the best way to destroy what made that work special in the first place.

Rapid Release turned writing into an assembly line as real as any other assembly line ... and what made our work worth reading evaporated when it did.

Horseman #2: Algorithms Replaced Readers

Most writers begin with a desire to please readers. That's the aim: *To create something that moves other human beings in the same way it moves us.* Maybe we want to throw readers into deep emotion, or maybe we just want to entertain them. Regardless, *readers* were where we began. *Readers* were our targets. Good stories are like telepathy: they let us send our emotions into the minds of others ... and those "others" are readers.

In fact, that's how self-publishing began. When the gatekeepers fell away and new Kindles needed filling, self-publishers were able to reach readers directly for the first time. The stories weren't always perfect and marketing wasn't always on-point, but everyone managed to find *some* readers in those early days.

Do you remember your first sale, if you've had one? Remember how it felt, to know some stranger had seen what you'd made and found it worth their time to read?

"Finding readers" was a great metric back when self-publishing's goal was to become real authors. But when the market changed and competition ramped up, focusing on readers was no longer enough. Now, instead of looking directly for readers, we started looking for ways to please platforms like Amazon that sold our books, because they were better at reaching readers than we could ever be. If you figured out how Amazon decided which books to promote to its customers, you could game their system and ride on their shoulders. Instead of reaching ten customers, the bookseller algorithms could put you in front of ten thousand.

For a while, we played to algorithms in order to reach readers. But then, as the market accelerated, we started playing to algorithms *for their own sake.*

Back when readers were our focus, we simply wrote the best books we could. It didn't matter what those books were, or how we positioned them. It didn't matter if the second book was different than the first, because readers are readers. Some are fiercely genre- or series-loyal, but many aren't. Every book is right for someone — and at first, our job was to find those someones.

But when we started writing for algorithms, all that changed. We altered our books and their positioning so the algorithms would favor them more. If the sci-fi algorithm was hot on military books at the time, we'd write *military sci-fi* instead of *sci-fi with a touch of military*. If our heart wanted to write a comedy after writing a thriller but the algorithms were rewarding sequels, we'd write a second thriller instead.

Year by year, individual readers became less important while the fat part of the reader bell curve — as a whole and combined entity, embodied by the algorithmic average — took over. Whatever the majority wanted, we'd be rewarded for producing. If we ignored the groupthink of it all and just wrote whatever came to us, we'd lose out even if our story was amazing.

In the age of algorithms, we were punished for writing what might have been individual readers' favorite books if there weren't enough of those individual readers to suit the algorithm. *The majority always won.* Cult hits became nearly impossible, because they didn't serve the average of the masses. Amazon could only promote so many books, so it promoted the surest hits ... and self-publishers, *en masse,* stopped focusing on individuals so they could try to become those hits.

You could be a millionaire if you contorted your books to ride the algorithms just right, but what about all the readers who *weren't* the majority? What about the career's worth of loyal readers we *could* have had, if we hadn't become so obsessed with riches and ignored them?

Horseman #3: Good Business Became a Race to the Bottom

I remember when authors first started talking about Amazon exclusivity. I thought it was absurd. Here we were with all of these options for places to sell books — including the ever-faithful neighborhood Barnes & Noble and smaller, local shops — but now we were supposed to ignore them so that Jeff Bezos could control every bit of our businesses, and reap the rewards.

What sensible company sells to only one client?

But exclusivity wasn't the only way that indie authordom

began flying in the face of every other logical business practice known to humanity. We were so desperate to ride those algorithms that we threw our figurative MBAs right out the window and began conducting business the way idiots conduct business.

What sensible company prices its products at a loss, gives away the farm for pennies, and chases business only on the basis of price?

What sensible company never engages its customers directly, but instead hands all customer interactions over to someone with interests different than their own — interests and goals that sometimes directly contradict *our* interests and goals?

What sensible company builds its business entirely on rented land? More and more, indie authors are building their empires purely on Amazon ground. Amazon controls the land, even if we're the ones who farm it.

Know what that's called? It's sharecropping. When you sharecrop as an author, you own nothing but the books themselves. Amazon is your land baron ... and they can — and have, and will again — change the rules at any time.

Horseman #4: Success Became a Trap

This horseman is my favorite — because at this point in the book, I know what your last greedy tendency might be thinking:

You say that Rapid Release fails a lot of people, Johnny, but what if it doesn't fail me? What if I play the game just right? What if I'm one of the winners? Why shouldn't I gamble on myself just in case? Rapid Release isn't always bad. Many authors have built their fortunes with it.

True. I know many Rapid Release big shots who only publish ebooks into KU. But if they're smart, they still live every day with two fears:

The first is that one day, the bubble will collapse. Amazon could decide to fold their book wing or drastically reduce royalties, and then everything those authors have built will crumble to dust ... and there won't be a damn thing they can do about it.

The second fear, interestingly, is that they'll succeed. They worry just a little that everything *will* click, their books *will* skyrocket, and suddenly they'll be earning a mint. The problem is, the rise won't last because Amazon's love only lasts about a month. To keep Amazon's love, they'll need to publish a new book, and it'd better be just like the last one so the algorithms can push it effectively.

No big deal, right? They can write a second book like their last one. They're writers, after all.

Except that a third book must immediately follow the second.

And a fourth book must immediately follow the third.

And so on and so on, for as long as they want to feed their families.

It's not like they can slow down. The tail of the algorithm isn't long enough to sustain real income if they do. And it's not like they can branch out and explore new creative ground, because new projects require a whole new algorithmic key — and even *that* assumes they write an inside-the-lines book. There are plenty of projects that will *never* suit an algorithm. I mean, consider my book *Unicorn Western*. That wacky fantasy/western mashup is one of my Artisan Author bestsellers because people love the weird of it, but it wouldn't get algorithmic support on Amazon in a thousand years. It just doesn't fit the mold we're all expected to stay in.

Take a moment, with that in mind, to reconsider what it means to be "successful" as a Rapid Release author.

The price of making bank is telling the same basic story in the same exact genre over and over again, all the time writing faster and faster, trying to outrun the deluge of books written by other rapid-fire authors and AI. They can't take a break. Can't branch into other creative areas. And all the while, they're courting readers who prefer not to pay for books beyond their KU membership — readers who won't follow them anywhere else, and who they won't even be able to reach if Amazon were one day to stop letting us publish there.

That's the price of success as a Rapid Release author. You can succeed, yes — at the price of insecurity, burnout, creative drought, and fear.

As Admiral Ackbar said in *Return of the Jedi,* "It's a trap!"

So sure. Enjoy your success, folks. Enjoy those golden handcuffs. Because if you want any chance at all of maintaining that success, you'd better keep yourself shackled to the production machine 24/7, with no time off to enjoy it.

The Dumbness of the Current Model

Despite the success trap, some authors are simply wired for Rapid Release. They can write without defying (or changing) genres or taking a break. They enjoy the puzzle of "solving" the algorithm, and get their creative kicks from making an often left-brained, marketing-centric approach to publishing work for them.

For those authors, the currently-dominant model of indie publishing can work. In fact, I know some for whom Rapid Release is perfect. There's nothing dumb about the way *those* folks (writers who understand exactly what they're getting into with Rapid Release and what to expect from it) run their businesses.

For *many* authors, though, following the rules of Rapid Release would be an idiotic approach to business ... because although Rapid Release logic works within the boundaries of Rapid Release, it's crazytown out here in the rest of the world.

By "crazy," I don't just mean "some authors are ill-suited to it." By "crazy," I mean that *taking a Rapid Release approach if you're not a Rapid Release natural flies in the face of logic.* I mean that outside of that very specific ecosystem, Rapid Release tactics don't make any sense. They are, honestly, just about the dumbest choices you could possibly make (with the most doomed-to-fail logic behind them) in any other arena of business.

Gee, maybe I should say what I'm *really* thinking.

From a strict numbers perspective, most authors aren't savants. Most are folks with a few books in them who just want their work to see the world. Or, they're career authors *in potentia*: people who dream of producing as much work as their idols, but don't want to do it like machines on an ironclad deadline, using a lot of constantly-changing marketing tricks. Most writers are story-first, meaning they'd rather write to their muse and *then* figure out how to sell, rather than beginning each book with its sales angle in mind.

If you're one of *those* authors but try to operate like a Rapid Release author, you're doing the equivalent of putting screen doors on a submarine. *They* can keep the water out so the submarine keeps sailing, but *you're* just setting yourself up to drown. It's like buying a house with only high shelves because you want your storage out of the way, then not being able to reach anything because you're 5'2" and afraid of ladders. It's entering a high-stakes poker tournament if you can't play poker. It's basing your basketball strategy on slam dunks when you can't jump, or hoping a stock market boom will save your finances when you don't own any stock.

If you're not *them*, you shouldn't operate like them. For *them*, it can work. In *your* hands, though, their winning tactics become moronic.

We've been sold a bill of goods, see. We've been shown a paradigm that only works for a minority of authors, then been brainwashed into believing it works for everyone. We've started to believe it's "Rapid Release or nothing" if you want to succeed as an author, but that's not true. There *is* another way (a completely different and often contradictory approach that, by the way, would be dumb in *their* hands), and we'll begin exploring it in the next chapter.

First, though, I'd like you to take a good, long look at the assumptions of the current model: one last glance at *their* way to see if you'd prefer it before you become an Artisan.

Read each tenet that follows, every one of which is something that Rapid Release implies or requires. Do *you* — in your unique Artisan Author shoes, with your own style and goals and dreams — believe them, too?

Quantity Matters More Than Quality

In the Rapid Release world, the number of books you produce matters more than their quality or uniqueness. It has to, because without volume, you won't have speed ... and without speed, the model stops working. It doesn't matter how great your books are if your business collapses.

Now to be fair, quality *does* matter in Rapid Release. Kind of. If your books are terrible, they'll get bad reviews and people will decide to skip them, or people who've been reading a series will abandon it after the first book. Quality matters, but it's a baseline sort of quality. Quality matters to Rapid Release books in the same way it matters to a Walmart mop.

Does this mop work without falling apart? Is it good enough for my kitchen floor?

Does this story work? Is it good enough for the day I'll spend blazing through it?

That's the kind of quality that matters in Rapid Release. Competency is necessary, but excellence is optional. Rapid Release authors *can* go above and beyond to make their books as great and twisty and cool as possible, but why should they bother? The difference between "fine" and "great" isn't usually enough to move the dial on sales in their world ... and time spent polishing one book is time they can't spend writing the next one.

I've heard authors admit that they stopped worrying about typos and perfect storycraft the minute they realized their target audience read too fast to care. I've seen authors dismiss cool ideas for their books because taking the time to make those ideas work would delay its launch.

Speed matters more in Rapid Release. That's a fact. Given a

choice between publishing a "just okay" book today to hit the algorithm's sweet spot versus releasing a *great* book a month later, successful Rapid Release authors always choose the former.

Now ask yourself: *As someone who likes to put care into your work, became a writer at least partially for art and self-expression, and who'd rather not be up against deadlines every single day, do YOU believe that quantity matters more than quality?*

In *your* world, is that something that makes sense to build a business around? Or, instead, does sacrificing quality for speed sound like just about the dumbest thing you could do from where you're actually standing?

Writing To Market Is Better Than Writing What Inspires You

If what you're inspired to write doesn't line up exactly — and I do mean *exactly* — with what the ravenous reader market is looking for, which force would you obey? Would you write what your heart wants, or write what the market demands?

In the world of Rapid Release, the answer is the latter. Faced with a choice between writing an on-market book that will ride the algorithm and an off-market book that won't, you always pick the market. The market is what sells. The tropes of your genre — confirming that market fit — are what sell.

Wrote a zombie book without a scene where zombies try to break into a human stronghold, like we didn't do in *Dead City*?

Wrote an alien invasion book that ends before the aliens arrive, like Sean and I did in *Invasion*?

Wrote a book that combines two genres like *Unicorn Western*, or a book written in third-person-past for a market that's usually first-person-present, like we did a hundred times over?

If you followed our lead and did any of those things, then congratulations — you've just tanked your book release in the KU world. Which will tank your *next* book release, because no KU reader will follow through or want the sequel to an off-market book. Which, in turn, will collapse your entire algorithmic advantage. And if you don't already have a perfectly-on-market book ready to replace the one that flopped, you're screwed.

Placed head to head with instinct or creative whims, the market's strict, unforgiving demands always come first for Rapid Release authors.

In your own Artisan world, is that smart? Or is disobeying your unique creative voice flat-out idiotic?

Cheap Customers Are the Best Customers

Here's something else that's dumb for most authors, yet is accepted as normal in the Rapid Release world: building your business around customers who won't spend more than a dollar.

Let's not price our books like books. That would be ridiculous! Instead, let's price them like expired Tic-Tacs. I know that novel took you forever to write, but that means nothing. Put it up for borrows, or price it at 99 cents. Who'd pay $3 for ten hours of entertainment? It's preposterous! Inconceivable!

It makes no sense at all. It's also insulting. I put a lot of work and thought into my books, dammit, and yet some readers balk at paying even three bucks for them — let alone the $6 or so that most of the world feels an ebook is worth. Do these people go to movies or subscribe to Netflix? Do they buy $5 lattes? You can find more money lying in the street than they're willing to pay for books.

Why have we built these people up as the only customers worth attracting — especially when there are so many readers out there who regularly and willingly pay more?

If your pricing is designed to attract KU readers but you aren't releasing at least 15 books into KU every year, you're being dumb. I don't blame you; the industry's group mind pretty much convinced everyone it was a good idea. It's not, though. Building a business around people who don't like to pay for things without a plan to earn your money another way is really, *really* dumb.

If you can rev the KU engine enough to generate a ton of page reads and don't mind doing it pretty much forever, fine.

If you're involved in some referral scheme wherein you give your books away so you can collect and then illegally sell readers' information, that's also fine if you don't mind prison.

But for all but the most die-hard (and lucky) KU authors, there *is* no secondary way to make money. You end up giving your book away with no plan for a long tail, or you get just a handful of page reads, or you make a 30 cent commission if your book actually sells for cash.

How is this business model sustainable? Pretend you're going on *Shark Tank*. Which Shark would nod their head with enthusiasm if you presented your author business to them, ready to invest in your idea to give your product away and hope for money to arrive ... somehow?

Hey, I've got an idea. I'm going to start selling wagons. What's my business model, you ask? Well, I plan to take them out to the street and give them away free to anyone who wants them. Alternatively, people can just borrow them. Not for free, if it's about borrowing. They DO pay to borrow. Not me, though. They don't pay ME to borrow MY books. That would be crazy. No, instead they'll pay a monthly membership fee to some billionaire who doesn't have my best interests in mind. That seems like a logical course of action.

It's like everyone started taking *South Park*'s underpants gnomes seriously.

Step 1: Write Books
Step 2: ?
Step 3: Profit

Step 2 matters, folks. You can't just underpants-gnome your way through the author business and hope that magic will connect your books to money no matter how flagrantly you fly in the face of the way that *every other business on the planet* is run.

In order for a business to survive, it needs a way to earn

money that's repeatable, reliable, and stable. Usually that means finding customers who value what you're selling and are willing to pay for it ... but hey, you do you.

This particular bit of industry dumbness is both dangerous and persistent. Most authors I talk to are afraid to break out of the *price-low, compete-on-price, advertise-only-with-a-larcenous-discount* way of doing business. And I get it; they *should* be afraid if they've only courted Rapid Release-type buyers. Those buyers are incredibly price sensitive. *Those* buyers will pass over a book they might like because a different book is cheaper.

As we'll see soon, though, Artisan Authors don't have to worry about pricing nearly as much. Within certain reasonable limits, Artisan buyers are *not* price-sensitive. They know that handmade, carefully-crafted work isn't cheap, and they're willing to pay for it. That's why the Artisan approach — not the Rapid Release approach — is so much better for authors like us.

But we're getting ahead of ourselves. Let's continue with the dumbness.

Putting All Eggs In One Basket Is A Good Idea

As we work our way through these last few truths of Rapid Release, I'd like you to keep reminding yourself that although writing can feel like magic, the business behind it is not. Capitalism doesn't invert and suddenly start acting like mist and fairies when books are involved. Business rules and good sense *always* apply, no matter what's being sold.

With that in mind, here's another question: Unless you're that dedicated, perfect-for-this, die-hard Rapid Release author we keep talking about, does it sound logical to sell your product at only one store?

Man, I can buy Coco Puffs in *any* supermarket.

I can buy Craftsman tools at *any* hardware store.

Looking for a Blu-Ray copy of *Miss Congeniality* to replace the one you played to death? You'll have no problem finding one, because it's not sold exclusively at one convenience store in Duluth.

Exclusivity without recompense or a plan is dumb. Some products are Target exclusives, but in exchange Target buys a bazillion of them. Some movies are streamable only on certain platforms, but you can bet your ass the rights holders were paid well for the privilege. Unless Amazon is willing to pay you buttloads of cash for going exclusive (and no, the vague hope that you'll break out and earn buttloads through sales doesn't count), you're violating a key principle of business: *If they expect something valuable from you (like exclusivity), get something valuable in return.*

As authors, we've been trained to go to Amazon first because Amazon *was* first: The Kindle, followed by KDP, is where the practical ebook market began. Because it's the biggest and most obvious, it becomes the lowest-hanging fruit. We figure Amazon is the "80" in the famous "80/20 Rule," so most authors hit it first and only then step back to ask if anything else is worth their time. Amazon, knowing the power they hold, found ways to convince us the answer is *No*. They created dubious benefits that only sometimes benefit exclusive authors, and we bought right into it — hook, line, and sinker.

For some authors — those who really work the Rapid Release system — Amazon-only benefits can be worth it. For most, they aren't. For smaller and slower authors, there's no benefit at all. You cut off your ability to sell in other places for a few bucks' worth of page reads. In the words of those old ladies from the 1980s Wendy's commercials: *Where's the beef?*

To be clear, "going wide" isn't magic, either. I'm absolutely not saying you'll sell a ton of books if you're available at Barnes & Noble. What I *will* say is that if you do go wide, you'll be operating like a sensible business. What if Amazon decides to change things while your books are there and nowhere else? Then where would you be?

No other customers on any other platforms.

No way to reach the customers you have, even if you have a mailing list. Most customers never join a mailing list, and it's not like Amazon will export your past buyers into a spreadsheet so you can reach out to them.

Amazon could cut author commissions in half.

They could delete your entire genre. Remember when that happened to a bunch of romance and erotica authors a few years back?

They could — and often do — change their bookselling algorithm. Your booming business today might collapse if they do. It's happened before. It will happen again.

Amazon's priority isn't authors. Amazon's priority is their customers. Amazon will never do what's best for authors unless it *also* happens to be best for their customers — and, ultimately, best for their bottom line. So here's a question: What happens when, one day, Amazon decides that what's best for their business conflicts with what's best for you? Do you think they'll be kind about it, and help you out at the cost of their own profits?

Is it wise to give one company *all the power* over your business and livelihood, considering they honestly don't care whether you succeed or fail?

Only eBooks Matter

Making an ebook is super easy. Just like Amazon KDP is the lowest hanging fruit of publishing, ebooks are the lowest hanging fruit of making books to sell. These days, it's a one-click thing. You click, you get a file, and you upload that file. Done and done.

Creating paperbacks is harder. You need at least a little bit of knowledge about PDFs and printing to make them, and you need to either expand your ebook cover into a paperback or pay extra to have your designer make one for you. Audiobooks are even harder than that. Recording an audiobook yourself — if you're suited to it and good at it — requires specialized equipment and a lot of time. Having a narrator record it is expensive. What's more, many indie authors sell very few paperbacks and audiobooks, meaning the time and expense isn't worthwhile in the end.

So I understand if you've only ever sold ebooks. I really do. On a lot of levels, ebooks make the most sense. Just as I'd never promise that you'll sell big if you go wide, I'll never promise that your paperback and audiobooks will sell.

Still, just as an intellectual exercise, let's ask the question:

Do only ebooks matter? Is it true that readers aren't interested in paperbacks or audiobooks?

Personally, I earn *far* more on paperbacks than I do on ebooks. Some weekends, I'll sell $5000 or more in paperbacks, versus a pittance in ebooks. It's not easy, and hitting those numbers took time and was far from automatic. I had to be a perfect fit for my way of selling, and I've had work my ass off. But yeah. I can tell you from experience that paperbacks still matter.

And do you know what people ask me about constantly, when I'm out selling paperbacks? *Audiobooks.* The audio market is booming right now. It's growing like gangbusters.

Weird and interesting things can happen if you make non-ebook copies of your books available. It's almost worth the effort just to see what comes. The other day, my dashboard told me that 16 paperback copies of *Winter Break* sold randomly into the United Arab Emirates. What's that about? I have no idea how it happened. There must be a Dubai book club or something, and they're Truant fans. You can certainly read ebooks when you're in a book club (that's what my wife does), but with die-hard book people, it's a lot more common to want a book in hand.

But are indie authors thinking about book clubs?

Or libraries, with their collections of physical books?

Or local bookstores?

Nope. The dominant model focuses only on ebooks. Ebooks and Amazon. The rest is irrelevant.

Only America Matters

Americans tend to think we're the center of the universe. We understand intellectually that there are other countries out there, but they're concepts, not real places with real importance, filled with real people who matter ... and who might enjoy a good read now and again.

There's AMERICA. Then, if there's time, there's everywhere else. Charming places, those countries we hear about outside the good ol' US of A:

There's the country where hockey happens.

The country featured in *Breaking Bad*.

The country where people drink tea.

And isn't there a country that makes good bread and cheese? Oh, and the place waffles came from!

Obviously I'm being facetious. America-only thinking isn't just myopic and isolationist; it's also bad business. American authors (and plenty of non-American authors, which makes even less sense) have forsaken the rest of the world in the name of hitting the biggest, easiest target. It's lazy ... and, as we'll talk about very soon, it's ignoring an enormous number of people who are underserved and still love books.

There are around eight billion people in the world, and less than 400 million of them live in the US. What's more, a lot of people in non-US countries speak — and more importantly, *read* — English. You don't even have to translate your book to reach those readers. I mean, my book purchased by the Dubai book club isn't written in Arabic.

But hey: The biggest self-publishing market is the United States, so that's where most indie authors focus. Why? Because America is the biggest and easiest ... and, usually, the most in-your-face.

But think about this for a second:

Maybe Amazon is the biggest self-publishing market.

Maybe ebooks are the biggest self-published sellers.

Maybe America is the biggest self-publishing country.

But if you add them all up, and you consider that the vast, *vast* majority of self-publishing authors focus on American Amazon ebook buyers and nobody else, what percentage of the worldwide reading market *aren't* we reaching?

Is it smart to focus only one one small segment of the market?

Authors whine all the time about how hard it is to stand out amongst the competition. Maybe expand to places that naturally don't *have* much competition. Maybe get your head out of your butt and understand that there's a *whole world* out there, and most authors aren't even trying to reach it.

Building a Fanbase Is Overrated

There are readers, and then there are fans. They're not the same thing.

(There are also *True* Fans, who are the #1 goal for an Artisan Author, but we'll get to them later.)

Rapid Release, when it works, attracts a lot of *readers* — people who will read your book and then, hopefully, go on to read the rest of the series. It doesn't attract many *fans*, though: people who truly love your work and will seek it out, go back to it again and again, consume bonus content, and so on.

Fans sometimes show up for Rapid Release authors, but more often than not they're what I think of as "lite fans." These kinds of fans remember your name and love your books ... but they'll probably only read them if they're in Kindle Unlimited, and/or if you can churn them out fast enough to stay at the top of their TBR pile. "Lite" fans are like nodding acquaintances. They'll wave when they pass you and might exchange a few pleasantries about the weather if you find yourself in a supermarket line together, but they won't go out of their way to schedule time to see you.

Call me crazy, but I think it's a good idea to have fans as an author — *real* fans, not the lite variety.

Readers are great, but if they don't particularly care about you or your book once they're done with it, you'll have to do the hard work of attracting them again the next time you want their business. Non-fan readers are the hourly jobs of the author world: You do the work once and you get paid once, and if you want to get paid again, you have to work again. Fans, on the other hand, are the passive income of the author world: You earn their trust and love *once*, and then with minimal ongoing effort they'll buy from you forever.

Rapid Release readers are almost entirely transactional: They get hungry for something new to read, they find a book, they read that book, and then they get hungry again and find a new book. Your book is just one in a long chain of books, so they form no special attachment to any of them. It's not uncommon that after reading your book, a Rapid Release "whale" reader will forget it entirely. Two months later, they won't remember its name, its cover, its author ... or often, its plot.

Artisan readers tend to be more loyal, and more likely to form fandoms. Because they're after quality more than quantity, they absorb more of what they read. They get to know the characters, the story, and eventually the style of the author. In other words, they transition easily from simple readers to fans.

You'll get less transactional behavior from fans. Each purchase is a careful choice: they think long and hard rather than grabbing the next cool-looking book that crosses their screen. Fans say *No* to a lot of books because they're sparing with their *Yesses*. When you have fans, it means that folks out there are waiting for an excuse to say *Yes* to you.

The dominant model acts like building a fanbase is overrated — in part because the go-go crowd can't afford much time to create and nurture readers into fans, but also because the readers those authors attract just aren't wired that way.

Treating fandom as optional is just one more way that Rapid Release is built on unstable ground. You've already given Amazon control over your business and curated a readership that's almost entirely in one country, in one small slice of the reader ecosystem. You've already cut out all diversification, hoping that the pastures that are green for you today will stay green forever. You've already spent all your time attracting customers who want things free, cheap, and fast. So why bother shooting for loyalty from your readers? Why shoot for fans?

Artisan Authors need fans. Our businesses are based on them. So for Artisans like us, this one is especially dumb.

It'll Stay This Way Forever!

Ah, yes. The *coup de grace*. This section is the hammer that rams home the stupidity of the current system for all but a small group of publishing outliers.

Throughout this section, I've tried my best to be fair. If we were talking about my own personal opinions, I would have said that every logical consequence of Rapid Release that we just talked about is dumb — no qualifiers, full stop. But hey, all authors are different. We've already talked about that. What's dumb for me is smart for someone else. So in writing this chapter, I've tried to give the Rapid Release crowd the benefit of the doubt.

Rapid Release absolutely can work for some people — and for those people, it doesn't matter that the system requires quantity over quality, that they must always write to market, that they find ways of making money that nullifies the whole "cheap customers" thing, and so on. For people who are truly suited for Rapid Release publishing, none of the statements I just made are *actually* dumb. Dumb for us, but for authors who go all-in and work the system to its utmost, Rapid Release and all its tenets can earn a fortune.

For now.

The one thing I have a hard time explaining away — the single dumb consequence of Rapid Release on which I can't give benefit of doubt — is its unstated assumption that nothing will ever change. Meaning this: You might be killing it in KU right now by publishing a book every two or three weeks. It might suit your personality and style perfectly. *But are you planning to do it forever?*

Because friend, you're building no equity at all.

Beyond the books themselves, the faster-faster approach doesn't create lasting assets — assets like fan loyalty (their willingness to buy from you even if they get distracted by another author), the earned ability to price higher (so you can make a living beyond page reads), direct connections to fans and a reason for them to talk to you (so they'll follow you if Amazon changed or shut down its book business), or diversity of offerings (so your income wouldn't drop to zero if something happened to the Amazon-only, America-only, ebook-only marketplace).

Amazon could shut down your KDP account or block all of your books. It's happened before. Sometimes, they won't tell you what went wrong when it does, so you have to guess until you get the right answer. I've been a full-time professional author since 2012, and in that time I've seen the publishing sky fall several times. It would be funny to watch if it wasn't so tragic: all these authors panicking like Chicken Little, wondering if their careers are over. You're blind if you think it hasn't happened before. You're naive if you think it'll never happen again.

But maybe I'm wrong. That could happen, right? I could just be *wrong*, and that means you'll be safe. If I'm wrong about things changing, you can keep operating under stupid-as-hell business rules and they'll never turn around and bite you with the scope of their abject and total dumbness.

Right?

Well, let's pretend and see.

Let's just pretend for a second that Amazon will never change, that the American ebook market will kill it forever, that you won't be swallowed by competitors or AI, and you won't do something innocent to get your KDP account banned. Let's pretend you're a Rapid Release author who's bathing every day in Moet and

Benjamins, and you've got a deal with the Devil that makes you certain that nothing about your situation will ever change due to outside forces.

Okay. Well, then what about *you*? Even if *the situation* stays the same, will *you* stay the same?

I know a lot of Rapid Release authors who aren't around anymore. Conversely, I know almost none with any sort of track record who still are. In practice, everyone burns out eventually. You might be able to keep the KU machine running and earning fat stacks, but we all know the machine will stop the second you stop turning its crank. If you stop rapid-firing books, the machine will stop giving you money.

So, sure: Your business will, in this particular thought experiment, work as long as you want to keep working it. But how long will that be?

I honestly want to know. I look at the hair-on-fire, wild-eyed Rapid Release authors who can't slow down and I wonder: *Do they plan to do this for the rest of their lives?* Are they counting on one day reaching a plateau wherein the principles that are so dumb outside of Rapid Release suddenly start making sense in the real world? Do they think they can convert cheap customers into higher-paying customers? Or are they just trying to work hard now, amass a nest egg, then one day walk away and let it all die?

Yes, I can give the benefit of the doubt. I can allow that everything I've insulted in this chapter still works for someone, and that in their hands, it's not dumb at all. But even so, what comes next? Will they hire ghostwriters to take over once they burn out? Lean on AI? What's the endgame, especially considering the fact that everything that's problematic today (especially competition and AI) will only get worse over time?

I'm willing to believe that smart, hard-working people can make Rapid Release work. What I don't believe for a second is that it will work for long.

There's no margin of error in the system. They're like a rocket car burning along at three hundred miles per hour, but all it would take to end them would be one small fault in the structure. One tiny pebble on the road. One little hitch in the engine. Rocket cars have a limited lifespan. You can't go at three hundred miles per hour forever, on and on until eternity.

I don't know about you, but I want a *sustainable* business — one I can happily and comfortably work in until the day I die. But that kind of business takes sanity. It has to operate like a real business instead of a short-term profit scheme.

Now that we've taken our tour of the past and explored the status quo, it's time to leave all of that behind. It's time to stop looking at all of the *insensible-for-most-authors* ways of doing things, and instead look at the alternative.

We've been through the muck in this first part, my friends, but I promise that skies are brighter from here on out. Goodbye and good riddance to the pressure-cooker treadmill that's become our ill-suited, house-of-cards norm. It's time now to explore the alternative — and *man oh man*, you have no idea what amazing revelations are ahead for you.

You *can* be happy and fulfilled as an author. You *can* make a side hustle or even a full-time living without Rapid Release, or Kindle Unlimited's reindeer games ... for once seeing Amazon royalties as a bonus rather than the end-all be-all to make your mortgage payment.

It's time, now, to explore the Artisan Author way.

The old rules are out.

A whole new world is in.

We're about to enter this book's second part ... and let the unbrainwashing begin.

Part Two
The Way of the Artisan Author

Chapter 3

Make Publishing Non-Dumb Again

When people ask for my best tips as an industry veteran, I bore the living hell out of them.

I say, "Write great books that people love."

I say, "Be nice to the readers you meet." Or ideally: "Be nice to everyone."

I say, "Answer readers when they send you emails."

I say, "Be professional, and do what you say you'll do."

When the frustrated person I'm talking to then tells me, *Yeah, yeah, I know all of that. What I want to know is how to make more sales!*, I say:

"If you want more sales, let more people know about your books and why they're cool."

Yeah, yeah ... but where? How? What's the trick? Do I need to be on TikTok? Do I need to run ads? Should I switch email marketing software? I hear list swaps and group promotions are a big deal. Should I do those? Should my books be shorter and faster-paced? Which keywords should I use? Should I collaborate with someone more popular? What genres are hot right now? Should I be in Kindle Unlimited? Should I run a Kickstarter? Should I offer different versions of my book cover? Should I push harder for reviews? Should I make my book free for a while?

And I'll answer, "Sure. You do you."

The thing nobody wants to hear is that there's no real answer to those questions. A lot of how-to is taught on the basis of something always working, but in truth the answer to *any* how-to or should-I question is "it depends." It depends on your books; it depends on you as an author; it depends on your customers; it depends on your brand; it depends on what you've done and said in the past and where you want to go in the future. It depends on your risk tolerance and whether or not setbacks bounce off of or shut you down. But nobody talks about how much *depends*, because when you say "it depends" too much as an educator, people stop buying the Easy Button you're selling. That's why a key focus of this book isn't about *what to do*, but instead to get you thinking deeply about *who you are and where you stand* ... or, in other words, on determining exactly what "it depends on" for you.

That's the bad news about being an Artisan Author: *There's no one clear path*. I'm sorry, but I can't draw you a sure-fire map. Instead, you'll actually have to think, experiment, and employ a bit of trial and error before you discover what truly works for you.

But it's also good news, because in reality, nobody believes in Easy Buttons anyway. We *want* them, but we don't actually believe in them deep down. Not at the core of our beings, where our deepest knowledge lives. When we chase Easy Buttons, we're operating on hope ... but hope is vapor; hope is smoke and mirrors; hope is powerlessness crossing its fingers and hoping someone else will come along to save it. But do you really want to be powerless in your author career? Do you really want to buy into "the newest and greatest thing" and then just *hope* it works despite your smarter self insisting it never will?

We can't achieve things that we don't actually believe. We can't work tirelessly and patiently toward an end that we sort of doubt will actually arrive. When you buy into some ridiculous, one-size-fits all Easy Button of a get-rich-quick scheme, you shut off your natural intelligence and ability and hand everything over to lunacy instead. Do you really think *you* don't know that *you* are doing something that will probably never work? Come on. You're smarter than that.

We can, however, achieve things that we *do* believe deep down. Once you truly grasp that selling books is and has always been boringly simple (not *easy*, but *simple*), you'll finally become internally coherent. The logical part of your brain will finally be able to work with its aspirational part for a change, instead of exasperatedly chasing it around as it embarks on yet another crazy hairbrained scheme.

Let's stop treating our logical brains as if they're stupid. They're not. Let's work *with* logic for a change, rather than thinking we're the one person out there who can defy it.

The weird, backwards strength of the Artisan Author approach is that it's boring, and hence completely believable.

Just like me, you'll soon be boring your friends to death when you tell them about being an Artisan Author. They'll ask, "How do you make money selling books?" and you'll say, "Through the patient and persistent application of tried-and-true principles that have always worked."

BOOOORING! There's no worse party-killer than sensible thinking.

They'll walk away, annoyed that your answer wasn't about a new social media tactic that ABSOLUTELY WORKS IMMEDIATELY FOR EVERYONE ALL THE TIME. You, on the other hand, will get back to work, actually believing for a change that what you're doing is sensible. You'll understand that what we do here isn't flashy at all, but is instead based on foundational stuff that never stopped being true — not even when it was buried under the bullshit ninja tricks that spent the last few years smothering the author world to death.

Let's try something, you and I.

As a thought experiment, let's set the last chapter's history aside for a moment. Just forget all about it. In fact, go ahead and forget everything else you know about self-publishing while you're at it. Nothing you've ever read, or heard, or seen, or been advised about writing and publishing exists right now. Make your mind a clean slate for a moment — a *tabula rasa*, as John Locke (no, not *that* John Locke) called it.

Okay. Now, as someone who knows nothing at all about selling books, pretend you have a book you want to sell. You wrote it, but without considering its marketability. You aren't so *rasa* that you forgot how to write, so it's a great book ... but it came from your artful heart, not your businessperson's brain.

How *would* you sell that book, with no knowledge of how to do so?

Well, the first thing would be to find someone who likes to read, right? Someone with at least twenty bucks or so of disposable income. No matter how vacant we are, that seems like a logical place to start.

Then, you'd tell them about the story. Assuming you *like* the story (which you should; otherwise, why did you write it?), you'd be bright-eyed and enthusiastic. You'd tell it with heart. With fervor. And sure, your introversion might get in the way for a while, but once you got into a groove, you'd have no trouble. You'd tell your audience about the cool twists, the amazing characters, and some of the other whiz-bang that inspired you to put it all down in the first place.

Eventually, you'd find a few readers who thought the story sounded interesting. More, though, they'd find *you and your passion for the story* interesting. And so they'd pull out their wallets, and they'd risk the cover price to give your story a shot — partly because you described a story that intrigues them, but partly because of the energy you clearly put into it.

Now: Was that an interesting thought experiment? I hope so, because it's the core truth of how books get sold. That simple, brainless, no-ninja-tricks approach is all that truly matters in the end.

Not the latest and greatest tactic being talked about in online writer groups.

Not ads.

Not social media.

Not writing to market, or refusing to write to market, or being wide, or being exclusive to Amazon, or being an Artisan Author. What matters is a reader, a writer, and interest shared between them. Nothing else. And sure: Tactics *do* enter the picture at some point to help authors sell better, but that's secondary, not primary. A tactic only works when it serves a deeper, more core ideal.

Social media works if it augments your natural style of sharing. Ads work when you're able to use them to put your book in front of more of the right readers in a way that works with your brain. Hell, Rapid Release works for plenty of authors, but only because it delivers the reading experience those readers want: high frequency, a specific style and content they can count on, and low prices. *Every* tactic is a vehicle for some deep and dead-simple core truth, not magic that stands on its own and therefore works for everyone all the time.

This is why I tell people "It depends." It's why, when I'm asked about my own strategies, I bore people. I have nothing mindblowing to share, and that includes the information in this book. I mean ... I have no love for Rapid Release, but should you use it? Well, that depends. It depends on the kind of author you are and the kind of readers you want to serve. *I* don't want to be that kind of author or serve those kinds of readers, so it's not for me. But is it for you? I doubt it, if you've read this far. But who knows?

Being an Artisan Author might feel revolutionary to some people, but that's only because so much pointless bullshit has accumulated between us, as authors, and the readers we serve. See through the bullshit, and you'll see the exact same elements that are at the core of *any* strategy that works for at least one author.

We write. They read. We're human and they're human. Humans want experiences, and good books deliver experiences. Humans want connection — if not to other people, then to a purpose, an ideal, or a temporary escape. Humans want to feel that they matter, too, which is why books that validate their experience tend to be loved ... and why the best tool in my fan-building toolkit is simply answering reader emails. If you don't answer emails and are successful anyway, it's because you're validating your unique fans in other ways: delivering connection through a fictional worldview they share, or delivering vicarious love in the pages of a romance novel.

No matter what approach you take to being an author, there are only a few root truths in play. We tend to forget that because being an author is hard and lonely, and clinging to someone else's strategy gives you company and a plan to follow. Problems come, though, when we follow without thinking. Someone else isn't you, so why would their strategy work for you? If their way *depends* on them, why wouldn't it also *depend* on you?

Let's all take a deep breath and back away from every strategy there is (yours, mine, other authors', or the strategies peddled as universal truth in your author group) and actually think for a second.

Think about you, and your work.

Think about the tactic you're considering, and its pros and cons — not universally, but to you and your career as individuals.

And most important of all, think about the core truths we discussed back when you were pretending to be a tabula rasa: about how *putting the right book in front of the right reader in exactly the right way at the right time* is all that matters. No one technique "works." What "works" is using *any* technique that best puts your book in front of the right reader in exactly the right way at the right time. What works is *anything* that, unique to you and your work, best teases and then delivers the experience that your specific readers are looking for.

The author community tends to focus on methods, which is a fair first step in deciding what to do. The problem is that few authors take the second step, which is the critical thinking described above. Instead, we get dogmatic. We decide — and then declare to others — that *this one thing* is THE WAY success gets done.

Will this method work? you ask.

And if you're smart, the answer should be: *It depends on me. It depends on my readers. It depends on whether that method, in my hands and delivered to my readers, will serve the core truths that underly everything. Will this method deliver the experience those readers want?*

No? Well, then you'll need to change yourself or your readers ... or find another method.

But we don't do that. We follow blindly. *Oh, I need to run Facebook ads. Oh, I need to write to market. Oh, I need to be on Instagram.* None of those things are true. What you need is to match your unique reader's needs to your unique writer's talent and disposition to the methods you employ. Maybe that *will* end up meaning Facebook ads, or writing to market, or being on Instagram ... or maybe it won't. Nothing is automatically right, and nothing is automatically wrong. *It depends.*

Here's another question: Which road should you take to drive from New York to Los Angeles?

Funny how nobody's dogmatic about roads, even though it's the exact same idea. *Which road?* Well, that depends. Do you want to avoid tolls? Take the scenic route? Get there as fast as possible? Are you a nervous driver or someone who handles high speed and gridlock with ease? Do you care about the world's largest ball of string? Because if not, why would you ever take that road?

And so at this point, we have to ask: *Is being an Artisan Author better than Rapid Release?*

Sure. Yes. No. Because *it depends.*

It depends even here, in this book. Even here, where Rapid Release is discussed as if it's a vortex of doom. Even in my mind — a guy who wouldn't do Rapid Release if his ass was on fire and Kindle Unlimited readers held the only bucket of water.

But it *does* depend. It's not *wrong*. It's just wrong *for us,* here in Artisan land.

If Rapid Release is perfect for you, and works great for you, and you've duly and critically considered its pros and cons and remained focused on the core truths of publishing instead of its secondary methods and dogma, then godspeed. You, oh Rapid Release author, should definitely keep doing you.

But for the rest of us — now that it's just Artisans up in this joint — let's talk about the truths of the world as we see them ... which are pretty different things from what Rapid Release says are true.

Quality Matters More Than Quantity

Here's a choice for you. You can have one of two things: Something good, or something that's crap. Which do you choose?

Quality always matters. *Always.* Even in Rapid Release (where quantity takes priority), quality is still a thing. The definition of "quality" might change from instance to instance, but it's pretty much universally true that given a choice, people want something good more than they want something bad.

In coming chapters, I'll explain how Artisan Authors can successfully put quality first — how we can flip the script so that better-than-average books are able to command better-than-average prices. Right now, though, your head might still be stuck in the old world. You might be thinking that taking the time to make better books would be awesome but pointless. In that old world, you can make the greatest books in the world ... but good luck finding people willing to pay more for them.

I promise you, those people exist. You just have to stop thinking like a Rapid Release author before you can begin to see them. You have to stop using that same old pool of readers — the one that 95% of self-published authors try to attract — as your frame of reference. Because true: *Those* readers *won't* pay more for quality beyond a certain point. If you keep fishing in the same old waters using the same old techniques and lures, you're going to keep catching fish who have only a middle-of-the-road bar for their books.

(Apparently these are smart fish, with their varied reading tastes. I'm going to stick with the metaphor anyway because the idea of fish reading books is hilarious to me.)

We'll talk a lot about how to fish in higher-quality waters later on, but for now let's just accept one simple truth: that in the real world, with all other things being equal, *quality stuff is better than crappy stuff.*

Artisan Authors know this. We don't just focus on making quality books because we want to — though as Artisans, we *do* want to. Nope, we do it because our new fish demand it. They won't accept garbage or slop, and if they care about quantity or speed at all, those cares are a distant second to greatness.

These are very smart and discerning fish, you know. They have little fish glasses and everything.

Price What You're Worth With Your Head Held High

It drives me crazy to see authors work their butts off to make great books, then get skittish about pricing those books as if they were actually valuable. So they price their books for cheap or free, or they put them in KU so readers can borrow them — not because it's a good strategy for them, but because they have imposter syndrome and can't imagine anyone actually paying for what they made.

There's so much fear in pricing. I get it, but if I can be real with you for a second, I'd like to kindly ask you to knock it the fuck off.

You're an artist. You're braver than most people. You dug deep inside yourself, dredged up your innermost thoughts and emotions, and put them on display in story form for the whole world to see. Who does that? Don't you think you should be paid well, if someone wants to read it?

Your pricing should be proud. It should say to the world, "If you want this, here's what it's worth and not a penny less. If you don't want to pay, that's cool ... but you don't get to read it if you don't."

I know. That's scary. You're worried that given such a hardline stance, everyone will choose the latter and nobody will ever buy. That's why artists flinch. It's why they cave and discount their books without a win-win marketing reason to do so. But how does that look to a reader?

I think this paperback is worth $25.
Not interested? Okay, the ebook version is only $5.99.
Still not interested? Well, what if it was $2.99?
99 cents?
Okay, okay ... will you please please PRETTY PLEASE read it if I make it free?

It's undignified. It's also a stupid business strategy for Artisans like us, because we don't have Rapid Release volume, speed, and personalities to make long-term cheapness work for us. As Artisan Authors, pricing cheap or free by default is a great way to end up losing.

Listen: *You made something worthwhile, and you deserve to be paid for it.* No matter what you charge for your book, unless you're delusional, it's going to cost less than your reader's cell phone bill. Hell, it'll probably cost less than their second mocha Frappuccino for the day. If readers balk at prices, an Artisan Author stands up tall and says, "Well, then go read something else." You have to be willing to say no — not to individuals, but to the market.

The dirty secret that nobody talks about is that *the indignity most writers exude has a stink to it that Artisan buyers want nothing to do with.* The best buyers out there see your desperation and lack of a spine as repugnant. If you come across as desperate and willing to sell cheap to make a deal, you're more likely to ruin an Artisan sale than to close it.

One thing to internalize as you embark on the Artisan Author journey is that Artisan readers are buying something different than non-Artisan readers. Specifically, they're not just buying something to read; they're buying a connection to the author behind it — something that's true whether they ever talk to you or not. They *want* to spend more on what they buy, because they want to prove to themselves that they support artists, believe in handmade items, and prefer individuals to big businesses. If you cheap out — if you act like they're doing you a favor by reading your book and price like an apology — you rob your Artisan reader of all of those things. Suddenly, they're not buying something that feels like quality. Suddenly they're not supporting an artist ... at least not very much. Suddenly, they might as well be a Walmart shopper looking for the next Blue Light Special.

(And yes, I know Blue Light Specials were a K-Mart thing (RIP) and that many readers won't have any more knowledge of them than they did about my "Where's the beef?" joke from earlier. But hey: I'm an artist and I'll say what I want.)

The more you stand behind your book, the more Artisan readers will want it. The more *you* act like that book isn't worth much, however, the *less* they'll want it.

The Majority is Not the Majority

Here's a truth that prevailing industry wisdom either doesn't understand or consciously ignores: *Targeting the majority actually means ignoring most readers.*

I've heard the arguments again and again: *If you want to make it as an indie author, you should focus on Amazon readers who live primarily in America, ideally in Kindle Unlimited and definitely with a focus on ebooks — or maybe exclusively on ebooks. That's the biggest pool of readers, so paying attention to other pools won't give you enough bang to justify your buck.*

It sounds right on the surface, but dig deeper and you'll quickly see how wrong it is.

"The biggest single pool of readers" is not the same thing as "*most* readers." In truth, Amazon-KU-ebook isn't the majority, even though we act like it is. It's not even close. From a strict numbers perspective — and you can do your own research and verify, if you'd like — there are far more readers in the world *outside* of the KU ebook pool than inside it. All you need to do, to see why, is to add up everything that's not KU ebooks. You probably won't sell a ton of paperbacks into Liechtenstein, for instance, but you *could* sell a ton of books in all non-US countries combined (including Liechtenstein), in all formats, on all platforms and places, if you focused on them.

Add up all the minorities, in other words, and you'll see that once combined, they dwarf the so-called majority.

The fact that something is called "the majority" doesn't actually make it a *true* majority, see. If 35% of all people are A, 15% are B, and there are 10% each of C, D, E, F, and G, you'd be tempted to aim for the 35% because you suck at math and think 35% is the same as *most*. But no. In this example, you're making a decision to focus on only about 1/3 of all people while ignoring the remaining 65%. See how math has failed you?

The question, then, is whether you should focus on any one of those little markets individually in order to tap the whole. That depends, because the answer to *everything* is "it depends." All I'll say there's a lot of potential out there in the world — a *vast majority* of potential, in fact — that almost everyone else is completely ignoring.

Anyone see opportunity in that? Anyone? Anyone?

Diversification is Good Business

Exclusivity without a plan is dumb. There are cases where it can work, but you have to have a larger strategy in place to *make* it work. Most authors have no such strategy. They just say, "Here,

Amazon! Control my future for me!" and walk away, hoping their flagrant denial of the way all other business is done won't bite them the way it bites everyone else.

Pretend I make hammers. So I go to the biggest home improvement shop in town — the shop through which all the other hammer-makers sell their hammers — and make a deal to sell my hammers in their stores. They'll put my hammers in with the thousands of other hammers sold there, and for the privilege, they make me promise I won't sell my hammers anywhere else. After this brilliant deal is completed, my next strategic step is to go home and begin hoping desperately, possibly while in the fetal position.

Sounds smart, right?

Um ... not so much.

Who works that way? As a consumer, it'd really piss me off. Maybe I'm in the market for a good hammer, but I like shopping local and would have to go to the mega-chain if I want yours. Or maybe I'm in a country the mega-chain doesn't serve. Hell, that's basically flipping me the bird. It's like announcing to the world that my country and I simply don't matter.

As an Artisan Author, you'll actually think the way most companies think instead of flying in the face of good business. You'll make your book available everywhere you can. You'll lose access to Amazon's promotional tricks, but you're here because you're tired of playing by their rules, aren't you? A lot of the best Artisan Authors I know barely pay attention to their Amazon sales. I know several who sell big from their own websites or in person (after years of building up to it, so wipe that get-rich-quick smile from your face, dear reader) but consider their Amazon sales to be "embarrassing." Amazon just isn't their jam, because their ideal readers don't shop there.

Stop bowing to Amazon, and stop being afraid you'll lose their favor. Amazon isn't in charge of your art. *You* are.

Isn't it liberating to consider a world where you could survive without them if you had to?

Sustainability Matters

The best thing about the Artisan approach is its sense of freedom. Once you stop playing the usual inside-the-lines game and stop relying only on its income channels, there will come a moment when something clicks and a world of possibilities cracks wide open for you. You won't instantly become a bestseller, but you will wake up with a liberating epiphany. All of a sudden, you'll realize you have freedoms you'd forgotten were possible.

One is the freedom to write what you want, as long as it's good and true to you and your style — meaning it's something your loyal readers (not just any old readers) will enjoy.

The other is the freedom to have a sustainable future.

Rapid Release flies in the face of sustainability. It ignores it, knowing burnout is always a bad day away, and keeps on chugging anyway. Rapid Release treats the inevitable failure of sustainability the way most people treat death: We all know it's coming, but we close our eyes every day and pretend it might not.

The need for sustainability is real. Nobody can keep running on empty forever — not while staying happy and sane, they can't.

All things being equal, you'll have more joy as an Artisan Author than you would otherwise. Maybe you'll sell more and maybe you won't ... but unlike all the stressed-out, red-eyed authors around you, you'll have bought yourself enough time in this business to persist until something works.

The reason the Artisan approach is sustainable is because you don't have to publish at rapid-fire speeds forever in order to survive. Instead, you can slow down. You can publish fast if you want to, but you absolutely don't have to.

I published fast (but not Rapid Release) for a long time, then slowed down to handle some other things. My readers stuck with me. They'll also stick with me when, soon enough, I ramp back up again.

There's a reason that Artisan Authors can slow down and take breaks whereas Rapid Release authors usually can't. It has to do with the different kinds of readers the two approaches attract, and the different ways that each approach connects with those readers. That, plus the fact that we haven't made algorithms our masters. We stand proud instead, refusing to let machines tell us what to do.

Sustainability means the freedom to not rush. To be patient.

Given enough time, long-term thinkers always win.

Loyal Fans Make You Bulletproof

Readers who demand Rapid Release typically only stay interested in your books for as long as those books are in front of them. If you take a break and your books leave their sphere of goldfish-like attention, though, good luck recapturing them.

That's not how Artisan readers think. Artisan readers have long attention spans and more loyalty to the authors they enjoy. Unlike Rapid Release readers, Artisan readers won't forget you the second you move out of sight. And remember: As an Artisan Author, your goal isn't to attract individual sales anyway, as epitomized by the *what-have-you-done-for-me-lately* Rapid Release culture. It's to create True Fans, who we'll talk about in the next chapter — and that's an entirely different ballgame. A *better* ballgame for authors like us.

True Fans are sticky. Rapid Release readers aren't, so you have to either trust Amazon's algorithms to keep them on the hook for you (you know: *Amazon?* That enormous company with goals that sometimes conflict with yours?) or entice them anew every single time.

Fan-building as an Artisan Author, on the other hand, is a lot like making friends. Maybe you get to know your fans directly like I sometimes do, or maybe your books and online presence are just so great and Artisany that fans "make friends" with your body of work instead. Either way, they're creating a bond instead of pushing through a one-and-done transaction before moving on to the next one-and-done transaction. It's inherently a more stable approach.

Customers come and go, but friends — meaning Artisan fans — stick around. A customer has to be re-found and lured back with a coupon after too much time away, but friends just need a reminder that you're ready to hang out again. That's why taking the time and effort to create loyal fans will make you bulletproof as an author: because once you have enough fans who love *you* instead of *the next book Amazon puts in front of them*, that relationship becomes portable and completely independent of Amazon or anywhere else. In the end, you can take your fans' love anywhere.

So: What if Amazon does something stupid to ruin your sales?

No problem. Just take your friends and go play somewhere else.

Chapter 4

Change Your Paradigm, Change Your World

There's a great bit in *Star Trek 2: The Wrath of Khan* (starring Ricardo Montalban, after whom my dog is named) called "The Kobayashi Maru."

In the *Star Trek* world, as part of their training, Starfleet cadets go through a tactical simulation in which they play the role of a captain. A call comes to save a civilian ship named the *Kobayashi Maru*, stranded in the neutral zone between Starfleet territory and territory controlled by their arch enemies, the Klingons.

In the simulation, these cadets-as-captains have two options: They can enter the neutral zone and fight the Klingons attacking the ship, totally outnumbered and outgunned, and try to save it ... or they can abandon the ship and allow it to be destroyed.

The game is rigged, though. If they try to save the *Kobayashi Maru*, *both* ships are destroyed. If they don't intervene, the *Maru* is destroyed while the cadet's ship watches. There's no way to win. It's meant to be a test of a cadet's mettle, to see how they handle a no-win scenario.

But the famous James T. Kirk — a rulebreaker if ever there was one — cheats. He hacks in and reprograms the simulation so it's possible to save the ship. His justification? "I don't believe in no-win scenarios."

I've invoked the *Kobayashi Maru* many times throughout my professional life — not because I'm trying to save spaceships, but because I want to keep in mind what the story represents. As my good friend and fellow rulebreaker Jon Morrow says, *If you can't win the game, change the rules.*

After reading what I've presented so far in this book, you might be full of objections. You might like the idea of being an Artisan Author (defying KU's rules, pricing what you're worth, and more) but can't see how it's possible.

If I price too high, people won't buy, you might think.

I don't want to pander to Amazon's algorithms ... but without them, how will I find readers?

I love the idea of writing more slowly, but how can I keep readers interested between releases? They'll forget me, won't they?

I get why you're asking. I understand why you have doubts — why as compelling as the Artisan Author Way might look, it just doesn't seem to jibe with reality. But if that's how you feel, let me ask you a question right back: *Which reality are we talking about?*

Are you still playing the original Kobayashi Maru, trying in vain to save a doomed ship? Or are you instead considering a *different* game with *different* rules — a game where maybe you *can* save the ship like Kirk did ... or maybe it's a game where the ship doesn't exist in the first place? In the game we're about to start playing, what if none of the "truths" upon which you've been basing your author career apply at all?

Seen through the "usual" lens, you're right; the Artisan approach *doesn't* make sense. If you see Amazon as your best or only option, believe that all readers buy based on price, and only look to what others say about acquiring readers, then you're right: The Artisan Way *won't* work. It flies in the face of the typical indie author's common sense.

But you shouldn't be looking through that old lens anymore. You should be looking through the lens of our changed game instead: a Kobayashi Maru where the rules are different, and in which different things are possible.

In this chapter, I'll show you the rules of the new world of publishing — although to be clear, there's nothing "new" about it. The way Artisan Authors sell books today is the same way artisans of all stripes have been selling since artisandom began. We're not forging new ground here. We're simply pulling our heads out of unreasonable gold-rush clouds and walking the sensible path that's been down here on Planet Earth all along.

You are no longer in the old, no-win scenario. Out here with rulebreakers like James Tiberius Kirk, we're artists. We're renegades. We've completely changed venues. We've altered our programming, the way Kirk altered his.

Consider this for a second:

When movies were new, theaters would show a film of a train steaming toward the camera. When audiences saw it, they'd scream and jump out of the way. Why? Because they were sure the train was going to hit them. The idea of a literal train was all that made sense to those audiences, because real trains were the only things that looked like trains.

Only after people began to grasp the idea of *a recorded image* did they see what was happening: It wasn't a real train; it was film of one. Before then, "film" wasn't a thing. There *were* no moving recorded images. If you saw a train, it had to be a real train. And so, the question people asked when they saw one onscreen was, "How did that train get into the theater?" "A recording of a train" simply wasn't in their vocabulary ... any more than "customers who barely care what a book costs" might not yet be in yours.

When you're an Artisan Author, Amazon only matters if you want it to.

When you're an Artisan Author, readers won't forget you if you take a break. They'll stand ready to buy whatever you sell no matter however long it takes, as long as you've kept them in the loop.

Artisan Authors don't care about becoming bestsellers. It'd be nice if your sales blew up, but it's definitely not necessary. My own ideal is "cult fame." I'd rather be a hip cult hit (like *Donnie Darko*) than a summer blockbuster (like a Marvel movie.)

Stop seeing the world the way Rapid Release sees it. We're playing by a whole new set of rules, baby. If you want to continue on this Artisan journey, you'll need to unlearn what you *think* you know so there'll be room for something new.

You don't need to play by the old rules of publishing anymore. How liberating is that? Let most authors do their thing over there, in the crowded pressure cooker. You, on the other hand, can begin playing a better game.

You're among artists now. And among the artists, we make our own damn rules.

The Bookstore of You

The biggest question that aspiring authors ask is how to write a book. To them, an author with even one finished book is a magician. The folks who desperately want to tell their story — but haven't yet — see the act of writing as beautiful voodoo. How could anyone take the complex and layered fantasy they see inside their head and make it real with words? What alchemy is this, to use letters and ink (or e-ink) to transport an entire world from the author's mind into the minds of readers?

The biggest question that *published* authors ask, on the other hand, is how to sell more books. Once our book becomes a product, marketing boots hit the floor and we go into salesperson mode whether we're comfortable there or not. For a lot of authors, the book remains a precious piece of their soul, and they can't be objective enough to sell it. For others — those who are best at selling — the book becomes a cold, hard product that must be tweaked and manipulated until it fits into the right niche, positioned just so to attract buyers in any way possible.

Traditionally published authors can avoid the issue entirely if they want. They can sit back and hope the publisher will handle all the selling, especially since most trad deals severely limit self-marketing options anyway. Independent authors like us, on the other hand, have to wear two hats: one for creation, and one for selling. We have no choice but to handle marketing, if we want to be successful. If *we* don't find a way to sell our books, nobody will.

Which venues and tools should you use for your promotions? How often should you plug your book, and in what way?

Should you spend money to advertise? How much? Which ads work best, and how long does it take for them to show profits ... if they ever do?

Worst of all, how can you possibly stand out in this day and age? More books were published in the past few years than in all of prior history, making your book one of competing millions. Between authors being told that Rapid Release is the only way to survive and the rising tide of AI-written books, the "standing out" problem isn't going to get better any time soon.

But what if you didn't *need* to stand out? What if you *had* no competition, no matter how many other books are published around you?

What if instead of fighting to be seen, your book was seen from its inception? What if instead of starting from obscurity, your book began its published life already in the spotlight?

I call this way of thinking about bookselling — your first lesson in our changed paradigm — "The Bookstore of You."

Close your eyes for a second. (Or maybe read all of this first and *then* close your eyes, unless you're reading in Braille.) I'd like to paint you a picture.

Imagine walking into a bookstore in your town. It's a small place: cozy and intimate, maybe with a little sitting area of overstuffed chairs and soft incandescent lighting. It smells of paper and old vellum. And it's dead quiet, save the soporific sound of turning pages.

In this bookstore, only your books are sold.

There's no James Patterson. No Sarah J. Maas. No Stephen

King. No summer reading books assigned for kids going back to school in the fall ... unless, of course, they've been assigned something you wrote.

If you only have one book, that book is on every row and endcap. If you have many, your catalog fills the shelves. If you're an Artisan Author who doesn't care about sticking to one genre, you might even have your own sections: sci-fi here, thrillers here, romance over here.

Your book covers are on every poster. You're on every recommended reading list. Every Staff Pick is one of yours, and if you were to ask the clerk for their new favorite, you'd get a gushing review of the last thing you wrote. Everyone is talking about you in the talking spots, eager to learn how the last book's cliffhanger will resolve.

Now let me ask you a question: How hard would it be to stand out in *that* store? How much would you need to advertise and market to the people who shop *there*? How hard would you have to push to sell? You wouldn't, obviously ... because in the Bookstore of You, everyone's *already* sold on your work. They didn't discover you randomly while browsing online, then had to be convinced to buy. No, these people "bought" in advance. They didn't go into Barnes & Noble to search around until they found a new book. Instead, they walked right into The Bookstore of You, knowing in advance which author they wanted to read.

As an Artisan Author, the usual promotional strategy flips entirely on its head. You'll still do outreach and marketing, but the goal is no longer to sell individual books to cold traffic. The goal, rather, is to sell them on *you*.

It's harder, yes.

It's slower, yes.

But if you put in the time to make it work, it makes you indestructible. How hard is it to get readers to buy your next book if The Bookstore of You is the first place they shop? How hard do you have to work to sell anything if readers, when they're ready for a new book, look *you* up instead of browsing Amazon? How much easier would life be if you didn't have to worry about keywords or placement or algorithmic visibility ... because the only search term that matters is your name?

When you market like an Artisan Author, you sell up front, sell big-picture, and put in the time to make those early bonds stick. A tiny percentage of the effort is done *en masse:* running ads, hitting social media and all the other things most authors do. You'll do some of those things, yes ... but instead of working hard to sell a single book now and then repeating it all from scratch when the sequel comes out, your careful nurturing will have created a growing snowball of people who no longer need to be sold.

Personally, I really like selling books in person. It's the ultimate *put-yourself-out-there, woo-people-who've-never-heard-of-you-before* move, but I like it because every time someone comes over and I talk to them face-to-face, I'm starting the process of creating a long-term, high-value bond. It's the opposite of leverage. Those interactions literally happen one person at a time, and I often talk to any given reader for five or ten minutes.

You read that right: *Ten minutes to reach just one person.* That's a lot more work than running a Facebook ad or Bookbub Featured Deal, where you reach thousands or tens of thousands of people by pushing a few buttons.

The way people normally promote their books is fast and easy ... but it's also middlingly effective at bonding. If you get a hundred sales from an ad, those buyers still don't know you. They don't have any reason to come back to you more than they'd come back to any other author they've read before.

By contrast, a higher-touch approach like mine — where the goal is to sell *yourself*, not just a single book — might earn five soon-to-be True Fans in a week. True Fans, as we'll talk about next, are the name of the game for Artisan Authors. I'll take five True Fans over a thousand casual readers any day because unless I betray them somehow, True Fans are mine forever.

What I'm describing is slow. It's a lot of work. But we've

stopped believing in quick fixes and Easy Buttons, haven't we? Good things take time, and good things take work. Sorry, but I warned you that although this approach is simple, it's definitely not easy.

As with all things Artisan, the goal is quality over quantity. You can use any selling approach you'd like (i.e. you don't need to sell in person like I do), but you must keep one thing firmly in mind no matter how you do it: *Your goal isn't to make single isolated transactions, the way most authors approach selling. Instead, your goal is to earn True Fans.* Or, to keep with the theme of this section, your goal is to score one more regular for The Bookstore of You.

You do that by being a real human being. By not thinking of your leads as leads, or as numbers on a dashboard. You do it by enticing readers to join your email list not with short-term tactics and cheap prices, but instead by being honest, open, and interesting to your new readers. You do it by asking people to reply to the emails you send, once you've lured them. You do it by answering their replies when you're lucky enough to get them — not in dismissive, 30-second standard responses just to clear your inbox as fast as possible, but by taking as much time to answer that email as you would one from a friend.

Because as I said earlier, that's what you're doing if you want to create regular customers for The Bookstore Of You: *You're making friends.* Not customers, not prospects, not leads ... but *friends*.

This is why Artisan Authors will have an advantage as "the usual way of doing things in self-publishing" gets worse and worse. Think visibility will get easier if you keep putting all your eggs in Amazon's basket? Think royalty rates will improve? Think the loyalty of KU readers will get better than it is, and those all-you-can-read readers will decide to ditch Amazon's buffet to shop only at The Bookstore of You?

Nope. Ain't gonna happen. The hands-off, non-Artisan way of publishing *will* continue, and I'm sure it'll work for some authors. But will it work for you? Long-term, do you have the stamina (to keep producing as fast as possible), the budget (to out-advertise the bigger players), and the shining uniqueness (to stand out in a growing flood of new books) to survive that way?

Or might it instead be better to slow down instead, focus on an entirely different crop of readers, and emphasize *quality* in your reader acquisition instead of always rushing for *quantity*?

You've made the right choice by leaning in the Artisan direction.

When all the high-churn authors start crying about declining visibility and sales, you won't have to worry. You'll simply throw open the doors of The Bookstore of You and keep treating the readers who came looking for you first — ignoring the wider market's noise entirely — like gold.

The Magic of One Thousand True Fans

Ah. Finally we arrive at the concept that makes all of this work: the Bookstore of You, the "if you can't win the game, change the rules" philosophy of the author's Kobayashi Maru, and the Artisan Author approach as a whole.

That concept is "1000 True Fans," as popularized by *Wired* magazine's founding editor Kevin Kelly.

As an Artisan Author, you'll need to throw away all of your old goals, along with the ways most authors strive to meet those goals. At minimum, those goals simply aren't relevant to you anymore. Beyond that, they're more likely to interfere with your *new* goals and methods than they are to help them. If you want to succeed as an Artisan Author, you'll need to undo the brainwashing perpetuated by the Rapid Release world and learn to think a whole new way. Remember our talk about paradigms? You can't build a Bookstore of You inside a whole new paradigm until you burn the tower of Rapid Release to the ground.

Your goal is no longer to sell as many books as possible.

Your goal is no longer to reach as many readers as you can.

Your goal isn't to hit a bestseller list, win an award, earn a flashy credential, go viral on the social media platform of the month, speak at conferences as an exalted six- or seven-figure author, or massage your earnings so you can brag about earning more than other authors even if what you're bragging about is technically untrue.

Your goal as an Artisan Author is extremely simple. *You have one and only one job, and it's to accumulate 1000 True Fans.*

"True Fans" are the bullseye at the center of any creator's target. They're the best of the best. True Fans are Team You, get-the-tattoo, *semper fi* until the end of time. These are the people who will buy anything you sell without hesitation — without even needing to look closely at what it is. They tell their friends about you. They sing your praises in public forums. If your reputation is ever attacked, True Fans are your constant defenders.

True Fans are a subset of normal fans, which in turn are a subset of other kinds of readers. Their value comes down to simple math. If you can amass a thousand of these all-in True Fans over time, you'll easily make a living. If you sell $100 worth of stuff to a thousand people every year, that's $100,000 per annum. Even better, you can sell next year's $100 worth of stuff to *the same people,* meaning you barely need to search for more. Once you have a thousand True Fans in your pocket, you barely need to advertise. True Fans will buy everything you make, and $100 per year spent on their favorite author isn't that much money.

As an Artisan Author, you'll write books with the intention of selling them to your True Fans. Forget writing to market; your True Fans *are* your market, and you'll write to them without effort because you were being your authentic self when they found you in the first place. Other readers will buy those books too, but with just the 1000 True Fans and nobody else, you'll be set. And that will remain true ... year after year after year.

What made Kevin Kelly's "1000 True Fans" essay so compelling was that it boiled success down to something so straightforward and simple, it suddenly felt achievable in ways the old definitions never did. I mean, think about it: What have most of us been shooting for? How many readers, how many books, how many reviews, how many sales? The answer is usually something nebulous and impossible to pin down, like "a lot."

How can you reach a goal you can't even define? How can you believe your goals are achievable if you have no idea what they are? You'll never succeed at something you don't believe.

1000 True Fans, on the other hand, is believable. It's a reasonable number (one that we can imagine easily) and it's quantifiable, unlike "a lot." The quantifiable goals that the indie author world *does* talk about are audacious — and, for many, ridiculous. If you've already got all of your author flywheels turning, maybe you can imagine hitting the six-figure or even the seven-figure mark, but most authors are nowhere near that. Most authors earn a few hundred bucks here and there, so how does an impossibly far-off goal like "seven figures" help them? It's like successfully climbing a stepladder for the first time, then planning to free solo El Capitan.

For most authors, it's hard to imagine achieving an income that huge. Even for authors who've reached those levels, it's hard to imagine *sustaining* an income that big for more than a few months or a year.

But a thousand True Fans? That's something we can wrap our heads around. We can picture a thousand people sitting in an arena. It's more than an intimate crowd, but it's not an insane crowd, either. My high school had about a thousand kids in it, and it's easy to picture my high school. But if you've been shooting for millions? What does *millions* even look like? Are you truly banking on reaching that many people, or is your mental picture instead of an amorphous crowd that can only be accurately described as "a lot"?

The idea of 1000 True Fans is *exciting*. It means that you can ignore the masses if you want, and focus entirely on growing that True Fandom. It means that each new True Fan is an extra $100 you can count on per year, if you stick to the average.

I'd heard about "1000 True Fans" for years before it truly sunk in. I understood the idea, but my mind took its sweet time applying it to my career as an author. Before then, I operated in a way that was sort of "1000 True Fans adjacent" rather than really leaning in to it. Like the goal of "a lot" of sales, my 1000 True Fans thoughts were nebulous at best. They sort of went like this: *I'll publish normally, try all the tricks to push my books on Amazon because that's where people buy most often, and accumulate a following over time. I'm sure some of the readers I reach that way will like me more than others. They'll buy more books. And that will, I suppose, make them True Fans. I guess.*

I made no deliberate effort. I didn't try to nurture casual readers into fans, then fans into True Fans. There was no real outreach, because I figured my books, always sold at arm's length, were outreach enough. My readers would morph into True Fans on their own, just because they liked my books. That's what I figured, anyway.

But I was wrong. You might get a person here and there who becomes a True Fan on their own after finding you randomly, but it's far from a sure thing. And so, throughout this book, we'll focus on better ways to find and create True Fans. You have to be deliberate about it — as deliberate and focused as you'd need to be if you were sifting through tons of riverbed dirt to find a few flakes of gold.

For now, though, I'd like you to sit with the idea of having your own 1000 True Fans. Really think about how it would feel if, instead of marketing blindly into the void, you instead started to find people one by one and usher them through the doors of the Bookstore of You. Think about what it would feel like to stop thinking in terms of SALES and think TRUE FANS instead.

No more revolving-door advertising, where you have to spend and spend to get readers every time.

No more obsessively checking your Amazon sales, hoping people will find your book in a sea of others.

Instead, knowing that when you have a new book for sale, you can simply send an email (or reach those True Fans in whichever other way you reach them), trusting that your core group will buy.

Imagine abandoning the need to cow-tow to whichever genre or keywords are hot right now so you can hit the algorithms just right. You don't *need* to hit algorithms when you have True Fans in your pocket. Or, imagine feeling safe during a vacation or market downturn, knowing your True Fans will eagerly buy your next book as soon as you have one ready — whenever that might be.

Imagine creating a special edition of one of your books, knowing in advance that most of your True Fans will want it.

Imagine resting assured that whatever happens in the rest of the marketplace, your True Fans will never abandon you for some other shiny object. You can buy ads or appear on podcasts or do whatever you'd like to blow up your sales if you want ... but even if those efforts fail, your True Fans will still have your back.

Imagine the feeling of relief that comes with knowing that you never — not even once — need to hit a bestseller chart to make a living. The mid-list is a powerful place to be, if you act like an Artisan instead of just one more author spewing words onto the pile.

True Fans are your ticket to freedom from all of the usual rules.

If you have enough True Fans (and that's "enough" by your own unique definition), you don't actually need anything else.

Meet Bob

The Artisan Author paradigm can take some time to work its way under your skin. It flies in the face of everything you've probably heard about how indie authors sell books. Fortunately, it *doesn't* fly in the face of common sense. (It's Rapid Release thinking that does that.)

To help ram the whole thing home (and enlist you in the greatness of 1000 True Fans), I thought an example might help.

My favorite musician is Austin-based singer-songwriter Bob Schneider — an Artisan creator if ever there was one. Bob's had some big popular successes. He's an Austin darling, has headlined many big events, received serious national radio play with a few of his songs (most notably "40 Dogs"), and spent time brushing shoulders with Hollywood elite back in the 90s when he was dating Sandra Bullock.

Still, I'm willing to guess that very few people reading this book have ever heard of Bob. Inside the Austin city limits, eight or nine people out of ten know his name, but if you drive an hour and a half south to San Antonio, that number drops to something like four in ten. When I first made this argument in Las Vegas, only two people in a room of a hundred or more knew who I was talking about, and one of them was someone who only knew Bob because he knew I was a fan.

Bob is famous in his home city, but virtually unknown outside of it. He doesn't have gold records. He's not going to play on Dick Clark's New Year's Rockin' Eve. He doesn't attend sporting events and attract as much of the camera's attention as the players, like Taylor Swift does. Bob's not going to be mobbed going through an airport. In fact, I saw him once in the Chicago airport, left him alone, then later wrote in to his podcast to ask if he hated being bothered in public. His response was that if I *had* come up, it would have made his day. Nobody recognizes Bob outside of Austin, so if I'd said something, it might have made him stop wondering if there was a point to what he kept doing with his life — if all that music-playing was maybe reaching a few people, and worthwhile after all.

Bob doesn't consider himself a celebrity. Outside of his own circles, he isn't one. He's just a guy who plays music his way, in his favorite venues, for his favorite fans. Because I'm a True Fan of Bob Schneider, I see him play all the time. I listen to his podcasts (and, apparently, write into them). I've heard him wax philosophical, unpacking the issue of why he's not more popular.

He'll admit that he's jealous. He'd *love* some of that big-time money and adoration. But then he'll say, "Yeah ... but I actually *do* know what it would take be more popular. I have the connections, the cred, and the foundation. There's just one problem: I don't want to do any of it."

The formula, Bob says, is simple. Just make the same song over and over, play to mainstream radio tastes, and do what his manager tells him. He'd need to pick a music genre instead of writing in all of them. He'd need to be on social media. He'd need to hit exactly the same kind of style and release rhythm that streaming platforms like Spotify favor. Spotify is kind of a race to the bottom for musicians, but you can chase its algorithms if you follow all the rules, work yourself ragged, and do all the right things.

Any of this sounding familiar? Spotify is the Kindle Unlimited of music, as it were.

The problem is, Bob doesn't like to do what he's told and doesn't want to stay inside the usual box. He prefers to play a country song after a disco song after a blues song after a reggae song. He likes to stop mid-set to ask his usual drummer, Kyle Thompson, how Kyle is doing in his legal battle with Sharon Osbourne over the one-man Ozzy show that Kyle created — a running joke that nobody but regulars understand at all. Bob likes to break his songs in half with long, often hilarious diatribes. And if those jokes don't land? If they're entirely ill-advised and inappropriate? Why, Bob then doubles down of course, offending a few people while others guffaw and the band squirms uncomfortably.

When he catches himself going too far outside the norm, he'll say, "I'm an artist and I'll say what I want." This is often followed by yet another risqué one-liner.

Bob can rock huge venues, but he's most comfortable in a small local pub where he has a weekly residency — a tiny joint with a capacity of somewhere around 150 people. When he gets to wishing he was more famous or richer, he'll usually catch himself and realize how different life would be if he got what he claims to want ... and ultimately, with all things considered, decides that he likes his limited fame exactly where it is. If he was bigger, he'd have to answer to the public. If he was known by everyone, he could no longer say and do what he wanted.

He could, in short, no longer behave like an artist.

And yet, Bob is doing well. He lives in a nice town that loves him, with a family that hasn't been twisted by the pressures of fame. (His father and daughter even join him onstage sometimes, both highly talented.) He spends one night a week in a spot as intimate as the bar in *Cheers*, playing for True Fans. If you look at his Patreon numbers and know what he charges for small shows and private events, you can guess his income. It sure seems to me like a good one. Now and then, he gets to step on a bigger stage and play for tens of thousands. He seems to know he got the best parts of stardom without its downsides. He can rock the mic and do what he loves for a living ... but he can still shop at the H.E.B. without getting mobbed.

To me, Bob Schneider is a perfect example of an Artisan creator — a model for those of us interested in Artisan Authoring to follow.

Make your art your way and break all the usual rules of other people's success ... and yet still make a damn good living.

The Beauty of the Side Hustle

Here's a paradigm-changer that nobody ever talks about: *You don't need to make a full-time living at writing to be fulfilled and happy.*

I literally never see this. Oh, someone here and there will bring up the idea of side-hustle income, but nobody gets on big stages, creates courses, or writes books about how to make a few hundred or a few thousand dollars a month. Nope — if you're new to this and didn't know better, you'd think from all the information out there that it's six figures or nothing.

It's not, though. In fact, I'll even go out on a limb and say that there are more "side hustle" authors out there than there are prospective full-timers. The reason we only hear about the latter is because 1) full-timers are the only ones who make YouTube channels and speak at conferences, 2) the kinds of authors shooting for full-time incomes and beyond are the loudest, whereas part-timers are quiet and don't make waves, and 3) you can't make as much money selling how-to to part-time authors. I mean, imagine you could have the profits of a course called *MAKE SIXTEEN BAZILLION DOLLARS WITH NO EFFORT AS AN AUTHOR* or one called *How to Sell Five Hundred Books Per Year*. Which of those titles sounds more lucrative for the teacher?

And yet, even though I pulled that number out of the air just now, selling *five hundred books a year* actually sounds pretty compelling for a lot of authors. Or a thousand. Or maybe just enough royalties to offset their car payment. Not everyone wants to nuke the world with their authorial success. Plenty just want to get their words on a page, then get people outside of their immediate friends and family interested in reading them.

As an Artisan Author, I hereby give you permission to aim for a side hustle or part-time income — or, hell, *no* income at all and only creative satisfaction — if it suits you.

Maybe you don't want to devote eight hours a day to learning all the ins and outs of cutting-edge bookselling. Maybe you don't want to write ten books a year ... or five books a year ... or even two books a year. Maybe this is a hobby for you. Maybe it's a bit more. But the way most author instruction acts like anything short of full-time is pointless, or the people interested in it don't matter?

Well, frankly that's bullshit.

The idea of side-hustle author income (whether it's your end goal or just a stepping stone on the way to full time) fits neatly into the notion of 1000 True Fans. It's not always easy to "scale down" the usual things authors say are necessary from full- to part-time, but 1000 True Fans scales *easily*.

Haven't gotten your 1000 True Fans yet or don't need that many? No problem. How about you shoot for 500 True Fans instead, and earn a half-time income?

Or what if you aim for 100 True Fans — enough for about $800-1000 a month?

Hell ... what if the first milestone you celebrate is the easy-to-hit number of *ten* True Fans? Remember, True Fans are your most reliable income, but you'll get a halo of less-than-True-Fan readers as a side-effect. Maybe ten True Fans are only worth about $1000 a year, but in gathering them you'll earn at least another $1000. That's $2k, or about $170 a month. Nobody's ever going to get onstage and brag about their $170 months ... but don't we all know someone who'd be thrilled to earn that much so they can have a nice dinner out every so often?

Approaching writing as a lucrative hobby or a side hustle is a perfectly valid way to be an author, and one that gets zero air time. If you see authors on YouTube talking about numbers that "small," they're usually documenting their journey to raise their numbers. Side-hustle income is never considered worthwhile in its own right, and yet I know many, *many* authors who don't care about making it big. It's not that they're failing in their attempts to go full time. It's that they honestly have no desire to do so.

Writing full-time sounds glorious to many people (myself included), but not to others. Writing is hard emotional work. Even as an Artisan Author, it's true that all other things being equal, you'll earn more money if you have more books, but many authors only want to write so much. Producing multiple books per year sounds daunting to a lot of authors, as does the prospect of exposing themselves that fully to reviews and criticism. My wife, were she authorially inclined, would *never* want to go full time because writing is an inherently unstable and scary business even *with* True Fans. Many authors only want to dip their toes, and yet nobody talks about them.

More authors than not still work another job. Plenty of those authors never plan to leave their primary job. What about *those* authors? Maybe you're one of them. If you are, I'm sorry that nobody pays any attention to you while they're waving the seven-figure dream.

If you're an author who doesn't aspire to full-time — or if you know any of those authors — then you're very much in the right place. Try to play the Kindle Unlimited game as a side-hustle author and your book will vanish without a trace, paying pennies within a month or two if it still pays at all. But as an Artisan Author, you can build Fan equity over time, grow rather than diminish with time, and make your own fate.

One size doesn't fit all, folks, even though that's what most author education implies.

Which, come to think of it, leads us naturally into another point worth knowing.

A Compass, Not a Map

There's no one right way to succeed in self-publishing. We've covered that already.

Every strategy you've ever heard about or can think of — as long as it's somewhat reasonable — works for someone. I was once at an event and met an author who hands out clothespins with tiny plastic frogs glued to them and his website address written on them. Not exactly something I'd do, but it'd gotten him at least a few solid readers.

At the same time, there's no strategy that works for every author, or should be used by every author. As I write this, everyone is soiling themselves with excitement over TikTok marketing. Personally, I want nothing to do with TikTok. It's wrong for me, and I get by just fine without it. If you're thinking right now that I *should* try it because it *might* work for me, my response is: No it wouldn't, because I don't want to do it — and "wanting to do it" is part of an Artisan's definition of "works for me."

Remember my Bob Schneider example? Bob knows exactly what he *could* do to raise his profile, but he doesn't want to do it. He's made his decision, and it's to choose less mainstream success over doing things he doesn't enjoy. Artists are stubborn. They have very specific opinions about how things should be done, which is the reason they make art in the first place. Art doesn't play by the rules.

I have four friends who do a lot of live selling. You'd think their strategies for selling well at live events would be the same because all live events are similar to one another (more similar to each other than any live event is to online sales, anyway), but they aren't.

One of my friends crams as many books into his allotted space as he can, including standing bookcases. The goal is to overwhelm people with a feeling of, "Wow, this guy is serious, so he must be good."

Another has created a smooth and polished brand, providing an upscale experience with all sorts of little touches. He's got a very consistent and cool feel that he brings to every element of his display booth, and that "feel" is ultimately what sells his books.

Another exhibits mainly at big conventions and uses a "get 'em in, get 'em through" philosophy based on quick, simple hooks for every book. The idea is that lines can get long at conventions, so you need to churn efficiently through buyers and not linger long.

The last of them, however, crafts story-based pitches for each book in those exact same convention environments: a little version of the story that can be told in 30-60 seconds. That's not a lot of time, but it's a lot more than you think when it's a *pitch* we're talking about.

And then there's me. When I sell live, I don't even have a single genre. My convention friends tell me that it's best to simplify offerings down to just a few books — and ideally only a few copies of each — to keep readers from being overwhelmed by all the different choices. I don't do that, though; I always bring everything I've got. Instead of refined pitches, I use open-ended hooks: "This is like the movie *Backdraft* with demons," or "This is an Agatha Christie style dinner-party murder mystery" ... or my favorite, *for Unicorn Western*: "This is like if Stephen King was on acid when he wrote *The Dark Tower."* When I'm selling live, I've found that the books matter (obviously), but not as much as my enthusiasm and level of engagement. They might buy my buddies' books because the story alone compels them, but half the time people buy from me with only the vaguest idea of the story, simply because they decide they like me. Sometimes I want to stop them: "Hang on ... don't you want to at least read the back copy first?"

If I hadn't yet started selling live, I can easily imagine my well-intentioned friends telling me not to do exactly what I've ended up doing. They'd tell me that I offer too many choices, and in their experience fewer choices work better. They'd tell me to focus on the story, instead of relying more on just making friends and having a good time. But what I do works for me. It works *well* for me. Just like what they do works well for them.

There's no one right answer.

Which is why, as you navigate the world of self-publishing — and especially if you're new to it — you should remember that the best metaphor for your journey's key tool isn't a *map*, but instead a *compass*.

To use a map, you need to know two things: where you want to end up, but also where you are right now. Everyone forgets that second part, but the big mall map won't help you find Auntie Anne's Pretzels if it doesn't have a big red dot on it that says YOU ARE HERE.

And yet, people give self publishing advice — and others follow it — with no regard for the YOU ARE HERE dot at all.

Someone will say, "You should run Facebook ads in exactly this way to sell your book." In the author world, that's a very specific directive: akin to "Turn left in ten seconds, then walk thirty paces." Those instructions work for the person giving the advice because from where *they* are right now, a ten-second wait followed by a left turn and thirty paces will get them to a destination called "Results." But if you're not *exactly where the advice-giver is,* those same instructions won't take you to the same place.

That's the thing about maps: They only work if you know exactly where you are at the moment. If you're using a map for street directions, you can at least look up at road signs to check your progress: "Oh, I'm at 2nd and Elm, so now I know what to do to get to 6th and Palm." But what's the equivalent for writers? Can you be that precise and specific: a "starting location" detailed enough to cover *every single tiny thing* that might affect the outcome of a given strategy? Every single little detail that, taken together, comprise YOU ARE HERE?

What's your personality?

What do you enjoy and not enjoy, and what are you good at and not good at?

What have your readers learned to expect from you, given your history?

Will the next move you're considering look brilliant to your readers ... or will it seem inconsistent with your past actions — or worse, will it seem like hypocrisy, like you're selling out?

Who are your readers? What are they like?

What's the tone of your books, your communications, your social media posts, your emails, your interview appearances, your Author's Notes ... your entire author brand? How well does that tone jibe with your next move?

I could go on and on, but it all boils down to one simple idea: *If ten authors want to end up in the exact same spot, no one set of directions will work for all of them because they're starting in different places.* (Or perhaps more accurately, most of the time none of them have any idea where they are, or if they're even on the map at all.) If you tell all of those authors to figuratively "turn left and walk ten paces" as map-thinking suggests, what are the chances that any of them will end up at the intended finish line?

Because every author, every body of work, every set of readers, and all the other things are different, expecting everyone to use the same map is a doomed strategy. In any creative venture — especially one with anchor points in both art *and* the selling of that art — maps can only be drawn after the fact. After you reach your destination, you could create a map to show how you got there — *you specifically*, not anyone else. Even then, it's an artifact, not a guide.

Instead of thinking in terms of maps, a far better metaphor for teaching any creative discipline (or the marketing and selling of that discipline) is a *compass*.

Compasses don't tell you how to get from any given spot to any other given spot. Instead, they give you information about where you are right now relative to certain universal truths like the four cardinal directions. It's not even *complete* information. A compass will tell you where North is, but that only helps if you know what *else* is North (like your intended destination), what the terrain is like between here and there, how far you have to walk, if you *should* keep walking given the time of day or if it's better to hole up and wait for morning, if something to the south requires your attention first, and so on.

In order to navigate using a map, all you have to do is blindly follow directions and hope the cartographer drew the map accurately. In order to use a compass, on the other hand, you need to know how to interpret data within a specific set of circumstances. You need situational acuity, a healthy respect for all the things you *don't* yet know that might trip you up, and the "why" behind what the compass tells you. If your compass's needle has somehow de-magnetized and no longer points North, for instance, you need to understand the principles involved enough to realize it. If your compass says North is directly in the direction of the sunset, you need awareness enough to say, "Wait. Sunset is West, not North."

You have to use your brain, in other words.

Instead of mindlessly following instructions, a compass-user needs enough critical thinking to know when the instructions they've been given are bullshit. The way people act in self-publishing (as if there's one and only one way to do things) they'd walk right off a cliff if the map said they should. In a way, that's exactly what Rapid Release is doing. A lot of new authors see up front how abjectly shitty life under Rapid Release would be for their books and their personality, but then they dive into it anyway — ignoring the precipice right in front of them because it's not on the map.

A map is literal. A compass is contextual. *Blueprints? Formulas? Also* sold often in self-publishing, and *also* taken literally by too many hapless authors no matter how many cliffs they walk off of because they aren't on the map.

Keep the compass metaphor in mind as you read everything that follows. I'm not telling you what to do at any point in this book; I'm giving you ideas for things you *might* do if they jibe with who and where you are right now. They're not directives. They're options.

When you see a specific tactic in this book, take a step back before you try it for yourself. Don't just ask "Am I ready to do this?" like a map-follower wondering whether or not to begin their pre-ordained quest. Instead, think like a smart outdoorsperson skilled in orienteering and ask, *"Should* I do this? Is this the best path up the mountain for me, or should I instead use my compass and my understanding of mountain-climbing principles to find a different path that would suit me better?"

If you're smart with your compass, you'll start to see that *you don't have to reach the same destination via the same path as everyone else.* Because you understand more than what the compass is telling you right now, you'll know that yes, you can walk due North for one mile ... but you could also walk due West for one mile, turn 135 degrees toward northeast, and then walk 1.4 miles and end up in the exact same place.

It's better to understand principles than accept someone else's instructions, because you can always adapt a principle to a way that *does* fit you if you understand its function, purpose, and intended outcome. Understanding — not blind following — is a far better method for finding your way through uncertain lands.

Now that we're clear, I'd like to introduce you to the six key principles — which I call "pillars" — that define what it is to be and operate like an Artisan Author. They're the cardinal directions you'll use as reference points when using your compass, because every tactic we'll discuss soon should fit within the pillars (from where you, not anyone else, are uniquely standing) to be worth doing.

Chapter 5

The Six Pillars of Artisandom

Okay, the number six is sort of arbitrary. What can I say? I'm an artist and I'll say what I want.

Aside from questioning my numerical specificity, you might see even the following guiding principles differently than I do. If that's the case, awesome! It means you're not blindly following me any more than you should blindly follow anyone else. Honestly, critical and borderline skeptical thinking could almost be a pillar in itself. We're rebels and rulebreakers, after all.

That said, what follows are the rules I live by now that my author business is 100% Artisan, and consider to be key for any Artisan Author.

Artisan Pillar #1: Art First. Profit Second

This first pillar is the big one.

Do note, though, that I said "profit second," not "profit never." You also shouldn't take from this first pillar that there's no art in non-Artisan philosophies, because I know plenty of frenetically-producing authors who put a lot of heart into their stories. They can and often do have a lot of art to them ... but by nature of their mode of business, that art must always take a backseat to speed.

Not so for us. It's the order, not the existence of either element, that differentiates us from them. *Artisan Authors always put art first. Period.*

Profit can come right after art, and for me it does. I'd write if I couldn't get paid for it, but I wouldn't write nearly as much because I'd need to put a roof over my head somehow, and those "somehows" take time. For me, profit is a really big deal even though it comes second. I don't believe in being a starving artist — not when it's relatively straightforward to be a profitable one.

As an Artisan Author, you'll consider your book's marketability, pricing, and all that jazz just like other authors do. You'll just consider it *second*, after the book is done. Alternatively, you could consider your marketing angle before writing the book — but if you do, be sure to stop at *considering*.

If you want to do that, go for it ... as long as you can be honest about your intentions. You'll need to develop that small, quiet artist's voice inside you and learn to pay attention when it speaks. If the artist within balks at your early marketing plans, drop those plans or stop thinking about marketing early to begin with.

I'll give you an example.

When Sean and I wrote our book *Invasion*, we decided to play a little game. We wanted to see if we could engineer a book that would hit the market just so. Even so, that didn't make it "writing to market" — not in the way others talk about writing to market.

For one, the directive ("let's see if we can write a very market-friendly book") *was in itself a creative challenge* for us, seeing as we'd never before thought about the market first and wanted to see if we could.

Second and more importantly, though, *Invasion* was only market-first in wireframe. The book's execution was entirely free-form, and its ending was *definitely* not on-market. Although we were gunning for short chapters with hard cliffhangers to make the book as much of a page-turner as possible, the actual writing followed the muse. When the muse wanted to take the story one way but the more marketable angle was something else, we always listened to the muse. That doubled in *Invasion*'s sequels, by the way: all six books that followed were entirely art-first (although still page-turners) because we couldn't keep up that "market" thing for long.

Don't ignore the businessy parts of your business. You *do* want to give your books the best chance of selling and earning a profit as you can, but those income goals must never be allowed to outstrip the art. Once your artist's intention for the story is fulfilled, *then* other considerations can have their way. Until then, nothing gets to get in the way of the art. If you create a book that sells well but that you can't stand behind as the best and most honest expression of your creativity, you've failed the first pillar of being an Artisan Author.

Art and creative expression come first. Every other consideration has to fit around them.

Artisan Pillar #2: Be Human

You'll be tempted to think that people buy books only for the books themselves. That's somewhat true — especially in certain cases, like selling outside of your True Fans — but it's not the whole story.

When people buy anything at all, they're actually buying an emotional experience.

If they buy perfume, they're buying the experience of feeling elegant. If they buy new carpet for their home, they're buying the experience of enjoying the home more, or being disgusted by the home less. Even groceries are emotional — and if you disagree, I'll remind you why it's a bad idea to shop the snack aisle while you're hungry.

Books are easy to see as the experiences they are, but it's easy to forget that any experience has many facets to it. If your customers bought your book online, it was because the cover and description promised them a certain emotional experience they'd like to have. If they bought from a store, they might have been wooed by the sensory experience of its weight, feel, or the smell of its pages. If they bought from you in person, part of that book's value — and the experience they'll remember and tell their friends about — came from meeting the author, who might even have signed and personalized their new book.

Maybe they found your book while idly browsing Facebook after a bad day, eager for a distraction.

Maybe they read your book while a friend was in the hospital, and it gave them an escape.

You can't know all of the emotional triggers your book will pull for a given reader. No matter how carefully you write your prose or craft your description or present your cover and hook, there's so much beyond those things that you can't control, and that neither you nor the reader will probably ever know.

Now consider this, as long as we're talking about experiences: *Today more than ever in recent history, people want to experience human connection ... and today more than ever, our world robs them of that connection.*

Everything is online. AI is on the rise. When you call a business, you get those damn call-response trees telling you to press 1 for the sales department. Most of us no longer touch our music because it's MP3s instead of CDs or LPs, and a lot of the time, we don't even *own* that music; we stream it instead. We text instead of call, and we call instead of just stop by when we're in the neighborhood. Gatherings are smaller. Covid killed a lot of human touch, for a lot of people, for good.

The more *human* you are as an author, the more you'll tap into the human experience that so many people badly want but no longer have — or don't even know they're missing, beyond vague feelings of malaise and depression.

To be clear, I'm not saying you should "be human" only as some sort of sales tactic. Nor should you be artificial or absurd about it. My argument also isn't necessarily anti-AI (I have no specific problems with AI), but it *is* anti-delegating-your-books'-soul-to-AI. The argument is that you should think, operate, and communicate like a genuine human being. It's easy and obvious enough, if you let it be as simple as it actually is.

Answer your own emails.

If you screw up, admit it.

If you have a family or pets, mention them from time to time. You don't need to get personal. Something as small as saying "I just got back from a family trip" in an email broadcast or Author's Note communicates it well enough.

Be proud of your achievements without being an asshole about it. I went to a concert once with my family, and the opener was a singer named Jake Wesley Rogers. Jake endeared me immediately (enough that I signed up for his text marketing, which I've never done before) because when he got onstage, he giddily told the crowd that this was his first arena show. There was no artifice in him at all. He was so proud and happy to be where he'd finally gotten, and he let that pride show rather than being a rock star who was too cool to show it.

If you're afraid to publish something, admit it. Fear that's eventually overcome is called bravery, and there's nothing more aspirationally human (and admirable) than bravery.

Tell the stories behind your stories. What inspired you to write a given book? I tell readers all the time about my book *Winter Break*, which I wrote for my daughter when she was 16. My real dog is in that book, by the way (including a photo of her at the end, and in the chapter headers), so I talk about that, too.

As an Artisan Author, I'd advise you not to overly systematize your business. You don't need an automatic reply to every email that says you're super busy and will get back to them if the email requires a reply. You don't need to be 100% polished and perfect all the time. You don't need a social media scheduling tool that sends blasts on regular schedules, though there's nothing inherently wrong with it if the posts are at least human in nature. And speaking of social media, I suggest handling it yourself rather than having an assistant do it — or, if you're like me and hate social media, don't do it at all. Tell readers about that, too.

Start a YouTube channel if it moves you, or start a podcast if that strikes you as fun. (But don't do either if you don't want to.) Any medium that lets people see and hear you equates, in their minds, to spending time with you. When I was on the Self Publishing Podcast, I met people all the time who'd spent innumerable hours "with me." Think that doesn't affect how much a person likes and trusts you, because they see that you're just as human as they are?

Every little thing you allow people to see of you makes you feel more human.

You'll start to feel like a friend to them. Buying and reading your books then becomes more than just reading. You, as the author, are in there, too. If you allow yourself to be fully human instead of robotic or "professional" at every turn, the more your Artisan vibe and convictions will seep into readers' awareness. They'll start to know your ethos, and the right kind of readers will appreciate it.

But in the end, you shouldn't be maximally human only to sell books. That's a nice side effect, but it's not the reason it's a pillar.

It's a pillar because you *are* human, and because when you're an Artisan Author, you get to stop putting on airs and connect with other humans who, in some way, want to connect with you.

Artisan Pillar #3: Treat Readers Like Gold, and Fans Like Diamonds

This one's the core of everything. It's also something that frenzied, faster-faster authors don't have time for. Your willingness to connect with readers as an Artisan Author is one big thing that sets you apart, and your willingness to treat your readers as more than anonymous transactions is the largest "sales asset" you have — in quotes because simply being cool to people who support your work won't feel like sales at all. (It has that effect, though. Wouldn't you want to spend more of your money with a business that actually appreciates you?)

Here's an easy way to start being cool to readers: *Actually answer their emails.*

You'll be tempted to ignore that last bit because it sounds so obvious, but I can't tell you how many times a reader has expressed shock that I answered an email they sent. To me, it's an of-course sort of thing: Why *wouldn't* I answer someone who took the time to contact me? And yet, the number of shocked responses I get can only lead me to conclude that most authors *don't* answer reader email.

Seriously? What a bunch of assholes.

If you don't answer every reader email you get, I'd like to kindly but firmly ask you to stop being an asshole. These people sat down and reached out to you — probably with some apprehension, because in their eyes, you're kind of a celebrity. They probably felt like they were out on a limb by emailing at all, and it's pretty damn cold if you let them keep feeling that way when it's in your power to make them feel so much better.

Don't just *answer* emails, by the way. Answer them *fully*, even if they're complicated and require extra time. You may have to gently draw a line with some verbose and over-enthusiastic correspondents, but in my experience that's almost never necessary. Authors act like they're Hollywood A-Listers sure to be flooded with emails they'll never have time to answer, but in truth that happens to almost nobody. If you get "too many" emails, consider it a quality problem. The rest of us should be so lucky as to be adored that much.

Yes, personally answering every reader email takes time, but in addition to being cool of you, it's also the best marketing you'll ever do. If it takes me an hour to answer my email, so what? I just spent an hour doing the very best marketing and conversion work I could possibly do. I wouldn't balk at the idea of spending an hour writing ad copy or lining up promo for a launch, so why would I balk at the idea of spending an hour nurturing the warmest leads I'll ever have?

I know what you're thinking: *But ad copy is one-to-many. Email is so low-leverage: just one-to-one.*

Right. It is. But remember: We've upended the old paradigm. Instead of worrying about numbers and leverage, you're supposed to be courting True Fans. People that eventually become True Fans might *enter* your world through ads and higher-volume marketing, but it's very hard to *turn them into* True Fans without getting your hands dirty — and by "dirty," I just mean not being a pompous asshole who's too good for the people who make your creative life possible.

I believe in one-to-one. An Artisan Author knows the value of abandoning leverage from time to time and being human (there's that word again) with your readers instead.

I met one reader in a casual, real-world setting. He fell in love with my books and bought dozens of them in paperback, direct from my store rather than Amazon. So I started bringing him free books — signed, of course. We even went kayaking together.

I have a reader who puts images of her favorite books' covers on paving stones in her garden. She asked if I could send her an advance image of my new book's cover so she could "get it in the garden" right away. Of course I leapt at the chance.

I've offered to meet any readers who buy my books from Austin's iconic bookstore Book People and buy them coffee. I've done that a few times, at the Book People cafe, and it's been amazing.

I always make exceptions for my best readers. Sometimes I'll send them bonuses. I got a prototype slipcover for one of my collections, then sent it to a fan who'd been the first high-ticket backer on three of my Kickstarter campaigns in a row.

I have a friend who *calls* his readers out of the blue sometimes. They enter their phone numbers when they buy from his store, so sometimes he'll pick up the phone and surprise them.

You're in the business of creating True Fans, each of whom is worth more than a thousand casual readers to your Artisan career in the long term. So when you see True Fan potential starting to bud, you'd better step right up and nurture it.

Be super cool to your best readers. These are the people who are saving you from the Rapid Release death spiral and making your career as an author possible ... and they'll *keep* making it possible for years and decades, no matter what the rest of the market does or how loudly other authors cry that the sky is falling.

But only if you treat them like the diamonds they are.

Artisan Pillar #4: Take Your Time

Does this one really need to be spelled out beyond the headline?

You're reading this because you understand that good books take more time than dashed-off books, and maybe because you've glimpsed (or nearly been eaten alive by) the rat race that is most of self-publishing. I don't think I need to convince anyone here that it's a good idea to take the time you need to make your art right.

Don't rush. You can move quickly if it suits you, but *rushing* is different from *moving quickly within your limits and comfort zone*. The latter is about your unique personality as a writer, but the former is twisting that personality because outside forces make you think you have to. You *move quickly* because you want to get a book out, but you *rush* because although *you'd* like to take more time with a book, *the market* demands that you release it now.

This doesn't happen to Artisan Authors. Oh, you might hear from some complainy fans here and there, but real Artisan readers understand that art shouldn't be hurried, and Artisan Authors refuse to hurry for anyone. Artisan readers believe in quality over quantity as much as you do, and almost always they're willing to wait.

Also, waiting builds anticipation and therefore has value to the right readers in and of itself. Have you ever been excited about a meal at a fancy restaurant, but been disappointed if the food comes too fast? I have. It makes me think that the restaurant wants me out of there quickly, rather than giving me the luxuriating experience I wanted. It also makes me wonder if they just powered through cooking my meal instead of taking the time to craft it with care.

If you'd like, take your time to write an Author's Note. You don't have to, but "I don't have time" is no longer a reason.

Take your time to create graphics, chapter images, or special formatting if you want to. My book *Pretty Killer* is a dinner party murder mystery that takes place in an elite, formal setting, so I created fancy cards to separate the different phases of the book with a pretty menu for each of the dinner's phases: *Appetizers, First Course, Second Course, Dessert, and Digestif.* There's a lot of clues in "found documents" in that book too, so I made up graphics of a police report, a coroner's report, and a ripped-out page from the Physician's Desk Reference. And of course, researching all of the police, coroner, and pharmaceutical stuff took a ton of extra time, too.

You might decide to create bonus material. Or character illustrations. Or side stories. Or you might choose to crowdfund a special edition of your book on Kickstarter … and let me tell you, *that* takes a ton of time, too.

As an Artisan Author, you're hereby commanded to take as much time as you need to write and release your books in whichever way *you* — not the market — want.

We just ran away from the rush-rush publishing culture, so let's be sure to stay as far away from it, in all ways, as possible.

Artisan Pillar #5: Think Outside the Box

Beyond just keeping an eye out for ideas that might suit you, I suggest ignoring what other authors are doing entirely — at least as far as their "shoulds" are concerned.

You're an artist now, and artists create. Yes, you're already creating just by writing, but this is a bigger definition of "create." I'm talking about *forging new paths*. About *doing things in new and different ways*. I'm talking about looking at a blank slate of possibility and saying, "I'd like to do this" without asking whether anyone else is doing it, too. You don't need others to do anything before you try it, because you can create it for yourself.

We're using a compass instead of a map, remember? Maps are anti-creative. Compasses, which give you information instead of hard-set directions, are creative. If you know how to use a compass, you can always cut a completely new path through the unknown because you know you'll always be able to find your way home again.

And by the way, you don't need to actively *avoid* what other authors are doing just because they're doing it, either. If you happen across a common tactic that might work for you, don't be a punk rock snob and dismiss it just because it's popular. You might want to write and promote reader magnets for a mailing list; you might want to do Facebook group takeovers; you might want to run ads or structure your launches in the usual ways. If it fits, consider it. Just don't do it *only because* you've seen others doing it.

In other words, think outside the box ... but even beyond that, *think for yourself*.

I love trying weird things that might not work. It's fun to forge new paths.

I once wrote a vote-as-you-go story with my email list. I sent them three potential story ideas and let them pick one, then wrote a beginning to it. I sent that beginning back to my list once I'd reached a crucial decision point in the story, at which point I asked them to vote, *Choose Your Own Adventure* style, on what my characters should do next. We worked through a whole novella that way.

I sent out a survey to see how long readers had been with me, which books were their favorites, how they liked to read, how much they read, and more. The results of that survey were interesting, but what was even more interesting was that several people emailed back to thank me for asking about my readers in the first place. No other author, they said, cared enough to wonder.

I always tell readers the behind-the-scenes of my books, giving them insight into my process. I once explained why I could never change the ending of a story even before it was published because in my mind, that story had actually happened. The ending wasn't arbitrary anymore. It'd become "what really occurred."

I do a lot of weird stuff. And why the hell not? Readers are with us because we don't play by the usual playbook, so why not step outside of that playbook even further whenever the urge strikes us?

Artisan Pillar #6: To Thine Own Self Be True

Think about this for a second: *"Normal" is nothing more than cultural brainwashing.*

Now, I'm not getting all conspiracy theorist on you. I don't think our society has been engineered by dark forces meant to erase our brains. (Reality TV did that. Dark forces were not necessary.)

What I mean is that for a long time, there were only so many media outlets in the world. TV was originally broadcast on three major networks, and everyone listened to the same radio. Even after channels multiplied (thank you, cable TV, Netflix, and the internet), most content was still only made by a small group of people. Movies and TV are expensive and take a lot of specialized talent, equipment, and money, so only certain groups can make them. That's even true today, as content has democratized and expanded.

Here's a question: Have you ever noticed how many movies are set (not just shot) in California?

That happens because the people who make movies primarily live in California, so they're best able to write what they know. It's not sinister; it's just a fact of human nature. It's the reason more of my protagonists are middle-class straight cis white guys than anything else: because *I'm* a middle-class straight cis white guy. That doesn't happen because I'm trying to push a viewpoint or agenda. It happens because like most writers, I draw most easily and naturally from the world I know.

If you knew nothing about the United States except what you saw in movies and TV, you might think that most Americans live in California, since so many movies and TV shows are set there. You might think that California took up half of the North American land mass, seeing as relatively few movies are set anywhere else.

I'm sure there's been some deliberate manipulation of TV and movies, but my maybe-naive belief is that most of our media's historically homogenous portrayal of the world comes from laziness and complacency, not evil intent. I think that most creators just wake up in the morning and write the world they see around them, because it's their world. And then, because the film and TV industry *broadcasts* that vision of that world, it starts to seem like it must be *everyone else's* world, too.

In other words, "normal" isn't actually the norm. It's more like a lopsided delusion. When we think of "normal," we're talking about what we think the world looks like ... and a lot of our "looks like" is created by the media we consume — media that was written by a group of people who aren't remotely the majority.

What we call "normal" is actually the worldview of a tiny minority who just so happen to have massive reach. Ten people in a Hollywood office work together to write a movie filled with people like themselves, doing things *they* do, surrounded by activities *they* enjoy, responding to things in the way *their* mothers and families always responded to things, aspiring to goals that make sense to *them*. Then that movie becomes a blockbuster, and everyone thinks that version of life is just "how things are."

I was forty before I finally understood something my father kept trying to tell me: that 1950s America wasn't anything like *Leave it to Beaver* or *Mister Ed*. Nope. Those were just versions of life and values held by the small group of people who made decisions in TV at the time. Sure, there were people like that ... but it was far from everyone.

I've taken you down this philosophical rabbit hole for one reason:

Think about what we consider "normal," along with all the pressures in the world — both overt and subtle — to conform to that normality.

Now, remember that if "normal" is actually the worldview of a minority with a disproportionately huge reach, that means "abnormal" people actually outnumber them. *Weirdly, "abnormal" is more normal than "normal."* Remember what Lewis said in *Revenge of the Nerds*? "We have news for the beautiful people: There's a lot more of us than there are of you."

Normal is a lie. By the numbers, the most "normal" thing you can be is atypical.

This matters to you as an Artisan Author because the Artisan ethos is all about being unique. It's about operating with a different flavor than the norm. If readers want mainstream, they know exactly where to find it. If they want something different — something off the beaten path, told in a different way — they come to us. It's our duty to give them that difference — to be brave enough to show them *our* way of peering through the looking glass.

All these years, everyone outside of our culture's definition of "normal" have been ignored and underserved. That's great news for you, if you're weird. If you've got a freak flag in your back pocket, then by all means get out there and fly it. There are audiences all over the world who've been waiting breathlessly for a worldview that better matches their own than the mainstream. All those people will see your outside-the-nine-dots books as a breath of fresh air ... but only if you've got the guts to go out there and be yourself.

I mean, shit. Look at Chuck Tingle. I won't list some of his early book titles because you might be listening to this on audio and there may be kids in the car, but do yourself a favor and look him up. I laughed so hard at the early Chuck books because it seemed he was walking a fine line between erotica and winking hilarity, and I couldn't tell which side he was on.

But then one day, I saw a book by the author of *Scary Stories to Tingle Your Butt* and *Handsome Sentient Bubblegum Who Is Also a Successful Landscape Architect* in all of the bookstores around me. Suddenly good ol' Chuck's got a horror book called *Bury Your Gays* running up the bestseller charts.

I'm telling you, man: There are bestsellers-in-waiting out there in the oddest places.

If you're far outside society's usual nine dots, you've actually got an advantage on this one. If you're more like me, though, you're a lot closer to the mainstream and won't stand out as easily as that aforementioned breath of fresh air. Fortunately, you don't need to be far off center to find your own special tribe. Every author's style is unique, if the author *lets* it be unique.

I used to back away from making the constant 80s and 90s references that find their way into my books. They were funny to me, but I figured a lot of people would either never get them or find them annoying. Then I realized it was more tiring and less fun to try to be mainstream than to just leave it alone, so I started letting me be me.

I used to wonder why I kept shooting myself in the foot by creating books that didn't cleanly appeal to any of the major genres. I mean, who was *Unicorn Western* for — western fans, or fantasy fans? Who was *The Future of Sex* for — sci-fi fans skeeved out by the hard-R rating, or hard-R readers who didn't appreciate the intense sci-fi? And forget about the several humor/erotica titles Sean and I had so much fun writing, the best of which was *Adult Video*. Who the hell were *those* books for?

Well, they were for me and Sean, of course. We loved all of them.

They were for my wife, who laughed until she cried reading *Adult Video*.

And they were for the folks here and there who emailed to tell me or to request more of the same.

Were there a lot of those people?

Nope.

Were there some?

Yep.

And those *some* — who hung in there through every one of my freak-flag books — have historically been my best and most loyal fans.

Because here's the thing: If you write a book meant to please everyone, you'll have to take out all the edgy stuff that makes it different. To write a book with maximally broad appeal, you'll have to smooth it out and make it bland, like unflavored ice cream. Giving a book *any* strong flavor at all means limiting its appeal ... but it also means *strengthening* its appeal to the smaller number of people who like it.

The fans of *Unicorn Western*, *The Future of Sex*, and *Adult Video* don't just like those books. They *LOVE* those books. They *RAVE* about those books. They become superfans. They jump whole-hog into my world *because I gave them something that nobody else could*.

An Artisan Author must be bold. Bolder than other authors, who are, in themselves, pretty bold. An Artisan Author has to be bold enough to say, "You know all those people out there who are brave enough to put their creative work on the line for all the world to see? Well, I'm going to be different from *them*. They're outsiders, but I'm going to be an outsider even among the outsiders."

Being an outsider isn't a bad thing. In practice, it's an *amazing* thing. Because the truth is that even if you're alone among authors, *you're not actually alone.* There's a whole tribe of readers out there who've been waiting for something only you can deliver.

Nobody else can be you. Nobody can duplicate what you uniquely offer.

It's your cheat code, and using it can be terrifying ... but isn't that true of all real creation?

PART THREE

MAKING ARTISANSHIP WORK IN THE REAL WORLD

Chapter 6

Producing Like An Artisan Author

Now that we've talked about the pillars of being an Artisan Author, you might be getting some ideas for how you'll start to apply them (as guiding principles, not a blueprint to follow) in your own author career. I think we're clear by now that the old "go faster, sell bigger" way of doing things isn't the ticket for people like us, and instead we're operating within a more deliberate, more personality-driven paradigm.

And that's cool and all, especially since I gave you a few examples of how I operate within the pillars ... but as we've abundantly discussed, you're not me and I'm not you. That's even baked into the last pillar: *To Thine Own Self Be True*. Will my specific ways of being an Artisan Author work for you? Probably not — not copied exactly, they won't, because we're not the same person.

In other words, the question *How should I apply Artisan Author ideas to myself?* can only be answered with that irritating but accurate phrase: *It depends*.

But no worries! Every "it depends" still has guidance behind it. Nobody can tell you how to express yourself as a chef, for instance, but it's fair bet you'll need a stove. Certain pans and knives are better for Artisan-minded chefs, even though nobody can tell you what or exactly how to cook with them. As a chef, you'd learn which implements are better and which are worse (although even those rules are meant to be broken. Think great chefs never use diner-grade equipment?), which flavors work well together, how to make various sauces without burning them, and more. The art, in other words, is unique to each creator ... but that doesn't mean that certain overall elements and guidelines don't apply to all of them.

In this chapter, we'll talk about *what to produce* as an Artisan Author, but we'll do it with guidelines rather than rules. You're an artist, right? Well, good news: Even within some best practices, you'll have lots of freedom to make your own choices.

In the next chapter, we'll talk about *how to sell* that stuff you made, using Artisan truths and principles.

And in the chapter after that, we'll talk about the lifeblood for all Artisan Authors: those wonderful True Fans. We'll talk about how to find readers as an Artisan — readers who may one day become True Fans. We'll then talk about developing those readers into True Fans, as well as keeping your True Fans happy so they'll stick around, keep buying your books, and tell all their friends about you.

But we're getting ahead of ourselves. First create, *then* sell to True Fans.

You're an Artisan Author now, so the question of this chapter is: What should you create, and how should you create it?

Amounts and Speeds

Before we talk about *what*, I'd like to detour into the second part of that last sentence and talk a bit about *how*.

In particular, we should address the question of how much and how fast an Artisan Author should plan to write. I've already told you that you can and should make your own rules, but you're probably still looking for a few hard-and-fast answers. You're thinking, *C'mon, Johnny. I know you keep saying "it depends," but there must be SOME sweet spot out there — at least SOME idea about how much I should be producing.*

Well, there's not. How fast you write — and how much you produce — doesn't really matter.

And oh, sure, it *technically* matters — but only within your individual authoring world. All other things being equal, you'll sell more books if you've written more books, but that's comparing you to you. That's holding "you" as a constant and changing only the volume. If you step outside your own bubble, though, how much you write and how fast you are doesn't matter at all in comparison to other authors. It certainly doesn't matter in the eyes of the Artisan market.

I'm making this distinction because thanks to self-publishing groupthink, you might believe you *should* go faster to earn more money, or there's some magical advantage to going fast and producing lots of work that doesn't exist for lesser producers. And I get it, because in the Rapid Release world, that's true. In fact, it's *beyond* true: MEGA-TRUE, as it were. Rapid Release tends to be all or nothing. You can't scale it down, figuring you'll earn half as much as a full-speed KU author by publishing half as much. Go half as fast in Rapid Release, and you'll be lucky to earn one-tenth as much.

For all practical purposes, Rapid Release *must* be rapid to work. It's all or nothing. Artisan Authoring, on the other hand, is much more linear. Write more and you'll earn more simply because you have more books for your fans to read. Write less, and eventually they'll run out of things to buy.

I know I'm not helping. Sorry. I told you there were no one-size-fits-all answers.

How much should you write? Well, in most ways that's up to you. If you must have something concrete, look to the pillars. What speed allows you to continue to put art first? What speed still allows you to express yourself fully, be human, and have time to interact with your fans? If you find yourself going so fast that art slips to second place or you're simply not taking your time, that's when you know you're doing it wrong. That kind of thinking will put you in no-man's land: the place where Artisan Authoring won't work well, but Rapid Release won't work, either.

C'mon. Are you a map-follower or a compass-reader? You're smart, and chances are you're an adult. I shouldn't have to make your decisions for you.

If you still want an answer, I suggest pretending you're a writer back in the good old days — before ebooks, before even the internet. Writing speed back then was guided in part by publishing companies and their marketing bandwidth, but ultimately it came down to an individual author's preference. Isaac Asimov wrote like three billion books (not an exact number) and Stephen King has written a smaller-but-still-impressive number of books that are absolutely massive. Others wrote very slowly or very little, like Harper Lee … or, for that matter, George R. R. Martin, who was so slow he got story-scooped by his own TV show — a feat comparable to being run over by a glacier.

Back in the day, authors weren't trying to game algorithms with their production speeds. Instead, they were making artful products that earned them more money every time they launched something new. It wasn't called Slow Release or Medium Release or Rapid Release. Instead, it was called "building a catalog," and it followed the same sound business principles as a woodcrafter selling more chairs whenever he made more chairs to sell. The pre-internet rules around publishing speed (a better parallel for Artisan Authors than anything in the indie world today) were a natural consequence of simply continuing to write over the course of a long and sustainable career.

As an Artisan Author, you'll grow because you're building a catalog, not because you're tapping into algorithmic voodoo. There's no point in growing simply to grow — not if it compromises the other reasons you became an Artisan Author to begin with.

So you should move at your speed. *Yours*, not anyone else's. If you naturally, comfortably, and happily write one book a year, then write one book a year. If, on the other hand, you're naturally and comfortably fast, you should write many books a year. Write however many you want to. However many suits your schedule, your style, and your goals. There's no right answer.

Artisan Authors can succeed at any level, from the one-time creator with a single book to a serial creator with hundreds. A one-book author probably won't earn as much as a hundred-book author, but that's just common sense. That's how math works. (It's also, in fact, the original message of *Write. Publish. Repeat.*)

Pick the speed and volume that works for you. Period.

No matter what those numbers are, there's a way to make it work.

Ebooks

There's no specific Artisan magic for ebooks beyond simply writing the best story you can, or writing the story you most want to write.

Which actually raises a point relevant to everything in this chapter: Just because we're Artisan Authors and have talked about ways you can take extra time and effort to make our books fancy, that doesn't mean you *must* do any of those things.

Your books can just be books. That's totally fine. You can write in Scrivener, import to Vellum, and use the stock styles to make books that are well-formatted but not particularly special. That's a very easy way to hit the minimum professional standard: a level of quality that might not make anyone *ooh* and *aah*, but that won't make anyone dismiss you as a fly-by-night amateur, either.

I seldom do anything terribly fancy with my ebooks. They're the adequate, get-the-job-done products they're meant to be — and, for some readers on non-ideal e-readers, they're all I can reasonably do anyway. I play with Vellum's settings and styles until the book looks cool and matches its overall vibe (curly chapter-heading fonts and flourishes for elegant books like *La Fleur de Blanc* versus stark fonts and hard lines for intense stories like *Pattern Black)*, and sometimes I'll add chapter images, backgrounds, or full-page graphics. Usually, though, it's just a book.

Where "Artisan" truly shows up with this most basic of formats is in the writing and the story itself. Consider it a commandment: You are hereby ordered to write the best and most honest story you can.

Here's a few Artisanal guidelines for those of you who like bulleted lists:

- **Don't skimp on editing or proofreading.** Artisan readers will forgive a typo here and there, but beyond a few they're going to start seeing you as a hack. You're providing a premium reading experience, remember, and in the next chapter I'll encourage you to charge accordingly. Premium experiences die pretty quickly when it feels to readers like you never bothered to check your work, and instead just dashed off the fastest crap you could.

- **Don't pull punches with the story.** Stephen King (he should really be paying me for as much as I'm mentioning him) wrote in his fantastic book *On Writing* that a writer should write about anything they want *as long as it's the truth*. This means not dulling the sharp edges and most niche aspects of your book just because you're timid about exposing your soul too much, or because you think that what you wrote might offend someone. Here's a newsflash for you: You probably *will* offend someone, and some people *will* hate your book. That's just the facts of being an author, and if you never ever get any negative feedback, it probably means you're not playing hard enough. Success comes with criticism. Get used to it and speak your truths anyway. That's what King meant about being honest. You can homogenize and sanitize your book into a bland and boring mess that won't bother anyone, but if you do that, you won't impress or move anyone, either. In order to truly blow some people away, you have to risk turning other people off. Think of it this way: The more you're afraid that your book will rustle some feathers, the more likely it is that it'll be someone's favorite book of all time.

- **Write the best and most authentically "you" story you can.** Really delve and layer your tale if it suits you to do so. If you like twists, don't pull back and worry that your book will become too twisty. If you're scientific like me, don't be afraid to add scientific detail that you think will bore some readers (or go over their heads) if it's natural for you to write that way. It's worked for me, but it also worked for a little author named Michael Crichton who had about ten of his books made into big-deal movies. It worked for Andy Weir, whose novels double as textbooks. After reading *The Martian*, I felt ready to maroon myself on Mars because I now knew exactly how to grow space potatoes.

- **Take as much time and care as you need.** Remember the pillars? Don't rush. At this stage, the most important directive is for you to do you. If you like writing bonus material, write it. If your muse tells you to draw a map or write up some character bios, go for it. A lot of Artisan Authors find Author's Notes both fun to write and a great tool for bonding with their superfans, who read those Notes and get to know them a little bit better.

If you want to actually *sell* your book, I'd also suggest taking the step of packaging it so that it appeals to your target readers. This is simpler and less tactical than we've been told it needs to be. Forget tweaking your title just so, keyword-stuffing your description and tagline, and creating vague boasts about the book that impress nobody. Instead, just keep a very simple truth in mind: *Books deliver an experience, so use the market-facing parts of yours (the cover, title, and sales description) to most accurately and flatteringly promise that experience to potential readers.*

Don't worry too much about "getting it just right" by the usual, Amazon-based standards. Like most things in the Artisan Author world, you'll make the best decisions not by learning new tricks, but instead by *un*learning the bullshit.

One packaging element that's *not* bullshit (and that I'd *very strongly* recommend for your ebooks) is a well-designed and professional-looking cover. If you're not a graphic designer, this is something you should hire out. Don't break the bank on a book cover, but don't be stingy, either. Trust me: In the world of book covers, "good enough" is definitely not *good enough*. People *absolutely* judge books by their covers. I've had people buy my books without ever turning them over, gauging them practically by the cover alone.

At base, book marketing is simple. All you need to do is to attract and then hook the right reader's attention.

Does your book cover draw people in? Awesome, then it's the right cover. Does your title arouse interest from that genre's readers? Perfect; it's a good title. Does your description or back-cover copy seal the deal, getting that right reader nodding with excitement? Great. That means you're on point.

Remember the second pillar? You want to be as *human* as possible. Forget about how machines will see and promote your book and focus instead on what draws individual humans.

If your ebook is well and interestingly written, as free of typos as you can make it, formatted professionally, and has a cover and other market-facing elements that pique interest, that's all you really need to get started.

Paperbacks

Nothing feels better than holding a physical copy of your own book in your hands. And honestly, because "Artisan Author" is a mindset as much as anything, there's a lot of value *just in your having that feeling*, even if you never sell a physical copy. The more you feel like an artist, the more likely it is you'll act like one.

When I started writing professionally in 2012, I focused primarily on ebooks like almost everyone else. Sean and I had paperbacks made of some of our books, but I seldom saw them. We uploaded the files to make them available for sale, but that was about it. My paperbacks felt like concepts, not real things.

Thirteen years later, I had an opportunity to sell my books at a book fair for the first time, so I scrambled to convert more of them to paperback and then ordered copies of each. The day they arrived was flat-out magical. I laid those books on the family game table at home, one title per stack.

And *Oh. My. God.*

I'd only ordered those paperbacks so I'd have some to sell, and I'd only arranged them on the table so I could inventory them. But something happened that I didn't expect as I looked at those books, laid out nice and pretty. I realized that for the first time ever (and remember, this was after *thirteen years* of writing full time) I actually felt like a real author.

For me, paperback books are the Artisan Author sweet spot. Because everything is always "it depends," that may or may not be true for you, but there's a fair chance this is something we'll have in common. Unlike with ebooks, paperbacks can be made cool and pretty in ways that actually make a difference — and yet doing so isn't nearly as difficult as "prettying up" hardbacks and special editions. Their in-between nature (not as simple as ebooks, not as complex as special editions) makes them an ideal middle-ground for Artisan Authors. Paperbacks are more than most indie authors do (which makes you stand out), they're ripe for aesthetic touches that don't really matter to ebooks (which makes you look and feel to buyers like an artist), they're a common and easy purchase for Artisan readers (who often like tangible books but don't always want to spend a fortune on special editions), and they're not terribly hard for authors to create, even if it means hiring someone to create them for you.

Do you need to make your books into paperbacks as an Artisan Author? *No.* Would I advise it for more Artisan Authors than not? *Yes.* The folks who appreciate Artisan goods overlap strongly with folks who want tangible things that they can hold. These are the people who buy vinyl records instead of MP3s and seek out handmade art instead of buying whatever catches their eye at The Dollar Tree. You'll find some Artisan readers who only want ebooks or audiobooks, but there's nothing — for many of them — quite like taking home an object they'll be able to put on their shelf and show off ... *especially* if they interacted with the author, and *especially* if that book is signed. Their connection to you turns that paperback from $20 worth of entertainment into a conversation piece. It stops becoming just a story and becomes a memory — and proof that they, as readers, are discerning people who appreciate fine and unique things.

Keep that in mind. Artisan goods have value to the reader beyond the specific item. *You're not just selling them a book. You're actually selling them a validation of their values. You're selling them proof that they're good people who appreciate fine things and support the arts.*

I tend to fancy-up my paperbacks while I'm preparing my ebooks, because most of those nice touches won't appear in the ebook anyway. Still, though, we're just talking about basic stuff — stuff anyone can do in Vellum, or InDesign if you're a pro. In the end, my paperbacks look clean and professional, but not necessarily that special inside.

(I do, however, love when I'm inspired to do the work of

adding something truly nice. The huge *Future of Sex* omnibus has beautiful custom new-chapter images that mirror elements from the cover, full-bleed individual images for each sub-book in the omnibus, and more. The people who've bought it appreciate it.)

The usual bookselling platforms allow a moderate amount of nice formatting without trouble, so it's easy enough to upload your paperbacks for on-demand paperback printing (to Amazon, to Ingram, to Lulu or BookVault for direct-store fulfillment) and be done with it. Do that, and you'll be able to say you have paperbacks available for those who want them at the very minimum.

If you're adventurous enough to try your hand at in-person sales, you can take the extra step of ordering copies of your books to re-sell. You might also order books to fulfill a Kickstarter, or if you run your own author store and want to send books out manually rather than having Lulu or BookVault drop-ship them to the customer. This is where my "I'm a real author" feeling finally kicked in: the first time I actually ordered books.

I get most of my author copies from Amazon and Ingram. Amazon is cheaper, but Ingram is faster and I've found the quality to be better, though seldom *appreciably* better. With certain better-selling titles, though, I'm able to order a short print run (at least 50 copies, but ideally more) and save a lot of money. Massive offset print runs (thousands of copies at a time) are the most cost-efficient, but obviously you have to find that money up front, and you have to know you'll be able to sell them all. Oh, and another bonus of ordering print runs — long or short — is that you won't have to pay sales tax. You'll have to *collect* sales tax from the end customer, but you won't have to pay it because there's no tax (in the US, and BTW I'm not a lawyer or an accountant, yada yada) on items you plan to resell. (Good luck getting *Amazon* not to charge you tax, though, even though you shouldn't have to pay it if you're reselling what you buy. It's friggin Amazon. They don't care.)

You don't *need* to make or sell paperback copies of your books, and you certainly don't need to order copies to your house to ship back out or resell. It's cool as hell if you do, though. I'm telling you: It'll make you feel like a real author in a way you never have before.

As with ebooks, your paperback's cover is extremely important. In terms of making the first sale, the cover is sometimes more important than the story itself. (The story becomes vital in making the *second* sale. Bad story = nobody interested in the sequel.)

If you haven't had your ebook cover made yet, it's smart to have your cover designer expand the ebook cover into a paperback cover for you while they're at it. The price difference is nominal. I pay over a thousand dollars for my ebook covers, then get the paperback add-on for around $150 more.

In the grand scheme of things, it's the most no-brainer money you'll spend. The difference between a good paperback cover and a mediocre one will *definitely* affect your sales ... and might even make or break them.

Audiobooks

Audiobooks are completely optional. In truth, you probably won't sell many. The rule of thumb for audiobooks is that if a book is already selling well as an ebook or paperback, it'll probably sell well as an audiobook, too — but if your ebook and paperback sales are struggling, chances are your audiobook will struggle even harder.

Some of my ebooks don't sell very well, but I have on my long-term to-do list to create audiobooks of them anyway. The reason? Because I sell a lot in person, I'm face-to-face with a lot of readers. I'm asked questions that most authors never get asked because of it, so I know what my readers want. And dammit if they don't ask for audiobooks *all the time.*

A lot of people want to read more but can't find the time. Or they travel a lot, and want entertainment. I have one reader who's a long-haul trucker — and driving that much creates a lot of dead air. Audiobooks are perfect for all of these people. Busy parents can listen to audiobooks during their hours upon hours of kid tasks; gym rats can listen while exercising; early-morning mall walkers can listen while they get their not-quite-a-sweat on.

There's a real hunger for audiobooks, but making them seldom pays off for indie authors like us. So what's an Artisan to do?

Personally, I opted for a two-phase plan. I only have a handful of finished audiobooks, so I was left with seventy books or so without an audio companion. I'll get around to making audiobooks of all of them in time, but it will take *years*. To bridge the gap, Phase One was to do something that might strike you as the least-Artisan thing I could do: I had Apple Books create AI-read audiobooks for me using their integrated tool at Draft2Digital. That way, readers who want to listen now can do so ... while in the background, I'll slowly create replacements narrated by me, one book at a time.

Creating human-narrated audiobooks takes either a lot of time or a lot of money, which is why I compromised with AI: It wasn't a choice between human audiobooks and AI audiobooks for me; it was a choice between AI audiobooks and nothing at all. The Artisan approach isn't anti-AI; it's anti-half-assing-your-job. You may disagree with my decision, but it felt permissible to me to create AI audiobooks as a stop-gap meant to please my fans, knowing I'll eventually swap them out with something better.

You can do what I did, or you can start with human audiobooks if you have a small catalog, a lot of time, a lot of money, or a damn good reason to do so that supercedes everything else — like an enormous readership ready to drop serious coin on the first audiobook you drop. Alternatively, you can partner with a narrator through ACX.com using a revenue-share agreement, wherein you agree to split royalties with the narrator for seven years. That process also tends to be time-consuming, and the best narrators won't do revenue share. Ultimately, it's up to you.

Choose your own path with audiobooks. Revenue-share

might work, but so might not doing audiobooks at all. If you're rich and want the very best, you can hire top-tier talent and pay through the nose for it, knowing you're unlikely to earn that money back. Or, like I plan to do, you can record your own audiobooks. The how-to-do-it-well on self-narration is beyond the scope of this book, but I have surveyed readers and found that most of them love the idea of author-read audiobooks, assuming the author isn't a terrible reader and has decent production value. It's a connection to the author, after all.

Hardbacks, Box Sets, and Special Editions

Ah, the fun stuff!

Almost nobody will buy hardbacks of your books without a special event like a crowdfunding campaign, so there's very little reason to go to the trouble of making them unless you find it fun and interesting. That goes double for box sets and special editions … which, by the way, you can't sell on the most common platforms and could only sell direct anyway.

You can definitely put plain, non-special-edition hardbacks up on Amazon and Ingram just for the hell of it even if you probably won't sell any, if it amuses you to do so. Both platforms can print on-demand hardbacks and drop-ship them to customers (or bookstores or libraries, in the case of Ingram) without your involvement. One caveat: If your hardback has a dust jacket, keep in mind that dust jackets require yet another cover design, and provide a boring answer to *"Why not* put them up anyway?": "because money."

If you're hell-bent anyway, you can either pay a bit more for a dust jacket design or simply have the cover file printed directly on the book's hardback boards. You'll need to modify your existing paperback design a little to make it fit a case-wrap, but it's not a true rebuild like a dust jacket requires.

For most Artisan Authors, the "above and beyond" formats of hardback, special editions, and box sets are created more for crowdfunding projects (like Kickstarter), direct sales from your website, or possibly in-person or convention selling. I've had moderate success selling all three in person, but they're usually gift purchases. The upside is that you might actually make some money if you can sell them in the run-up to Christmas.

The nuances of — and many possibilities of — premium editions are far too tangled to explore here. The bottom line is: Try them if it intrigues you or if you have superfans who've been asking for them, but otherwise maybe don't bother. It's a lot of work to create special editions. If they're done well, though, they're infinitely cooler than garden variety editions. The first time I hold a new special edition in my hands, I'm always very happy. It's amazing to see your work in such a high-end format.

I'll add a caveat: If you enjoy the art of authoring, you might choose to create premium books *simply because you want to make them*. If that's the case, go for it! You'll enjoy it more if you release any expectations of sales, and instead just love the process for its own sake. (That's something I'd recommend for your entire writing career, actually, especially as an Artisan Author. Of course you want to sell some books, but you should love the process even if you never sell a thing.)

The sky's the limit when it comes to special editions. You can — and should — let your creativity run wild.

Certain touches like sprayed edges (solid color or custom), foil stamping, ribbon bookmarks, decorative head and tail bands (the "stitches" at the top of the hardback binding), spot UV (to make one part of a cover shiny), custom endpapers (the first spread, which ties the "book block" to the hardback boards), and more can actually be done today as print-on-demand, meaning you can literally order one copy at a time. Same for box set slipcovers, actually. BookVault does all of those things, and I'm sure there are others.

Other touches require a bit of planning and an often-sizable investment. You can emboss or deboss your cover (sunken or raised sections, creating texture), have your binding sew-bound instead of glue-bound ("perfect bound"), or do crazy crap like die cutting, where sections of your cover are actually cut away. For these more elaborate touches and more, you'd need to order a larger-scale print run as of this book's writing. That means ordering *at least* 50 copies of your book at once, probably many more. Ordering hundreds of copies of books that fancy will cost a fortune per copy (meaning you won't make much profit unless you turn around and charge customers a fortune, too), and ordering *thousands* or *tens of thousands* at a time to lower the per-copy cost will cost a fortune overall. If you choose either of those routes, I suggest either being rich so you won't care if they sell, or creating sales demand *before* you place the order (which you can do through pre-sales on a direct store or by running a Kickstarter).

The book formats in this section are beyond optional. For many (or most) authors, they could even be an actively bad (or at least pointless) idea. That doesn't stop them from being fun and cool as hell, though, so if you've considered the pros and cons and want to make all sorts of special fancy books, I say go for it.

I'll add one last thing here, but be careful not to give it too much weight and get yourself in trouble: *As an Artisan Author, there's real value in serving your True Fans disproportionally.* If only the Truest of your True Fans will buy a given special edition, making it *might* be worthwhile on that basis even if it only means selling ten copies.

There are two main reasons for this: First, True Fans are worth making an effort to over-serve. Remember Pillar #3? You're supposed to treat your fans like gold (or diamonds). Second, though, exclusivity is a big deal in itself. It might not be a great deal for *you* to do all the work to make something that only ten people will buy, but that same low number is *wonderful* for collector-types like True Fans. I mean, think about it: They now have something that *only nine other people in the world* have.

It's super cool, and it's a great way to make your True Fans love you even more (or turn a normal fan or two into a True one), but be sure to consider carefully before hanging yourself with this idea. Ordering ten special editions to resell at break-even might be worthwhile fan service for you, but ordering a hundred and selling ten (or even ordering ten and selling zero because you miscalculated your readers' intentions) will set you back more than it moves you forward, especially when you factor in the time it'll take you to put those special editions together.

Thinking Beyond the Book

If you're craftier and more motivated about such things than I am, there are all sorts of other neat products you can create as an Artisan Author. I haven't explored many of them, but that doesn't mean you can't or shouldn't.

As with special editions, the only real limit when you create "beyond the book" is your imagination. Ask yourself what sorts of merchandise would make your worlds more compelling for your readers, then consider taking a stab at creating those things.

You could make mugs. I've considered a mug for my *Fat Vampire* world that has blood dripping down one side. That would be rad.

You could make maps. My worlds never really work for maps (partly because I don't write fantasy and partly because I never know where anything is geographically in my stories anyway).

You could make board games. I know some people who are actively considering this one. It's pretty far out of my own wheelhouse, but it might be perfect for LitRPG or fantasy authors who are already board game naturals. If that's you, maybe you'll want to lean into it, seeing as it's something that's *uniquely you* but that others with different skill sets (present company included) would be downright stupid to do. (Board games make great crowdfunding projects, by the way. The game community loves Kickstarter.)

Character cards. Concept art. Digital wallpaper. I saw one author who made socks. My friend David Viergutz makes badass stainless steel bookmarks with his logo etched into them. You could do T-shirts. Posters. Custom hats, for shit's sake, if there are cool hats in your story. My friend Bill wants to help me make 3-D printed Rollards, which are demon-fighting weapons from my *Gore Point* series. I thought it sounded cool, but there's just one problem on my end: despite describing them over and over in the books, I only have the vaguest idea what a Rollard actually looks like.

If you're hands-on and crafty — and if you carefully consider the financials of these kinds of items — they might be perfect for you. If you're not hands-on or crafty, though, you could create "beyond the book" experiences that don't require images or building anything: creating an online scavenger hunt, digital bonus content, Easter eggs, or whatever else.

Have fun. The sky really is the limit ... and as an Artisan Author, you practically have a mandate to be cool. You're an artist, after all!

Chapter 7

Selling As An Artisan Author

So now you've got your stuff. How exactly should you sell it?

Just like we talked about in the last chapter, your imagination is the only limit when it comes to creative sales strategies. In fact, here's something that shifts the paradigm so hard, it'll break your brain: *Try to think of sales and marketing your work as being part of the art.*

Gross, right? You want to create, not sell. You're an artist, not a huckster. But does it have to be that way?

Time and time again, friends have asked me why I self-publish in the first place. They say, *You could land a traditional deal, Johnny, so why don't you try to get one?* The answer I give is, "Why would I want to? Solving the puzzle of 'How can I package and sell this?' is half the art — and half the fun!"

Here's what I mean:

- When I noticed that most new readers would buy one book from me but didn't particularly care what it cost, I created a huge paperback omnibus containing all six *Fat Vampire* books. That omnibus sells for $45: great profit for me, and a $30 savings for the reader versus buying the books individually. It was a creative problem with a creative solution, and it's made a lot of deposits to my bank account since I solved it.

- When I noticed how influential my recommendations were on which books people bought, I started experimenting with recommending some of my hidden gems: books I love, but that aren't the usual suspects. It worked, and I learned something about my unique audience and my unique strengths as a seller. I learned that I can move just about any book I want to — a trick that comes in handy when I sell out of something popular.

- A lot of times when I sell in person, I get the same reaction from lapsed readers that everyone gives to the dental hygienist when they ask how often you floss: a guilty "I don't do it as much as I should. I keep meaning to, but just never get around to it!" And so over time, I've learned to help those people out. They want to read but can't get through books, and obviously I want to sell to them. So instead of shrugging and bidding them well as they walk away empty-handed, I now suggest a page-turner like *The Target* or *Namaste*: books that are fast-paced, short, and engaging enough that even out-of-practice readers burn through them quickly, getting them back on the reading horse.

It's a mindset shift, nothing more. You could *choose* to like selling. All you need is to keep an open mind, then make that choice.

And honestly, it makes sense. When you think about it, writing books is a process that involves facing and solving problems over and over again. Writers tend to love *that* aspect of problem-solving, but balk at packaging, marketing, and sales ... which are *also* problem solving. Why *wouldn't* you be interested in finding the best ways to earn money from that book you poured so much time into — *especially* as an Artisan Author, where there are no rules and you can do whatever you want? It's fascinating and a great intellectual challenge ... and when you solve the puzzle, you get money for it. Who wouldn't want that?

Oh, you might need to stretch your comfort zone a bit, but I hope you'll try. Dismiss your knee-jerk reaction to the boogeyman of SELLING. Instead, Kobayashi Maru style, remember that *you're playing a different game now.* What used to repel you can — if you keep an open mind — become a huge part of the fun of this Artisan thing. It certainly has for me.

Besides, you're likely to run into some cool "a-ha" moments with Artisan selling *[resists an urge to make an A-Ha! "Take On Me" reference that nobody under thirty will understand]* that I promise will be delightfully eye-opening. You're going to start seeing ways to promote and sell your books that nobody ever told you were options before. You're going to have revelations, if you stick with it, that feel like you're one of only a few people who see through the Matrix and into the real world behind it.

For me, it was when I realized that I didn't need Amazon anymore.

I remember the day fondly. I was adding up profit forecasts for all of my upcoming in-person events, tossing in a few planned Kickstarter campaigns to boot. (A formula that's perfect *for me*, by the way, but definitely not a formula for you or anyone else to follow because I'm me and you are you.) At the end of those calculations, I reached a number that made me happy ... and *only then* realized I hadn't added in my online sales. Not Amazon, not Draft2Digital, not IngramSpark, not any of the audiobook distributors. Hell, I hadn't even factored in my own direct store, because I hadn't gotten around to optimizing it yet.

All I'd added up were in-person sales and Kickstarter. And it was enough.

I thought: *Wait. I don't need Amazon anymore? Is that really a thing?* But then I remembered at least two people I know who've said plainly that their Amazon sales are garbage, and yet *they* make full-time livings from their books, too. So yes, it really is possible.

Now, let me be clear: In no way am I saying that you should remove Amazon or anything else from your bookselling vocabulary. I'm saying that was *my* revelation, and that you will have different revelations of your own. I'm saying there are possibilities out there that even I'd never considered — not even after a dozen years in this business. I'm not planning to leave Amazon or the other online retailers (quite the contrary; my next problem-to-solve is ramping them up), but the point is: *I don't have to do any of that if I don't want to ... and more importantly, I have no reason to worry if Amazon does something dumb..*

When you learn how to sniff out Artisan selling opportunities in the strangest and most previously-unseen places, you won't "have to" for any single channel, either. The freedom of that sort of revelation is exhilarating. Realizing you can find readers almost anywhere, all on your own? It's an amazing feeling.

As you read this chapter, I'd like you to do two things.

First, discard your preconceptions and prejudices. Adopt what martial artists call "beginner mind," meaning you're willing to let go of your ego and accept anyone and anything as a possible teacher.

Second — and I hate to be a buzzkill — keep your expectations in check. I've worked with enough authors to know that although I shared my "I don't need Amazon" story above only to make a point, some of you are already slobbering over the idea of 1) copying my approach exactly even though I've told you about ten times not to and 2) finding untold new riches between the cushions of the great bookselling couch.

I'm telling you right now, it won't work that way. My unique book catalog, personality, skill set and strong suits, and the fact that I've been through the ringer in this business for a long time makes my approach work for me. I had an enormous head start, and I also worked for two years solid to rebuild even my well-established business to work up to what I've just described. But you aren't me. You'll be able to do things I can't if you really lean into the "you do you" of this Artisan approach, so don't bank on doing things that *I* do well that aren't right for you.

But who cares if sales start out slow? Hell — who cares if they *stay* slow, as long as they're reliable and give you something to build on, patiently, over time? You're an Artisan Author, remember? *Art first. Profit second.* I want you to sell your wares and have fun doing it, but if profit was our primary driver, we should all be in another profession.

Don't think in terms of "riches." Think in terms of "a whole new world of possibility."

And man oh man, are there possibilities out there for authors who are willing to work hard, think creatively, and persist.

The Usual Suspects

Sometimes I run into authors who decide they're going to buck online sales completely. They won't upload to Amazon. They won't upload to Draft2Digital, PublishDrive, Kobo Writing Life, Barnes & Noble Press, IngramSpark, or anywhere else. These authors announce with pride that they're going to instead row this boat all by themselves. If Amazon is such a shit show, they figure they'll just walk away entirely.

I'm not here to tell you what to do, but not selling on "the usual suspects" of bookselling strikes me as a terrible idea. It's true that Amazon, B&N, Apple, and others may yield mediocre (or downright bad) results for a lot of Artisan Authors — especially where the "upload and wait for sales to happen" approach is concerned — but there's also very little downside. Uploading your books to a few different retailers or aggregators will cost you nothing but your time. You'll pay a commission when you make a sale on any online platform that you don't personally control, but so what? Those are sales you wouldn't get otherwise.

Don't fall into the trap of thinking you can lure Amazon buyers into buying from you directly instead, thus negating the need to publish on Amazon to get them. Technically it's possible, and it does happen, but it's such a small minority that counting on it amounts to throwing the baby out with the bathwater. Typically, Amazon buyers remain Amazon buyers, Kobo buyers remain Kobo buyers, and the people who will buy from you in other ways were *always* willing to buy from authors in other ways. You'll change very few reader habits. Refusing to sell on the usual platforms because you're planning to recapture those people through other channels will only cost you sales.

We'll talk more about this in the next chapter, but not every reader you'll attract as an Artisan Author will become a fan, let alone a True Fan. You'll also get casual readers, people who read one of your books and then never read you again, and more. You shouldn't base your entire sales strategy around the usual booksellers, but that doesn't mean your books on those platforms won't still attract readers. Some readers — even those who primarily read in Kindle Unlimited — will run across your book thanks to some also-bought or algorithm, see the cover and title, and want to read more. Some of them will even buy it.

My retailer sales kind of suck right now because I don't fit into their boxes, but I do get sales there. You may even find, like many of my Artisan friends, that your off-Amazon promotional activities increase your Amazon sales. While selling in person, I run into readers all the time who don't read paperbacks for one reason or another: the type is too small, they have too many books already, or they're trying to spend less money. Those readers *do* look me up, though, on the bookstores they're comfortable with — stores like Amazon. And that's how it happens — how deliberate Artisan selling will get you sales in places that aren't very "Artisan" in nature, too.

So yes: I *do* suggest publishing your books in the usual places. There are no upfront fees or extra expenses to do so, with just a few fringe exceptions. Again: *All it costs you is time.*

Put your books in the places below and your foundation will be covered. You'll look pro to readers, too, because they feel that "real authors" are those who are available everywhere. You don't need to focus on selling Amazon copies if you don't want to (though you may very much want to! Just because I don't focus there doesn't mean anyone else shouldn't), but at the very least, they'll be there.

Let's talk platforms, beginning with a bit about what it means to be "wide" with your books.

Wide Means Wide

If I have one maxim about book availability, it's "be absolutely everywhere." Where do people look for books? Got it? Okay, put your books there — in *all* of those places.

Online bookstores. Your own direct store, if you have one. Brick and mortar bookstores. Libraries. In ebook, paperback, maybe audio and hardback formats. Not just in your own country, either. Make sure your books can be purchased all over the globe.

And by the way, everywhere can truly mean *everywhere*. Sometimes it means places that don't even earn you a profit.

For instance, Austin, where I live, has a big used book market. People tell me they've seen my books at Half Price Books, and even though I won't get a penny if those books sell (presumably I got paid when they sold the first time), I very much want them there. Why? Because having my books where other books are sold just makes sense. I haven't done it, but I've toyed with the idea of taking even more of my books into HPB and selling them like anyone sells any used books. If they'll pay me at least as much as it cost me to print them, it might be worthwhile just to have more on the shelf.

Hmm. Now I'm thinking about that one again. Weird? *Yes.* Clever and something no other authors do? *Also yes.*

When a reader goes *anywhere* for a book — or runs across books out in the wild — you want your book alongside the others. *Where are books? Okay, put your books there.* Stop me if this is getting too complicated.

Artisan Authors are long-term, big-picture thinkers. We want to earn money from our books, but profit alone isn't where the buck stops. We don't think *now-now-now* like our Rapid Release friends. Instead, we're in this for full careers. We're grounded and patient authors, trusting that fanships — and the money that comes from fanships — will eventually follow.

I've left copies of my books in public places for others to read and take.

I've given my books away, especially to people who I think might show them off. I have a friend who runs one of the biggest TV shows in history, so you bet your ass I gave him a copy of *Unicorn Western* when he was in Austin. He was already a *Fat Vampire* fan. What if he shows *Unicorn Western* around to his buddies? It only cost me $11 to gamble and find out.

One of the libraries here is so small, local authors have to donate their books if they want them on the shelves. I gave them as many copies as they'd take. Why not?

In fact, right about now the wiseasses among you might be thinking, "Okay, Johnny — so what about Kindle Unlimited? Does *that* count as somewhere my book should be, if there are other books in KU and I want my books everywhere books are sold?"

Touché, wiseass. *Touché*.

My answer is technically maybe, but almost certainly no. KU isn't like Half Price Books because it refuses to play well with others. HPB doesn't care who else carries my books, but KU does. KU doesn't expand your reach; it severely restricts it. You can't sell ebooks *anywhere* else if you sell them in KU.

But even so — and even though I'd never put *my* books in KU as part of an Artisan strategy — that doesn't mean it's off-limits for all Artisan Authors. If you've looked at your unique situation and decided to try KU as part of your strategy (using KU books to get attention, maybe, or attempting to drive paperback sales through witchcraft and alchemy), then hey — you do you.

As with everything, it depends.

There are as many intriguing ways to get your books out there as there are stars in the sky, but don't let the number of options bog you down. Even though I just said to spread your books far and wide, you won't be able to reach every nook and cranny of the world in practical terms. So instead of obsessing and trying to be perfect, just follow The 80/20 Rule and do your best. Keep the big-picture in mind, get as close to it as is reasonable for you, and you'll be just fine.

That rule is: *Be everywhere.*

Below are a few ideas for "everywhere" to get you started.

The Usual Kind of Wide

There are two definitions of "wide" in the indie author community. The most common means "available on as many online bookselling platforms as possible rather than just Amazon." Instead of finishing an ebook and uploading it *only* to Amazon, "wide" authors upload to other places as well. Apple, Barnes & Noble, Kobo, and Google Play are the big ones, and you can hit most of them in one fell swoop using an aggregator like Draft2Digital if you'd rather not upload to individual stores one by one. Personally, I love Draft2Digital. They take a bigger cut of your profit than the individual stores do, but time and convenience are more important to me than earning a few extra cents per sale.

As for the second and less common meaning of "wide," credit goes to Monica Leonelle and Russell Nohelty for explaining it in the easiest-to-understand way I've heard. To emphasize the "even wider" scope, they usually insert an adjective: Instead of just "going wide," Monica and Russell suggest "going *aggressively* wide." "Aggressively wide" lines up with what I said about putting your books everywhere. "Wide," in other words, doesn't strike me as wide enough.

The remainder of this chapter will introduce some of those "aggressively wide" options, but first we should cover the basics: what most authors mean when they say "wide" in the first place.

Below is my own "the normal kind of wide" checklist. It's a good starting point for Artisan Authors, but my choices won't be the best choices for everyone. Be sure to consider your own situation before simply copying my approach like a mindless map-follower.

With that disclaimer out of the way, I upload my books to the following places at a minimum — even when I don't get around to being all *aggressive* about going even wider.

Ebooks

- **Amazon KDP.** This is almost everyone's first stop, to make your books available on Amazon. When you publish, you'll be given the option to enroll your book in KDP Select, which will put your book into Kindle Unlimited and require making your ebook exclusive to Amazon. **Unless you have a very good reason, *do not* choose to enroll in KDP Select.** Select and KU are the *opposite* of wide, and the wrong choice for most Artisan Authors.

- **Draft2Digital.** This is my aggregator of choice. There are others, but I've known the people at Draft2Digital for my entire career and would vouch for all of them. For no upfront charge, publishing once at D2D will put your book into Apple Books, Barnes & Noble, Kobo, the library system, and a ton of other (often international) bookstores.

- **Google Play Books.** Draft2Digital used to upload to Google Play Books along with all their other partners, but they don't anymore. Now, I just do it myself. The Google Play app is standard on Android phones, which vastly outnumber iPhones worldwide. This means that putting your book into Google Play Books gives you the potential (though not the inevitability) of reaching far more readers. I don't earn much on Google Play yet, but it puts me in front of a huge portion of the globe that I'd miss otherwise.

- **BookFunnel.** If you sell your books from your own online store (or if you offer any free ebook downloads anywhere at all), you'll need a service to easily and seamlessly deliver them to your readers. I use BookFunnel for this, to fulfill ebook and audiobook sales after they're purchased on JohnnyBTruantBooks.com. You won't find a cooler, more customer-centric company in the indie pub world than BookFunnel.

Paperbacks and occasionally hardbacks

- **Amazon KDP.** They'll handle your paperback as well, and they'll pay a higher royalty on physical books sold through Amazon than books sold off-Amazon through Ingram (below). One note, though: If you're at all serious about selling paperbacks, **I strongly suggest *NOT* checking the "Expanded Distribution" box when you get to the pricing page.** Amazon Expanded Distribution makes your book available for off-Amazon sales through the Ingram network ... but does so at terms unfavorable to bookstores, so none will ever buy it. (Besides, bookstores hate Amazon anyway.) For off-Amazon physical book sales, you're far better off skipping Amazon's Expanded Distribution and going directly to Ingram instead.

- **IngramSpark.** This is the self-publishing wing of Ingram, the largest US bookseller network, and the best choice for reaching that network instead of doing it through Amazon Expanded Distribution. Uploading to IngramSpark will make your book available to brick-and-mortar bookstores and libraries, and will make it possible for customers in those stores to special-order your book. There are some pricing and discount considerations with Ingram that are beyond the scope of this book, though, so do your research before uploading.

- **BookVault or Lulu.** As of this writing, these are the two best services for printing on demand and drop-shipping paperbacks, hardbacks, and even special editions (BookVault only) ordered through your website, assuming you don't want to print in bulk and ship them yourself. BookVault is a lot cheaper, but in my experience Lulu's customer service is a lot better. I've used both, and have smart friends who swear by each. Your call.

Audiobooks

- **INaudio (formerly Findaway Voices).** These guys function as an audiobook aggregator — sort of like Draft2Digital for audiobooks. They'll distribute your audiobook to Audible, Apple, and many other audio outlets.

- **Spotify for Authors.** If you want to be available on Spotify, this is where you'll upload.

- **BookFunnel.** They also handle audiobook delivery, for both free distribution and direct sales.

If you make your books available in multiple formats (which you absolutely don't need to), you'll hit the 80/20 of "wide" bookselling by uploading to the places above. Your books will become available in most places an internet browser or mobile user will ever look for them — at least in the English-speaking market.

To be clear, I'm not saying you *should* do all of the above. Like everything in this chapter, they're only options. Audio can be an unprofitable boondoggle for Artisan Authors (see the last chapter), so you might not want to do it. You might not even do paperbacks, if you don't have a good way to move them or if they don't fit your strategy.

For most indie authors, though, the above list is pretty comprehensive. It's a good starting point for "going wide."

Go Global

We've talked about this before, but it bears repeating: *The United States isn't all there is.*

I'm a little insulted that it needs to be said. Most of the world's population — and most of the people who speak and read in English at least some of the time — live outside of the US. And yet what has the hive mind of self-publishing chosen as its primary strategy? Why, to serve the US market almost exclusively, of course.

Now, I know what you might be thinking. *Amazon distributes outside of the US, so uploading to Amazon IS going global!* And ... okay. Sort of. Maybe a little bit. But ask any high-selling indie author to check their stats and tell you what percentage of their sales happen outside the US, and you'll see the truth.

Amazon has sister stores in a handful of countries — mostly Canada, the UK, and across Western Europe. In those countries, though, Amazon is secondary or lower, not primary. Canada, for instance, gets most of its online books from Kobo. In other countries, Amazon doesn't exist or might as well not exist.

So how do you *really* reach those markets, meeting readers in the places they find their books? My answer has always been offering more options. There's no guarantee that putting your book on Google Play Books (far more "authentically international" than Amazon) will get you non-US sales, but I *can* guarantee that your chances of being found on Google Play are zero if you don't put your books there. Why not at least give readers some choices? Once you're non-exclusive to Amazon, you can put your books *anywhere*. So why not put them *everywhere?*

For me, going global is as much ideological as it is practical. To put it plainly, I make my books available to as many people worldwide as possible because it's the right thing to do. Isolationism is bad. Communication and cooperation are good. Cultural myopia is bad. Being willing to consider people different from yourself is good. And besides, it's also the Artisan thing to do. Since when do Artisans think in terms of "the minimum required effort"? Artisans are proud about behaving different from the purely-capitalistic norm. We do things because we want to share our art, in other words, not just because we want money.

To truly maximize the whole "go global" thing, you might choose to explore translating your work into other languages, but I haven't tried it yet. It's a bit too far in the other direction for me, currently requiring more expense and time than I'm willing to invest — and even then, you sort of have to know the nuances of marketing in those other languages. But if you've had success with translations, by all means keep at it!

Selling Direct

The topic of selling books directly from your own online storefront — like all of the other "aggressively wide" topics left in this chapter — is a deep field about which entire books have been written. If you want to know how to sell direct and the best practices for doing so, search out one of those other excellent guides.

Oh, and another important thing to mention about selling direct and the remaining topics in this chapter? They're *possible choices*, not things you should definitely do. My aim is to give you a "grab bag" of options for your Artisan Author sales strategy — a handful of things you *might* want to try, or maybe just mine for ideas — and to explain how those options can fit into the way of the Artisan Author.

For the right authors at the right places in their author journeys, direct sales can be a great sales choice. You can keep things simple by creating plain buy buttons for an existing website, or you can go whole hog like I did and create a Shopify store (mine is at JohnnyBTruantBooks.com if you'd like to take a look). If there's a way for customers to give money directly to *you* for books rather than an intermediary or a bookstore, you're selling direct.

Despite the way it's sometimes talked about in the author community, direct sales is neither your unequivocal savior nor a magic boon that will suddenly make you a millionaire. For the vast majority of direct-selling authors, the maxim "if you build it, they will come" does not apply. If all you do is create a website, sales will not just show up on their own. Moreover, it's harder than you think to get your existing customers to buy directly from you. Even your best fans are likely comfortable buying where they've always bought, so they'll need a damn good reason to change their ways.

There *are* ways to entice them, involving discounts, special perks, and exclusive items not available anywhere else. Most successful "direct" authors, though, need advertising to drive traffic ... and ads are a whole expensive and complicated mess in and of themselves. Do ads work if you keep at it and do them right? Oh yes. Fortunes have been made that way. But will it work just because you heard it's the newest and greatest thing for self-published authors? Um, no.

That said, direct sales is a great end goal — a worthy thing to aspire to, over time and eventually — for many Artisan Authors. It's not because you'll make bank selling direct (you might, but you also might not ... and definitely not without work, patience, and investment). It's because the ethos of selling direct is so perfectly in line with the ethos of an Artisan. Artisans want high-quality, often-direct connections with their fans, and the fans are often *seeking* that direct connection as an antidote to buying corporate. For the right buyer, there's a ton of value in *buying directly from the artist* that transcends even the item itself. Given the choice of buying a *good* necklace from a local artisan jewelry maker and an *excellent* one from a big-box jewelry store, the truly Artisan shopper almost always chooses the former.

Remember, we've changed the paradigm. All my talk about the Kobayashi Maru should have rammed that home by now. It's a mistake to assume that the buyers you're trying to attract as an Artisan Author think the same as KU buyers. They don't.

By default, you're likely to believe that the average buyer's reasons for buying are those we've been taught are universal: They buy a lamp because they need light, or they buy a book because they need to be entertained. That's not always the case, though. Sometimes your ideal buyers will buy from you specifically because they like the idea of supporting the arts. Sometimes, they'll buy because they like you. Perhaps most interestingly, sometimes an Artisan buyer will go out of their way to buy something overly expensive *just so they can brag about how expensive it was.* It's called the Veblen Effect and it's very real. Look it up.

The point is, *selling* direct has value simply because it allows certain high-quality readers to *buy* direct. A lot of people find psychological value in that sort of thing. They go to farmer's markets to support local farmers. They buy Artisan cheese from a local dairy because they visited the dairy once and liked the cows. They often buy for the *story* of the item — not the story in the pages of the book, but the story of how they found you somewhere as an author, liked your vibe, made a connection, then bought directly from your cute little store instead of Big Bad Amazon.

There's a huge learning curve in selling direct. If you decide it's right for you, know what you're getting into and set realistic expectations. I'd never do without a direct store myself, but it's far from required ... at least during your Artisan beginnings.

Kickstarter

Like direct sales, Kickstarter has become THE THING in the author community as I write this. It's a sales channel that tons of authors are flocking to because our culture got everyone excited about it as if it's a panacea. It's not, though — not universally so. Kickstarter (or any sort of crowdfunding for your book) isn't for everyone. It's tricky to learn and a ton of work, and for plenty of authors it doesn't pay off.

That said, Kickstarter it can also be an absolute game-changer if you approach it with the right mindset and for the right reasons. It's another version of direct sales: direct sales on steroids.

If you've never heard of Kickstarter or haven't looked into it enough to be familiar, it works like this: You offer different formats or variations of your book (and possibly some related items) for sale at discrete pricing tiers (EX: Join the $9 tier and get the ebook, or join the $30 tier and get the ebook *and* the paperback). Customers (called "backers") then pledge whichever of those tiers they want. The campaign runs for a limited period of time (usually 2 weeks to a month) and then ends, at which point nobody is able to buy it anymore. The pledge money will then be dumped into your bank account, and you'll set about giving your backers the items they purchased.

There's a lot of energy around a Kickstarter campaign. Because time is limited and because successful campaigns are an "event" for creators and their backers, they tend to create excitement. Because good campaigns often offer stuff that's not sold elsewhere (special editions of books that can't be sold on Amazon, bonus stories, author commentary, posters, etc.) and/or offer early access that non-Kickstarter buyers have to wait months longer for, they're ideal for the readers who want more of you than "just the book" and are willing to pay for it.

Because so little of my own Artisan Author business relies on sales through Amazon and the others, I tend to use Kickstarter as my primary launch vehicle. I eventually publish all of my books in the usual places, but more and more I see those places as secondary — as "nice to have" sales that barely matter in the grand scheme of things. Kickstarter allows me to offer all the cool bonus stuff my best fans want. I prioritize Kickstarter because *those* fans (the ones who want all the cool bonuses, want my books early, and want to support me directly) are the fans I choose to prioritize anyway.

If you're interested in Kickstarter, by all means try it! Don't just jump in, though; do your research instead. I'd suggest reading *Get Your Book Selling on Kickstarter* by the aforementioned Russell Nohelty and Monica Leonelle. Russell's Substack, at theauthorstack.com, is also an amazing Kickstarter resource.

Carefully consider the pros and cons realistically. Ask yourself if those pros, cons, benefits, and drawbacks align with you and your larger plan. If they do, go for it.

Live Sales

Ah, welcome to live sales — the cornerstone of the Johnny B. Truant Artisan Author strategy!

It's weird for me to write that, because as I type this, I've only been selling live for six months. And yet, in that time it's completely taken over my business. I write and build other parts of my machine during the week, then spend around half of my weekends behind a table in a sales booth, meeting readers and selling books face to face.

Live sales is a perfect match for my place and personality. I'm at least half extrovert, I genuinely enjoy talking to people (often for long periods of time, and often without a sale), I like the empowerment and control that comes with active selling instead of the passive selling we normally focus on, and I was willing to make a substantial financial and time investment on the hunch that live selling might be the thing I've been looking for all my life. It goes without saying that my experience in and alignment with live sales are far from universal — moreso, even, than anything we've discussed before.

If you're introverted and not interested in learning extroversion, you may not want to bother with live sales. Customers can tell if you're into it, and they won't want to talk to you if you're there grudgingly.

If you don't want to haul a bunch of books, racks, tables, signage, and equipment back and forth into convention centers or parking lots, it's not for you. I get my workout on selling days. It's not like owning a store, where you lock the door at night and simply show up the next morning. No; you need to set your "store" up every single day, and it ain't always easy. Hell — a lot of my events are outside, and that means I need to set up a tent, too, and weigh down the legs with cinderblocks (and then hope there's no rain and not too much wind).

And if you don't like the idea of standing up and proactively engaging with the people who walk by (not like a carnival barker, but inviting those who seem interested to have a conversation), stay home and spare yourself the effort of hauling out and setting up. I've been at live events beside authors who sit down the whole time, look at their phone, and wait for customers to browse on their own until they finally say, "I'd like to buy this." Those authors do terribly.

Remember, Artisan buyers want *you*, not just your books. They want *the story of meeting an author*, not just one more anonymous thriller from a bookshelf. If you want to sell at a live event, you have to be willing to be on your feet more often than not, smiling and friendly and willing to chat with just about anyone — without resenting the many people who, after chatting, still won't buy.

For some people, the idea of selling live is worse than a nightmare. If that's you, just skip this section and move on.

But if you suspect it *might* be for you but aren't sure (you're shy and nervous, but interested in getting to know some readers and regain some control), I suggest starting as small as you possibly can. The first time I sold outdoors, I borrowed a friend's 10x10 canopy and a folding table and set up at a farmer's market. Farmer's markets are wonderful entry points for live sales. The atmosphere is low-key and low-pressure, the other vendors are friendly and typically willing to answer questions and help if you need help, foot traffic isn't overwhelming, and a lower-than-average percentage of passersby will be interested in books, meaning you won't have to engage with as many people as you would at "better" events.

You probably won't sell terribly well in relative terms at a farmer's market, but with practice you'll sell enough to know whether it suits you — and with luck, maybe you'll sell enough to *excite* you with possibility. I typically grossed around $300 at my early farmer's markets and kept about half of that after paying for the books and the entry fee. But hey ... it excited the hell out of me to earn even $150 that I wouldn't have otherwise — $150 that I didn't have to hope would show up in an online dashboard, but instead that *I made happen*.

For me, live sales are empowering. They give me visibility into my ideal customers' buying habits and preferences that I'd never have otherwise. But that's me. It might not be you. That's why I suggest starting small if you're interested, then growing from there.

I quickly found markets where I grossed $500. Then $1000. Then beyond. I eventually tried conventions as well (like Comic Cons) and did even better. I know plenty of authors who regularly gross $4000-$7000 at conventions. The price of books, sales tax, an often-substantial entry fee, and travel costs come out of that amount, but just think about it for a second: They're getting hundreds of people who may never have heard of them before to buy physical copies of their books, and giving those customers a unique author/reader connection and story to tell. How valuable — how Artisan Author — is *that*?

I'm uniquely suited to live sales. I'm outgoing, love the rush, don't mind the time suck, and have an enormous catalog for buyers to choose from — enough that pretty much anyone can find something they're interested in. Thanks to that particular alchemy, my live sales income quickly eclipsed my online income. At my current pace (which is still maturing, by the way), I'll soon be making enough selling live that it'll technically be the only thing I'll ever need to do. Not that I'd stop doing other things, but it's a pretty cool factoid to know.

If the idea of live sales intrigues you, I suggest picking up *Power Author* by Ben Wolf. Ben is super helpful and willing to answer any questions you have after reading the book. My good friend and industry legend Mark Leslie Lefebvre also has a live sales book called *A Book in Hand,* which hopefully he's released by the time you read this. (I do keep bugging him).

Substack, Patreon, and Subscriptions

Welcome to the part of the book where I talk out my ass!

I don't jibe well with this section's trio of sales channels at all, but it would be conspicuous of me to skip them. Plus, it gives me one more chance to make a point: I'm giving you choices to consider, not a blueprint. My own success with subscriptions won't tempt you to follow my footsteps this time, seeing as I have none.

Honestly, I'm a case study for what *not* to do with membership-based income streams. I just can't make them work, and I don't like them at all. For others, the value proposition is exactly the opposite: Artisan Authors who do very well with memberships, and who love them to death. It all comes down to a fit between methods and personal style.

Authors who sell their books through paid membership on Substack, Patreon, Ream, or any number of other monthly subscription models produce content on a regular basis, then give that content to their members — sometimes with every member getting everything, or sometimes with different tiers of membership with some getting more or less than others. For a non-author example, I'm a Patron of Bob Schneider, the musician I mentioned early. At my tier, I get eight new songs every month and an early shot at buying show tickets. Higher tiers also get even cooler stuff, like dedicated seats at his venues, backstage privileges, and more.

If you'd like to learn from my bad example, I suck at membership because I can't produce interesting content on a regular enough basis to serve my paying members. My style is very different than that: I work on one project at a time, and I write it straight through and polish it before anyone else is allowed to see it. I could probably create a Patreon and give my members my finished new books when they come out, but I don't produce fast enough right now that it feels like enough of a benefit. And besides, how am I supposed to "tier" my approach? Frankly, I don't want anyone involved in my process or peeking over my shoulder. I'm all about showing up to sell books in person, but I frankly want everyone to stay the hell out of my office.

If you're the type of author who produces enough ongoing artifacts of your work to interest avid fans, some sort of recurring membership or subscription model might be great for you. If you write short stories regularly, it also might be perfect.

As with anything, look into it, maybe experiment, and see how it goes. Trial and error is part of the Artisan Author way of working, after all — seeing as nobody gives us a map.

Bookstores and Libraries

I've only dipped my toe into this one, so right up front I'll refer you to yet another book on the topic if you're interested: *Working With Libraries and Bookstores* by the aforementioned Mark Leslie Lefebvre. Mark has one of the widest breadths of book-related experience I know of. He's worked in libraries, in bookstores, in distribution, at Kobo and Draft2Digital, and more. Mark *knows* books ... and relevant to this section, he knows brick and mortar.

If you're interested in having your books in stores and libraries, they should be available for said stores and libraries to purchase in the ways those places like to purchase books. They won't want to buy from you, for instance. Instead, they're far more likely to acquire your books through the channels they use for all their other titles.

Libraries get their ebooks from services like Overdrive, which your ebook will be submitted to by default if you publish through Draft2Digital. They get their print books from Ingram, which you can upload to directly through IngramSpark. Don't try to get a library or a bookstore to buy your book from Amazon. They will tar and feather you, because Amazon is the death of bookstores — and, to some degree, libraries.

Libraries are great because they're simply how some people read. Making your books available there takes you one step closer to our mandate to "be everywhere." There's another benefit, too, and it's that you'll have an answer to give readers who tell you they can't afford your books. If they sincerely can't afford $5.99 for an ebook or $20 for a paperback (more on my pricing suggestions in the next section), cool. They can get either for free from the library instead. Requesting your book from the library has benefits for both you *and* the reader. You get paid and you get some exposure, and they get to read for free. It's win freakin' win!

To get into libraries, start local. Libraries are run by people who love books and tend to love authors. I simply walked into a few nearby libraries, introduced myself, and told them I was a local author. I then asked if they were interested in carrying some of my books. They vetted me (have to make sure the books are good and look decent), and soon enough I was able to walk back in and see my books right there on the shelves, covered in that weird library lamination wrap they put on everything.

Or, more accurately, I was able to see *some* of my books on the shelves. Most of what the system had was checked out. That thrilled me. People were browsing the library and picking out *my* books even though they may never have heard of me before!

Seeing your books in libraries is a trip, but seeing them in bookstores is practically bucket-list for many authors. I've had zero luck walking into my local Barnes & Noble stores and asking them to carry my books (they always invite me to email a supervisor, but despite emailing several many times, I've never once gotten the dignity of a reply), but I do know that people have found my books in chain bookstores in other places, so it must happen organically from time to time.

You'll probably have more luck with small, independent bookstores than trying to wrestle the B&N behemoth. Those outfits tend to be indie friendly because they're indies themselves. You're up against big-box authors, and the little book shops are up against big-box bookstores. You're simpatico, the small bookseller and you.

The first store I know of that carried my books was Studio Moonfall in Kenosha, Wisconsin. It's run by one of my favorite people in the world: Donovan Scherer, who was a fan of *The Self Publishing Podcast* from way back when. Years upon years later, I decided it might be a good idea to try and be in more than one store and doubled my footprint by going after a second: Book People, an iconic bookstore here in Austin. Donovan did the heavy lifting for me by simply putting books on his shelves, but Book People is probably a more instructive story because it didn't happen automatically.

The story goes like this: I walked into the downtown store one afternoon and talked to Thomas, the friendly guy at the info booth that day. (Book People, like most indie bookstores, is a friendlier environment than places like B&N. You can simply get a job at B&N, but you need to be a card-carrying book nerd to work in an indie store.)

Thomas gave me two names and email addresses: Consuelo, who does their buying, and Michael, who handles consignment. Consuelo was intrigued by *Fat Vampire* because it had cred: a million downloads, tons of online reviews, and a TV show adapted from it. Michael, however, didn't need as many credentials. He was interested in *Pretty Killer* and especially *Unicorn Western*, because they have great covers and looked intriguing. But more importantly, Michael didn't *need* to be as interested as Consuelo, beyond wanting the books to look good on his shelves and please the people who bought them. Consuelo was laying out the store's cash money to buy my books to resell, but Michael was taking consignment. If they didn't sell, he'd just give them back to me.

Every so often, Book People will send me a check for my consignment purchases. It's a nice cut, too — far more than I'd get from an Ingram sale like Consuelo handles. After enough books sell, Michael emails me and asks me to bring more. I grab some from my home inventory, drop them off, and the store handles the rest. Book People takes their cut when one of my books sell, then gives me the rest.

Like I said, I've only dipped my toe. Getting into bookstores and libraries is a one-at-a-time job, excepting the organic sales that happen when readers request books without your involvement. (That happens all the time, by the way. Someone told me they found a bunch of my books in some random LA bookstore once. How did *that* happen?) So far, I haven't been able to spare the time to get into more bookstores and libraries, but I'm dying to.

Pricing Like an Artisan

Before we move on to talking about attracting and nurturing your True Fan base, there's one last topic we should hit in the sales arena ... and that's pricing your books.

Pardon me while I take a deep sigh. This subject exasperates me. It's sad and exhausting to see so many authors on bended knee, begging the world to read their books.

That's what chronic, no-good-reason-for-it low pricing does: *It begs.*

If your book is cheap because you're running a sale, fine. If your first book is free as a loss leader intended to get people to pay for the second, fine. If you're pricing low to build your email list, or entice people through ads, or some other thought-out strategy, also fine.

But setting an everyday price of 99 cents?

Or bundling an entire series and selling *that* for 99 cents, without some greater strategy behind it?

Or cultivating a reader list who came to you on a free deal and will now only buy if you make books free or super-cheap again?

Not fine.

Not fine at all, my friends.

I understand why authors are insecure, which is what chronic low prices scream to the world. We're not a bold bunch by nature, and chances are we weren't Prom King or Queen, always adored by every one of our peers.

(Fun fact: I actually went to prom with the Prom Queen. She wasn't remotely your typical Prom Queen, and we went as friends, but it's still fun as hell to say.)

Authors, on average, are introverts. We're quiet. We vanish into crowds, drowned out by louder people. And then, atop all of that, we spend our time writing stories that come from deep within us — that sometimes make us feel naked when others read them. Many authors are so grateful to be *able* to publish in the first place that they take that ability as the reward. When you're already so grateful to be able to express yourself creatively, it feels greedy to ask for money, too. What's more, there's *so many of us* these days. It's not just our own reluctance that makes us want to practically (or literally) give our books away for free. It's our sense of business as well, arguing that nobody will pay more for us if others are cheaper.

If you feel the way I just described, then with all the love in the world, I'd like you to get the hell over it. Stop allowing yourself to feel less-than. Stop letting the world make you feel like you don't deserve to be paid well for your work, or that what you do doesn't matter. Remember our talk about the farce of "normal"? Part of that is a truth that your unique kind of work is exactly what someone has been looking for. You don't need to be ideal for everyone. You can't be. You're ideal for someone, though, and you need to let that someone pay you what your work is worth.

See, payment for anything is an exchange of value, and that value goes both ways. If you charge almost nothing, what you're selling *feels* like almost nothing to the person who receives it. I'd argue you're being disrespectful and borderline cruel to your own perfect brand of weirdoes by denigrating your own worth. You're *exactly what they've been looking for,* remember. Are you really going to turn around, look them in the eye, and tell them with your pricing that "exactly what they've been looking for" is worthless?

Come on. You're better than that.

Using price as your primary sales driver helps nobody. Certainly not in the world of an Artisan Author. You're not exploiting anyone. You're not coercing anyone. The prices an Artisan Author charges won't break anyone's bank — or, if they somehow do, those people can get your book from the library.

You did good, difficult work and you deserve to be paid fairly. Period. End of sentence.

Your own pricing choices will (wait for it) *depend* on a number of factors, but as I write this in 2025, my standard-length ebook price is $5.99. I'll drop to $4.99 for novellas, but that's about it. Extra long books cost more, and collections and omnibuses hit $9.99 or higher. Those numbers are near the top of where most indie authors feel comfortable pricing, but I'm honestly considering pricing even higher on Amazon and the other stores. Why? Because I don't sell too well on those stores anyway. Raising might lose me a few customers, but those who pay despite the price will likely be Artisan readers (the kind I want), and they'll make up for the drop-offs. Besides, pricing higher on stores lets me price a bit lower on my own site, to reward fans who buy direct.

Now, that's all unique to me. Don't take *my* situation and use it as a reason to change *your* prices.

The point is, *price what you're worth*. Price what earns you a respectable profit. The way that Ingram physical sales work, you have to offer bookstores a steep discount or they won't carry your books. Plenty of indie authors find that after the discount and the cost of printing the book, they earn less than a dollar from an Ingram bookstore sale. Knock it off, man. Get over yourself and raise that price until you're making at least three.

I'll say it again: *The kinds of buyers we want as Artisan Authors aren't price sensitive*, so using price as a lever won't move the needle very much. Discounting your book slightly to reward people who buy direct is a thank-you, not a move required by the market to make sales. People *appreciate* bargains when they come, but Artisan readers don't base their purchase decisions around them. If you price your books too low, you might even alienate readers who want a high-class experience, whereas you keep trying to give them a Walmart clearance experience. Raising prices seldom affects sales if you have the right readers.

To make this point, try a little thought experiment with me.

Imagine you're considering watching a movie. It's a must-see masterpiece, and all of your friends — who have your same taste in movies — have been talking about it nonstop.

Now, pretend that you go to a theater to watch that movie. You discover while you're at the box office that there's another movie playing, too: a deal-of-the-day situation wherein another film — one that's so-so to you; one you could take or leave — is offered for a few bucks cheaper.

Do you go to see the movie you know you'll love, that you've read up on and are interested in seeing?

Or do you instead say, "Meh, *Ernest Goes to Camp* costs $2 less, so let's see that instead."

Nobody does that. Nobody who's interested in movies, anyway. Similarly, nobody that you want as a reader considers two books and chooses the one they're less interested in just because it's cheaper. Do you really want readers who buy on price? Or do you instead want readers who buy on interest?

When I sell in person, nobody even asks the price. *Nobody*. It happens so reliably that I've had to train myself to tell *them* the price before they tap their credit card, just so my conscience is clear and they know what they're getting into. Not once have I had a reader interested in a book, then had them turn it down at checkout because it's too pricey.

I'm not shy about pricing. My paperbacks average about $25 each — a good deal more than I've seen even other hand-selling authors charge. I have several that cost $35, and one that goes for $45. People routinely buy three books or so at once, and I ring them up for over $100. And does anyone bat an eye? Nope. They walk away saying how excited they are by their purchase — how they can't wait to start reading.

Now, I'd be remiss if I didn't add a caveat to all of this before cutting you loose to set your own prices: *I'm suggesting that you price what you're worth, not price high.* (After the hive mind twisted "Write. Publish. Repeat." into "Rapid Release," I've learned to be clear about what I actually mean.)

Price what you're worth, but be reasonable.

Personally, I think traditional publishers are unreasonable in their ebook pricing. They don't do it for reasons of artistic dignity; they do it because they're trying to protect their paperback sales. In a logical world, paperbacks *should* cost a fair amount more than ebooks because they have to be printed, shipped, stocked, and so on. There are hard costs with a paperback, but no hard costs with an ebook. Everyone understands that. The formula "ebook + hard costs = significantly higher price" is one we can all agree makes sense.

The inverse, then, should also be true: "paperback - hard costs = significantly lower price for an ebook." When that doesn't happen — when I see a trad ebook priced at $15 and the paperback at $20, which isn't enough difference to account for the costs — I don't think "artistic dignity." I think "manipulation and greed" instead, and it pisses me off. At that point, my resentment of being screwed overwhelms my desire to get the book I was interested in, and I walk away feeling insulted ... and with a bad taste in my mouth about that book and author, by the way, which isn't fair but happens just the same.

I call it "The Panera Mac and Cheese Effect."

My kids like Panera mac and cheese, but I hate buying it because a little cup costs $8. Can I easily afford $8? Yes. But do I think *any* tiny cup of mac and cheese is worth $8? No. Because it's *fucking mac and cheese*. Similarly, when a plain old ebook (i.e., not a collection or omnibus) goes above $10, my gullible radar starts pinging. It's not that I'm unwilling to pay that much; it's that I feel like a sucker doing so. And I *hate* feeling like I've let someone play me for a sucker.

One last thing on keeping prices reasonable — not too low, but also not unreasonably high:

One of the great benefits of being an indie back around 2010 was that we could operate more lean than big publishers, without all their infrastructure, and therefore could easily afford to price our ebooks in a way that offered a benefit to the buyer while still protecting our profit. So while trad publishers were stumbling around like fools and asking $15 for an ebook, we could offer ebooks for $5-7 and everyone would win.

So let's not throw the baby out with the bathwater. Let's not throw away an advantage if we can keep it.

Price what you're worth. Don't be an ass about it, but price what allows you to sustain your author business at whatever level (part time, full time, *Adventure Time*) you've set your goals. If you have to stop writing because you can't earn enough to justify it, do you think your fans will be happy? Of course they won't. They want you to stay in business ... and to make sure that happens, the right readers are happy to pay what's fair.

Chapter 8

Finding Readers and Creating True Fans

Now that you've leaned into creating Artisan books and have a bunch of ideas about where to sell them (and how to price them with dignity), it's time to move on to the aspect of Artisan Authordom that makes it all work: gaining Artisan readers.

Without attracting and slowly accumulating Artisan readers, none of what you've read so far will work very well. They're the anchor of the paradigm: the folks who appreciate all those artisanal books you've been making, and who shop with quality and connection — not just price — on their minds.

Simply acting like an Artisan Author isn't enough to succeed as one. If you don't also change your readership (or, more accurately, *expand* it; more on that in a second), all the Artisaning in the world won't do you a bit of good. If you simply take the dominant self-pub model — the one that includes Rapid Release — and just try to slow down, add more love to your stories, and charge what you're worth, you'll crash and burn. The customers that the Rapid Release crowd serves *won't* care about the extra love you put into your books. They *won't* want to pay more than a few bucks. And forget about special editions, Kickstarters and the rest; the old paradigm's readers won't give a crap about them. Changing reader behavior is nearly impossible, and changing reader preferences is *flat-out* impossible. Have you ever announced a live event to an audience that's only ever bought ebooks from you online? I have. Guess how well it went?

You'll always have readers who want nothing more than basic ebooks and prefer to get them on sale, and there's nothing wrong with that, or with them. But you can't base your business solely around those readers — not as an Artisan Author, you can't.

In this chapter, we'll talk about finding your ideal Artisan readers, who make it all work. These are people who care what's in a book's backstory. They don't mind paying more for early access, special touches, bonus material, or physical goods including beautiful special editions. They won't all travel to see you if you appear live, but they'll wish they could. They'll read your newsletters, if they're real and honest and interesting. They'll read your Author's Notes. They'll notice Easter eggs, references, and clever allusions.

They're discerning, too. It might take them a long time to comb through books before settling on one that sounds perfect. Books, and the precious time it takes to read them, matter to these people. You'd better impress them if you want to keep them. Lucky for them, you're an Artisan Author. You know that impressing your best fans — all of whom have the potential to become True Fans and get you $1/10^{th}$ of a percent closer to your goal of 1000 (if that is indeed your goal) — is what this Artisan Authoring thing is all about.

If you're having trouble imagining the idea of Artisan readers, here's a little more to work with. Obviously not all of the below will be true of every reader, but the spirit of what follows is likely true:

- Artisan readers may or may not collect vinyl records in the age of digital music, but they're the type who would.

- Their predilection for Artisan goods likely extends beyond just books. They might buy their produce at a farmer's market, have backyard chickens for fresh eggs (or know someone who has them), drink microbrew beer, attend shows by local musicians, or prefer high-concept TV shows over the more popular mass-market shows.

- Slogans like "buy local" and "support small businesses" resonate with them, even when they can't do those specific things. (Tip: This is why I made a sign for my event booth that says LOCAL AUTHOR in big type.)

- They *LOVE* books. And I do mean *LOVE*. I know I've got a real Artisan reader when they approach my display with a gleam in their eyes, when they touch the books with affection, and when they seem overjoyed to browse titles and meet an author, regardless of whether or not they buy.

- Perhaps most importantly, *their Artisan tendencies are part of their identity.* This is something few people understand, but it means everything. Artisan buyers take great pride in being the kinds of people who do the things I just listed. Selling these people on your books does matter, but they're *already* halfway sold once they understand that you're an Artisan creator. It's *in their identity* to support people like you, so lean into that. Let them know that you care about your work, that you're independent, and that you do things your own way because you don't like Big Business's way. Once they see you for the Artisan you are, they're probably *already* trying to find a way to say Yes to you. If they can give you a legitimate Yes (by buying something), it validates *them* and makes *them* happy. At that point, your book is almost a bonus.

Let's delve into building your audience of Artisan readers, with the goal of turning some of them into those oh-so-valuable True Fans — starting with an important caveat:

They Won't All Be Artisan Readers, and Won't All Become True Fans.

By this point in the book, I might have accidentally given you a false impression. You might believe this philosophy to entail something that it doesn't, in fact, entail at all.

I should clear that up.

True Fans are the center of your bullseye. They're your end goal, and you should keep them in mind with every crowd-facing thing you do as an author. If you know Stephen King's idea of the "Ideal Reader," to whom you quietly write your books, your True Fans are that. You should write for your True Fans only after you write for yourself.

Write your email newsletters to appeal to True Fans. If you're on social media, post things your True Fans would be interested in, and preferentially act with people that strike you as having True Fan potential. Craft your advertising toward True Fans, too. This means choosing True Fan favorite books to advertise, writing your ad copy the way you'd talk to True Fans, and not being afraid to be snarky or sappy or sentimental or scary, if those moods are on-brand for you: if they're things your True Fans love (or likely will love) about you.

Do that. Do all of that. Align your author machine toward True Fans. Make them your moon, your sun, your everything. And I shouldn't need to say this, but be authentic about it, too. If your natural and preferred way of writing, communicating, and being is fundamentally different from the ways you talk to True Fans, you're doing it wrong. In fact, here's another way to look at it: *You should be your own True Fan.* That's why talking to, bonding with, and nurturing True Fans is so easy and comfortable if done correctly: because all you're doing is being the way you already are. You're letting your hair down, letting your guard down, and *just being you*, with all your humanity and foibles.

Do that and be that ... but — and here's a possible misconception I'd like to clear up — don't make your other readers wrong if they don't quite vibe with the full extent of you. Your attitude should be, "I'm going to be myself and try to meet my True Fans," not "It's True Fans or nothing!" Instead of becoming a True Fan snob, stay open to all the other non-True-Fan readers you'll meet along the way.

You will have readers who adore you.

You will have readers who like you.

You will have readers who don't particularly care about you, but enjoy your books.

You will have readers who ran across one of your books randomly and read it, but who will never read you again.

All of that is okay. It's fine. It's natural. True Fans may be the center of the bullseye, but they aren't its totality. From a numbers perspective, your *non*-True-Fan readers will vastly (and I do mean *vastly*) outnumber your True Fans. If ten thousand people read your books, maybe ten of them will be True Fans. Maybe less.

So let's be clear, shall we? You want to act in a way that maximally attracts and appeals to your True Fans and repels people that are actively wrong for you, but what you *don't* want to do is repel the people who are somewhere in the middle.

Now here's the good news: If you do this right, all but the most casual readers will at least be on the True Fan spectrum. This means that although they might not get excited and fan-ish when you lean into your unique quirks, they'll probably find them at least somewhat engaging. They may never become more than occasional readers, but they'll feel more warmly toward you — and be more likely to buy from you again — because although your unique flavor might not be 100 percent their jam, they'll respect that you *have* a jam and are brave and self-assured enough to stand by it.

To give you an example, I've mentioned that I make a lot of 80s and 90s references in my books. My Truest Fans love the hell out of it. They laugh when someone says "Don't call it a comeback" like LL Cool J or when *Big Trouble in Little China* is referred to as a cinematic classic in a book set in the future . They'll point out the little mentions I make, even when I assume nobody will notice.

My regular readers might not laugh too hard at my jokes or contact me with tidbits I might not have known about my references, but they'll snicker a little. Or they'll nod with nostalgia.

One ring farther out on the target, my casual readers might not do any of those things. They won't mind my quirks, though. They'll understand that they're the things that give a Truant book its unique flavor, different from other books. I mean, I'm not into women's feet like Quentin Tarantino clearly is based on his filmic choices, but I acknowledge it's a Tarantino hallmark, and I enjoy any creator cool enough to have hallmarks.

See what I mean? If you operate like an Artisan Author, your spectrum of readers (those who get through at least one book and like it at least a little) may not be universally gonzo-thrilled about every little thing you do, but they'll either not mind those things or will like them a little. This is why aiming for your True Fans first is so effective: Yes, some will become True Fans ... but for those who don't, you're still being you, still casting your unique flavor out into the world, and still earning their loyalty in a similar (but milder) way than True Fans.

Aim for the center of the bullseye. You'll hit readers all over the target if you do that, but at least you can rest assured that it's *your* target, and that as long as you keep firing at it instead of *someone else's* target, you'll be building a readership on all levels that will grow and support you for the long term.

The bottom line is: *You need readers.* No matter what else is true, you need readers — of any sort at all — to make it as an author.

I shouldn't be lighting any epiphany fireworks by saying that, but I'm saying it anyway because as ridiculous as it sounds, author groupthink sometimes seems to forget that readers are the name of the game. A lot of authors really only count *sales,* and some count *page reads.* They track *downloads* and *ad clicks* and *conversions* ... and if those numbers seem low, they'll tweak their *keywords* or *categories* or *ad targeting* or *ad creatives* to improve them. They'll enter group promotions with authors who have *large lists,* and sometimes they'll talk about *customer avatars* or *lookalike audiences.* Compared to all of those buzzwords, talk of *readers,* as real people with real human lives, is almost nonexistent.

Remember, becoming an Artisan Author is less about learning than it is about *un*learning. There's nothing groundbreaking in the book you're reading right now. Boiled down, all it says is "Write good books, find readers who appreciate good books, then sell your books to them at a profit." I could have saved you whatever you paid for *The Artisan Author* by sending that sentence as a Tweet.

So it's worth an incredibly obvious reminder that readers are what matter. When you get a sale, it's because a *reader* wanted your book. When you get an ad click, it's because a real human *reader* thought the ad was interesting. When you swap lists with another author, it's so you can reach the *readers* they've interested in their work, hoping you can interest them in yours, too.

Really think about that. Go ahead. I dare you.

When you truly — and I do mean *truly* — comprehend that every single interaction, outreach, and effort you make as an author has a real human being on the other end, it changes the way you approach everything.

You stop thinking in aggregate and start thinking of individuals. You stop worrying about "what's right for this faceless market" and instead have thoughts like, "You know, *I* think this ad tagline is funny and I'm a human being. That means there probably are *other* human beings who'll think it's funny, too — and if they do, they'll be perfect for me."

It'll make you think outside the box. It'll make you stop dismissing your instincts just because something doesn't seem to work by the usual metrics, because maybe your metrics aren't the usual ones. It'll give you the freedom to be yourself, which is how you'll attract True Fans and readers for your target's outer rings around them.

And remember: *In order to create True Fans, you need readers first: the right kinds of readers, unique to you.* Readers are the raw material you need to make those wonderful diamonds. The more of the right kind of readers you have, the more chances you'll have to grow your True Fanbase. Fewer ideal readers, and you'll have a far harder time.

So let's talk about readers. Readers as people, readers as individuals rather than market averages. Averages don't matter nearly as much to Artisan Authors, because we're not looking to siphon as many random statistics as possible from the fat part of the bell curve. Instead, we're looking for the oddballs who jibe with our oddballness perfectly ... and you can only find those crazy folks one by one, using methods different from authors chasing the majority.

I've divided reader acquisition into three main buckets, described in the following pages. There's nothing official about these buckets. All I know is that they feel right to me, and they cover the three main ways to think about readers without getting all bogged down in aggregates.

Bucket #1: Discovery (Author is Passive)

This bucket contains all the ways readers just sort of "run across" you or your book. I'm including anything wherein the author sets the book up at the beginning, but then has no real control thereafter.

In this bucket, all you can really do is to set your book up in such a way as to give it the best chance of being seen. After that, you have to trust something or someone else (an algorithm, search, luck) to take what you put into the book's packaging and positioning and use those things to show it to the right readers at the right time.

At base, the author is *passive* in this bucket. After you set your book up or make a change, all you can do is sit back and hope it will sell.

There are really only two options within the Discovery bucket: Either the customer (reader) is as passive as the author, or they're active.

Passive Customer

In some Discovery cases, your customer is almost as passive as you are. You're waiting for sales to happen with no ability to control whether or not they do, and the reader is just sort of browsing somewhere (bookstore shelves, a bookseller website like Amazon) without a specific aim in mind. They're looking for *something*, but it's not terribly specific. Or, alternatively, they *are* looking for something specific, but they're not looking for books like yours ... until your book catches their eye.

Either way, they aren't *looking* for you. They just sort of *happen across* you instead. It might as well be random, for all you can do about it.

The passive author/passive reader scenario is something to keep in mind, but it's nothing to base an Artisan Author strategy around. You will find people this way, but it's scattershot and no more likely to yield ideal readers than anything else. Because the other two buckets involve things you can control more directly, I suggest putting your limited time, effort, and attention on those things rather than this one after the book is live and in the world.

This doesn't mean that your "mostly passive after launch" elements don't matter. They do. Your goal when launching a book is to make that book maximally attractive to readers who find it, so do that: Make it as attractive as you can to readers who might randomly see it. Most of the elements you'd optimize at the outset to maximize this scenario double as conversion elements to attract *any* reader through *any* means, so it's no extra work to do these things right:

- **Make your cover attractive and professional.** Don't skimp on covers, because people absolutely judge books based on their covers no matter what their mother said about not doing that sort of thing. Covers make ALL THE DIFFERENCE. A good cover promises an experience that accurately reflects the book's contents and that feels compelling to prospective readers. If your cover doesn't hook readers' attention in an OMG sort of way (or doesn't match the experience the story actually delivers), you're doing something very wrong.

- **Use a compelling title for your book.** Don't try to keyword-stuff it, if you're on a platform that allows keyword-stuffed titles (which most don't). Artisan readers think keyword-stuffing is stupid. It makes you look schlocky, like someone more interested in gaming the system than someone they'd actually want to read. Do, however, make your title intriguing. It matters.

- **Write a good description.** This is more art than science. It's also an area where personally, I don't mind AI assistance at all, as long as you refine the teaser rather than just cutting and pasting what ChatGPT gives you. Run any prospective description by people who read books like yours and ask if it makes them want to read on. Sometimes what *they* want in a description and what *you* put in yours don't match up. The description, along with any existing reviews for your book, tend to be the final gauntlet before a reader buys, so write it to push them over the enthusiasm edge after the cover and title have gotten the ball rolling.

Those are the important elements that must always be firmly in place: elements that are typically only set up once, then become passive attractors for the rest of the book's life. You can change them later, of course, but that just re-starts the cycle. It's always *set up, then wait and hope.*

At this point, the passive/passive scenario should drop firmly into the less-important part of the 80/20 equation for an Artisan Author. You'll do a bit more initial setup, but you shouldn't sweat it too much and shouldn't worry about getting it perfect or optimizing later. You'll be glad that you get a few readers this way, but because it's all so hands-off (and because an Artisan Author is hands-on), doing more than setting your book up for success in the ways above usually isn't worth your time.

But, *do* try to pick accurate categories for your book when you upload it. *Do* choose keywords that seem like things readers might be searching for, or that might help the algorithms decide who to serve your book to. Don't worry too much about it, though — as in horseshoes and hand grenades, close is good enough for our purposes.

Active Customer

The other "passive author" category of reader acquisition is one in which the reader is actively searching for something — a certain category or style of book, a certain trope they enjoy, or books similar to other books they've liked in the past. The goal of this category, for the author, is to set things up on our end such that we maximize our chances of being found by readers searching for the kinds of books we write.

On the surface, it makes sense. If you wrote a vampire book, you want to show up when readers visit an online bookseller and search for vampire books. The problem is, there are a *lot* of vampire books out there. There's the books that just so happen to have been written about vampires, but there's also the many books that were written-to-market about vampires: books created specifically because vampire books were popular at the time, and the author wanted to capitalize on a trend.

When there's that much competition for vampire books, it's not enough to have written a good one if you want to be found by a searching reader. You need a lot of other algorithm-driven things going for you as well. You don't only need to have a searchable title and description; you also need a big-time sales record, a lot of good reviews, and more. On Amazon, you'll tend to be more findable if your book is in Kindle Unlimited. They *absolutely* prioritize their exclusive authors over traitors like us who dare to give readers more than one option.

See the problem? Being found by actively searching readers — like being found by the passive ones that just stumble across books — is no longer about being a match to what people are searching for. A *lot* of books are a match. To claw your way to the top of that search, you have to do more than organically present your book. You have to delve into the complex and cutthroat world of Ninja Tricks.

And that right there is where an Artisan Author loses interest: when instead of simply describing your book to appeal to its best reader using metadata, you suddenly need to work ten times harder to manipulate a system. Is it really worth it for us — lots of constantly-shifting plotting and scheming and game-playing just to maybe get a few more readers who probably aren't perfectly suited for us anyway?

C'mon. We're rule breakers and change-makers for our own careers. We can find better uses of our time than to play the algorithm chess game, can't we — especially when the other ways are so much more interesting, so much more likely to find us ideal readers, and often so much more fun?

And okay: I sense an objection at this point. I know what at least some of you are thinking.

You might be wondering why everyone talks so much about nailing keywords and selecting categories if I'm telling you it's not very important. I mean, there are *entire courses* about keywords! Entire *expensive software packages* to help you choose your keywords!

The answer is: Nailing metadata is *extremely* important ... for the Amazon-centric, algorithm-centric crowd, but not for Artisan Authors.

I remember talking to Ed Robertson on one of the earliest episodes of *The Self Publishing Podcast*. Ed wasn't the first to talk about bookseller algorithms, but he was the first I heard — the first who spoke about them in ways that made sense to me. We were all fascinated, hearing Ed talk about ways he'd optimized the listings for his *Breakers* series so that Amazon would push them better. Our listeners became fascinated. We talked more about algorithms, eager to learn more. The community — some because of us and some on their own — talked more and more about it, too.

Because optimizing algorithms sounded so much like the legendary Easy Button everyone was looking for, the subject of algorithms exploded. Algorithms, like hot trends, became something authors could play to. That's when books started becoming less about pure expression and became a lot more about business ... which is exactly the balance we're trying to correct now, as Artisan Authors.

Bucket #1 is where the Rapid Release author spends most of their time. They also visit Bucket #2 (advertising), but for them, that's really just an extension of all that's happening in #1. *That's* the reason so many people fret the details of playing algorithms — because it's the primary way the non-Artisan finds readers. It's also the reason that we, as Artisan Authors, can — and should — largely ignore it in favor of more personal ways to find our fans.

Bucket #2: Advertising (Author is Active)

Functionally speaking, advertising is anything that is initiated and controlled by you on the creative end, and that you usually have to pay for. It differs from the first bucket (Discovery) in that it's more active on your part. After setup, there's very little you can do to get more readers out of Bucket #1. Because the driver for Bucket #1 is either blind luck (less often) or the work of an algorithm serving your book to the bookseller's customers (more often), you can't control the important parts almost by definition. All you can do is hope you've set things up in a way the algorithms (or luck) like best.

Advertising, on the other hand, is a way for you to "push" your book. Instead of putting your book out there and hoping someone sees it, your payment *ensures* the book will be shown. There's no hope to that part. You shift from hoping someone sees your book to hoping the people who see it will want to buy it.

I've subdivided advertising into two main methodologies: mass advertising and targeted advertising. I'm sure the pros would tell you there's a lot more than *two*, but because this isn't an in-depth advertising book, simplifying to two options keeps things straightforward and covers the main points. Good enough for our purposes.

Mass Advertising

Mass advertising is sort of "spray and pray." The idea is to blast your book out to a whole lot of people who may or may not be ideal for it or for you, then sift and sort the readers you get from it until you find the gems.

BookBub Featured Deals are mass advertising. If you've ever bought one, you'll know that they're pretty expensive but will put your book in front of a ton of readers. The flip side is that the most granular you can get on the "will these be my ideal readers?" spectrum with a BookBub deal is to choose a category. Your romance book goes in with all of the other books that could be classified as romance, as far as readers are concerned.

If you've searched around, you've probably seen other newsletter-based advertising in this vein: Written Word Media, Freebooksy, RobinReads, Red Feather Romance, E-Reader News Today, and a dozen more. All will sell you a spot in their email broadcasts (with a concurrent feature on their website) for a fee that's usually under a hundred dollars. They're cheaper than BookBub, but also less effective.

The thing about all newsletter-based promotion is that they all require or strongly suggest a very steep discount in price — usually to 99 cents or free. Their readers are, therefore, bargain hunters. That's not necessarily a bad thing, because a big enough spike in sales will, to some degree, nudge the algorithms to make your book temporarily more visible for others to buy. For BookBub, if you get lucky (they're not as strong as they used to be), you can even make good money on sales at only 99 cents simply because there will be so many of them. Lastly, if the book you advertise (even for free) is part of a series, you'll get at least some buy-through: readers who finish the first book and are willing to pay full price for the sequels.

The fact that newsletter promos attract bargain readers still isn't necessarily a bad thing even if you didn't get any of the benefits above. You're bound to pull some of those people into your own circles (if you entice them onto your email list or to follow you on social media, or to otherwise start paying more attention to you), and that gives you the chance to do the "sifting and sorting" I mentioned earlier. You basically take a lot of silt from the river bottom, then pan through it until you find the few flakes of gold buried in all the muck. Do that, and you'll discover that some people are both bargain readers *and* Artisan readers. They may be Artisan readers who like to grab deals when they present themselves, or they may know from experience that good books often come through those channels, so why not treat on-sale books like free samples at the grocery store — a "try it and see if you like it" sort of approach?

If you're planning to sift and sort ideal from non-ideal readers anyway (there's a section on how to do that coming up), you can also buy less-aligned mass-advertising promotions than the list promotions already described. These sorts of promotions don't necessarily center on your book, though they can. More likely, they'll go to an audience that will likely contain a whole lot of noise: folks who won't stay with you long, if at all. I'm thinking of KingSumo promotions, Humble Bundles, BookSweeps, and so on. You can get a ton of attention from these, but it's like a shotgun blast. Maybe you'll hit some good future readers, but you'll hit a lot of crap, too.

I'll tell you what to do with these readers shortly. For now, the idea is that you want to get new people to read one of your books, to join your mailing list, or to do both. Get them in your orbit, then let the sifting and sorting into ideal readers and cast-offs begin.

Targeted Advertising

Mass advertising is scattershot. You put your book (or yourself) in front of a whole lot of people and hope some of them at least read more of your books, or ideally stick with you for the long term. Targeted advertising, on the other hand, is ... well ... *targeted*. Instead of blasting your book at everyone who *might* be interested, you zoom in on a subset of that group who's *more likely* to be interested.

So we're talking about Amazon ads. Facebook ads. Possibly BookBub display ads. Maybe Reddit ads will work for you, though for me it was like throwing a thousand dollars into a garbage disposal. Either way, you choose a book, write some sort of enticing copy to go with it and/or create an image to go with it, and try your best to target that ad at people who will 1) be intrigued enough by the ad to check out your book and then hopefully 2) be intrigued enough by your book's sales page to buy it.

There's enough instruction out there on all forms of advertising (and so much constantly-changing nuance to learn) that I won't give many details. Here's what I will say, though, for Artisan Authors who want to try targeted ads:

- **Be careful.** The Artisan Author paradigm is, on average, a smaller and more intimate paradigm than the monster of KU and Rapid Release. For that reason, Artisan Authors should be extremely cautious with paid targeted advertising. We publish less often, so we usually have smaller backlists. Bigger backlists (i.e., more books to buy) are one thing that makes paid advertising worthwhile in the long term, since it's often a loss in the short term. You can really lose your lunch money on paid ads, and the gambling feel of it can make them hard to quit even if they're not working for you.

- **Know that it takes time.** This is related to the first one: You should be careful in part *because* it takes time for even good ads to work. I'm grateful to my friend David Viergutz, who told me when I was about to launch my first Facebook ad, "It will suck away all of your money and give you nothing for about three weeks." I sort of wanted to punch him in the face after he said that because the idea of wasting several hundred dollars didn't sound so hot to me, but I'm grateful because his disclaimer sent me into the fray with realistic expectations. With ads, it's not at all unrealistic to spend thousands of dollars before something starts to work a little bit ... *maybe*. (The good news is that when it finally clicks, ads can be a huge difference-maker. I know many people for whom ads provide almost all of their income-generating traffic ... and those people end up doing very well.)

- **There's no formula.** You can and should get advice if you embark on targeted advertising, but know that even the smartest ads expert can only give you guidance. Nobody can tell you exactly how to craft ads for your books that will definitely produce results. If all of Artisan Authordom is like walking through fog without a map and trying to find your way, then ads are like walking through thick black syrup with a blindfold on and earplugs. You will absolutely fail many times with ads before you succeed because the nature of the thing is trial and error ... and lucky you: You get to pay money for every single error.

I do have one last blanket suggestion for Artisan Authors looking to advertise. Use it at your own risk, and know that many ad mavens would argue with me and say that I'm being irresponsible by even saying it.

At the risk of having tomatoes thrown at me, I'll say it anyway: *In your ads, be yourself.*

If you decide to try targeted advertising and weren't dissuaded by my three dire bullet points above, I figure my final advice can't hurt you much more than the ad machine will hurt you already. I think it's worthwhile to be yourself either way, and here's why: *Readers are human beings.*

Remember my incredibly obvious diatribe from earlier, about how somewhere along the way we started following sales and page reads and link clicks but stopped thinking of readers as singular humans with their own minds and lives? That applies here, too. Maybe an ad you create will be "wrong" by some official metric, but you can't shake the feeling that it just might work for your ideal readers. That happens because you're a human being, and your readers are also human beings. If *you* think an ad is interesting, others might, too.

Dangerous advice, I know. Don't be stupid about this, kids, and don't come back to yell at me if it fails. I'm just giving you my thoughts. Take or leave them at your own expense.

I'll give you an example. I've yet to have sustained positive return-on-investment with an ad, but I got closest with an ad set for the paperback version of my *Unicorn Western* omnibus. I used the ridiculous gunslinger-riding-a-unicorn image from the cover, with text on top espousing the tagline I mentioned earlier: "Like if Stephen King was on LSD when he wrote *The Dark Tower.*"

I ran that ad because *I* thought it was funny. Because it would make *me* stop scrolling. Because *I'd* be amused and interested enough to click on it. If I thought those things, there must be other people out there like me. And again: I lost money on that ad, but I lost the *least* on that one out of my many other losers.

I have a theory. It's that people hate sterile advertising. Not *all* advertising, but *sterile* advertising. I think that nobody likes the usual sales games — and, in fact, I think they see right through those games and resent the advertiser for insulting their intelligence. We're savvy these days. Everyone's looking for the hook, the angle, and the con.

If you disagree with what I said? If you think that most people fall for boring, inside-the-box, standardized advertising and aren't smart enough to see through the tricks? Well, then, let me amend my statement. It's not that *everyone* is that way. But it is that *my ideal readers* are that way.

I don't want dumb, gullible readers. I want smart, discerning readers. I don't want readers who will leave me the second someone else writes a mindless book with no soul. I want readers who roll their eyes and say, "I'll stick with Truant, thanks."

As with all things Artisan, we're after quality over quantity. That means your ad-satisfaction metrics will be different from those of other authors. If I have a choice between spending $100 on ads to get $50 in sales from two high-quality readers with True Fan potential or spending that same $100 to get $125 in sales from random buyers, I'll take the first choice all day long even though it costs me money. Two True Fans are worth a lot more to me than $50 in long run.

Use with caution. Your mileage may (and absolutely will) vary.

Bucket #3: Creating Fans Out of Nowhere (Author is Basically a Friggin' Wizard)

Let's recap, shall we?

Bucket #1 is a Discovery model of reader acquisition, wherein you as the author are passive. All you can do is set your book up for success and hope it'll be shown to (or randomly found by) readers. This is where Rapid Release types focus most of their effort, but where we should focus the least.

Bucket #2 is Advertising, wherein the author is active: You control what's in your ads and some of where they're shown. You can also, with time and practice and an investment of money, get better and better at putting those ads in front of readers who are perfect for you. Mass advertising is fairly affordable and will almost certainly "work" to some degree assuming you sift and sort the leads you get from it to find your best readers out of all the noise. Targeted advertising, on the other hand, can be *very* effective but it can also rob you blind. It will, in fact, almost certainly rob you blind along the way even if it becomes effective eventually. Artisan Authors at more advanced levels can really thrive with advertising (it's how many drive readers to their direct stores to sell primo versions of their books), but beginners should tread carefully. All of that means that this bucket goes even more into the "it depends on you" category than everything else. You might dive deep and get a lot of readers this way, or you might stick with the occasional mass promo and get fewer.

But now we're on to Bucket #3, which I call "Creating Fans Out of Nowhere." If authors are *passive* in the Discovery bucket and *active* in the Advertising bucket, we're flat-out *wizards* in this bucket. Creating customers out of nothing? That's some alakazam shit right there.

Of course, you're not *really* creating customers from nowhere. You will neither turn non-readers suddenly into readers nor manifest human beings from dust like some sort of god. You will, however, find yourself fishing over and over again in ponds where no other authors are fishing. You'll end up selling to people who didn't even know they were in the market for a new book. Your currency will become surprise and delight as much as the thing you normally use as sales leverage: a compelling story. If readers were literal money, most authors looking will go to the equivalent of banks: the big booksellers, the usual advertising spots, and so on. You, however, will find your "money" between the cushions of life's figurative couch.

There are a lot of ways to find customers as an Artisan Author, and despite the way I set this method up as king (because personally, I think it is), you might instead focus on Buckets #1 and #2, and it's fine if you do. Depending on your goals, you might do just fine operating by the usual rules: Upload your books to all the places, buy a list ad now and again, write more books, and dote on the readers you have — and especially on any True Fans who pop up. There's nothing wrong with those ways. They won't work as well for you as for Rapid Release authors, but they'll work. You'll need to be patient ... but that's okay, right? You're an artist. You know that good things take time.

The methods in this section, by contrast, are weird and unconventional. They might make you uncomfortable, and the amount of nonstandard-for-authors work involved might put you off. You might be like I was between the Wolf and Bear badges in Cub Scouts, when I realized my den mother would no longer put badge requirements in front of me and I'd instead have to proactively chase a list of unpalatable activities if I wanted to advance. I never did get that next badge. I remember looking at the big book they gave us, considering the things I enjoyed and didn't enjoy, and saying, "Sorting shoes with circus performers to earn one stinking Arrow Point? Hard pass."

If you don't want to do any of the things in this final Bucket, that's fine. Honest. An Artisan Author is not made or broken by the ways they find readers. They're instead defined by the quality they put into their work, their attitude toward the business of writing, and their relationships with the readers they already have, no matter how many (or how quickly) new readers find them.

But I *will* say that once I discovered this way of operating, it's become my True North. It fits me very well. It made me realize that even though I'd been in this business for a dozen years, I'd been missing a huge part of it. I'd been passing mindlessly by people every single day who could reduce and eventually eliminate my reliance on Amazon — the master to which virtually our entire industry feels it must bow. I will say that once I started looking for readers in unexpected and unexplored places, I found a degree of control over my author business that I'd never felt before. I realized I'd never have to worry again about something I couldn't control (bookseller whims or algorithms, tech and tactics that change every month) taking everything away from me. I realized that if one day I suddenly found myself needing a few hundred extra bucks, I could just go out that weekend and get it.

Nothing is universal. What works for me may not work for you. Everything works and nothing works depending on the situation, as we've already discussed. You might totally crap out on this section. Or, you might find like I found that it's the pool of readers you've been looking for your entire professional life.

Let's begin.

Let Them See You

Artisan selling is inherently human in nature. That's not a knock on AI. It's more fundamental than that.

You can be a flesh-and-blood human being without acting very human — and honestly, that's what a lot of authors do. We're predominantly an introverted group, and the machinelike ways of self-publishing have made us moreso by removing the human interactions that even introverts normally have to engage in to do business. We've been trained to become faceless, because supposedly only the next book matters.

For an Artisan Author, human connections are important. In fact, they're damn near essential. In certain cases, they're *all* that matters, because Artisan buyers of anything often want a direct connection to the creator.

Throughout this book, I've argued for putting as much *YOU* into your books and public image as possible. There's a reason for that. It helps attract your ideal people, but it also adds the human connection that Artisan readers want. Everything you do — and everything you do *differently* than Rapid Release — humanizes you for your ideal readers.

Your unapologetic humanity shows in the confident and unique voice of your books. It's in the Author's Note you write at the end. It's in the way you send and answer emails. And, if you really want to supercharge your ability to sell Artisan books, it's in your physical presence as well.

I suppose we should formally get something out of the way. If you're going to run screaming from this section, you might as well do it now and save yourself some reading time. And that thing is: *Most ways of attracting the readers no one else is reaching — the ways I call "creating fans out of nowhere" — involve being visible and interacting with other human beings, ideally in person.*

Which means that if you want to maximize your Artisan Author potential, you're going to have to come out of your shell and learn a little bit of extroversion.

As I already said, you don't have to. You can create great, beautiful books and gather your tribe of readers, albeit more slowly and deliberately, using the techniques in Buckets 1 and 2. If that's what you choose, you'll grow slowly but can grow deep at the same time: not just finding readers, but moving them more deliberately along the path toward True Fandom. If you avoid Bucket #3, you'll focus more on nurturing relationships than growing new ones. Depending on your goals, that just might be enough.

But this right here is the secret sauce for any Artisan ... and I'm sorry, but there's really no way to avoid putting yourself out there if you want that sauce. *Your abject, in-sight, often-in-the-flesh humanity is what the Artisan reader values most.* They may never interact with you directly, but they'll want to see that you interact with others directly — that you're accessible, in other words. That you're a person like them, not a corporation. That you make by hand, rather than through an assembly line. There's no way to do that without letting your readers see you in ways you might be uncomfortable being seen.

If that scares you, good. Fear is healthy in a case like this. It means you're up against your limits, and being against your limits is how you grow. But you know what they say about bravery, right? Bravery isn't about an absence of fear. It's about feeling the fear, then acting anyway.

As I said in one of my early Substack posts about Artisan Authoring, your best fans love you because you're brave. They love *you* — not just your books — because they see that you are willing to do something they are not. They aspire to the energy you bring. They don't just want a book — it's your human energy (your *brave* energy) that they seek.

In the sections that follow, I'm going to throw a bunch of options at you: things you can experiment with to shake those valuable reader coins from the big couch of life. Some will fit you better than others, but most of them involve some degree of vulnerability or exposure. That's what I mean by "let them see you." Guarding yourself — including holing up in the usual writer's cave — won't maximize your Artisan image. Think of any creator you consider to be an Artisan. Are they anonymous, or are they accessible? Are they confident or timid? Take notes. What you see in them will work in you, too.

Take small steps. Choose the easier options in this chapter and build from there. You'll be surprised by what a few low-pressure wins will do. If you find the guts to talk confidently rather than timidly about your work to one person, their response will be good unless they're an asshole. If they're an asshole, accept it and move on. But if they're not, you'll believe just a little bit more that you can actually do this.

Not every Artisan starts out brave and willing.

The good ones, though, end up there in the end.

Guest Appearances on Podcasts and Blogs

Let's start with low-hanging fruit. Appearing on podcasts isn't the most effective way to act as an Artisan Author, but at least it's virtual and fairly nonthreatening. I figure it's a good option for introverts.

If you want to try this one, think first of the podcasts you listen to and enjoy, and therefore are probably compatible with. If you don't listen to podcasts, hunt around. I've hosted many podcasts, and they're beasts that are always hungry. Hosts always want new and interesting guests in their field, and that includes fiction genres and fiction in general. Really into sci-fi? Then find some sci-fi podcasts that aren't so popular you'll never get on them. Make sure they have guests, then pitch yourself to be one of them.

The trick to making this work is to be interesting. Be yourself in your introductory email, but be professional, too. Share any accolades you have, or if you don't have accolades, share some aspect of your journey that might fit the podcast. So for instance, maybe there's a podcast out there about creativity and self-expression — a small show just getting its footing. If you can be outgoing enough to share your story without obvious fear, you'll actually help some of their listeners. You're an author, for Pete's sake. Authors are fascinating to non-authors. You'll inspire them just by talking about what you know.

Not into podcasts? Well, maybe there's a blog out there you could guest-post for. Or be interviewed for. I once interviewed my friend Lance on my Substack because he'd dumped a career in corporate sales to try his hand at acting. People dig stories like that. You could be one of them.

Now: Will you get a lot of readers this way? Honestly, there's no way to know. Remember, this isn't the "how to sell" section of the book. We already talked about selling, and this section is about getting readers. Readers are a far squishier metric than sales. People could read your book (or just parts of your online presence, down to social media or your website) without you even knowing.

You can't track that sort of thing. Because you're using your humanity and personality as your major points of reader attraction, whether or not you win readers over comes down to nothing more complicated than making people like you. There's no way to track likability. It may happen in stages, and it happens with a network effect. Get out there and be cool and interesting often enough, though, and your stock as an author will grow ... in time.

Say Yes to Everything

Credit to my friend Todd Fahnestock on this one. In Todd's excellent book *Falling to Fly*, he talks about a low point in his author career when his wife gave him simple advice that ended up making all the difference: "Say yes to everything."

In Todd's case, it meant agreeing to sell books at an upcoming Christmas fair — something he failed terribly at the first day, then killed on day two after realizing all he needed to do was lean into his ability to tell a story. Todd has since parlayed that revelation ("I don't need to be a carnival-barker-style salesman; all I need to do is tell stories") into mastering conventions and an off-Amazon career selling books all by himself.

Your path won't be exactly the same, but there's worse advice out there than to say yes to everything.

I've said yes to speaking at a library.

I've said yes to talking to schools.

I even said yes when I got a completely out-of-the blue email from a guy who does fundraising at my old college. I told him I wasn't currently in a position to donate to scholarship funds; did he still want to meet me? The answer was a definite yes. Now I might end up speaking to students at the college, as someone who's published in the real world. Will anything come of it? Who knows? And really: Who *cares?* There's not always a direct line from action to results in this business. The best seeds often take years to develop.

That library talk I mentioned above? I learned after the fact that they paid speakers $300. I said yes, and then they gave me unexpected money. But I still didn't get any new readers, you say? I beg to differ. After my talk, several of the group I spoke to checked my books out from that library. When other books they wanted weren't at the library, they requested them, and the library bought.

I've said yes to guest-writing for various websites, including smaller ones. I don't always have the time for that, but I do it whenever I can. I say yes to almost any interview. Who cares how small the audience is? A reader is a reader, and any one of them could be a True Fan down the road.

Say yes often enough and you'll find your readership starting to creep up.

But my advice is still too slow, you say? Well, I guess I might as well fire my big gun next.

Live Events

I already talked about selling at live events. Now, let's talk about using them to gain readers.

The lines blur, of course. If people buy books from me in

person, I sort of expect they'll read them. But from a strict reader-engagement standpoint (rather than a sell-them-another-book standpoint), meeting new potential readers in person is the ultimate hack. Those readers *start* our relationship with a good impression of me. It's like they skip all the way to the front of the ideal reader line, because they got to know and like me before they even pulled out their credit card.

Every single live event I attend gains me a few more readers on my email list — my main method of coaxing them toward True Fandom, which I'll discuss at the end of this chapter. Sometimes I add just a few to my list. Sometimes, it's over a hundred.

Some authors use a passive signup form to collect email addresses at live events, but I don't find that active enough. Nobody likes getting more email without a reason for it. My way actually makes email-collection part of the sales process, meaning that by the time I ask them if they'd like to join my list, they've already bought a book and we've usually already had some banter. The mood of it (and again, this is unique to my personality) is more like a half-joke. I'm saying something more like "You obviously want to join my list because you understand now that I'm awesome, right?" than "Do you want to get my random dull author newsletter in your inbox along with all the other garbage?"

They know my emails will share my personality, in other words. It's an easy sell. 90% or more of the people I ask enthusiastically say yes. And by the way, I don't ask everyone. If I get a purely transactional vibe from a customer (someone who wants a book but doesn't share my energy), I don't even ask. If I do and they say yes, though, I hand them my phone, and they enter an address to which their sales receipt will be sent. At the end of the day, I export those folks and add them to my list.

Hundreds of new people on my list every month. Hundreds of high-quality, high-touch readers who already know and like me, because I'm never purely transactional when I sell books. I am always, 100% of the time, exceedingly friendly. I want them feeling *great* when they leave my booth.

Do this sort of thing long enough and soon you'll have thousands of people on your email list who are already at the "engaged reader" phase rather than the "maybe saw a book somewhere and gave it a shot, and signed up for my list to get the next book free" phase.

We all understand how incredibly valuable a list like that is in terms of creating True Fans, right?

Talks and Readings

Small bookstores, libraries, and local interest groups are always on the lookout for ways to bring new people through the doors. You could be one of those reasons.

The bad news is that this one may feel like introvert Kryptonite. The idea of standing in front of people and reading your work (or giving a talk about your work) may be terrifying. However, keep in mind that the venue brought you in as an attraction, and that means they want you to succeed. Keep in mind too that the kinds of people who listen to author readings and talks *also* want you to succeed. Nobody sits down for a reading with a chip on their shoulder. They do it because authors interest them.

It's often difficult for authors — even local authors, and especially new authors — to land book signings. I know; I've tried. It's *not* hard, however, to donate your time. If a library, small bookstore, or other interested group won't let you set up a signing table or pay you for your time, do it for free instead. All you want is to get in front of book lovers ... who, by the way, no other authors are even trying to reach.

School Visits

I've done this in the past, but only twice because most of my books aren't for kids. If your books *are* for kids, though, talking to schools can be a great way to get the word out.

My friend Mike (who you may know as one of the co-hosts on my *One Drink Book Club* podcast) does this. Mike writes children's poetry and a bit of middle grade fiction, and just the other night he told our group that he was "gearing up to start doing school visits again," like he's done in the past. He'll visit local schools, read a bit to them, talk about the story, and earn some new readers in the doing.

And remember Todd Fahnestock? Todd tells a story about visiting so many middle schools in the past that kids who lived in his area at that time *absolutely* got a visit.

One other bonus: Turns out kids grow up to be adults with their own credit cards. Whether or not school visits get you new readers right away, you're priming plenty of new readers for the future.

Facebook Groups, Discord, and More

I don't do social media, but I hear there's this thing called "Facebook" out there. Apparently it's pretty popular.

Despite my loathing of it, social media can be a solid way to earn new readers. Artisan Authors go about it a little differently than other authors, though. Specifically, Artisans eschew immediate sales from social media and instead just hang out and be cool. They'll talk about their mutual interests, but will stop short of saying, "Buy my book." Nobody likes to be pushed, especially once it starts to look like the "just hanging out and being cool" vibe was all an act, and the hard-press salesperson is that "cool" individual's true face.

Try to focus on communities on social media, rather than just blasting your thoughts into the void. There's a Facebook group out there for everything — ditto Discord servers on every topic plus a whole host of social media happenings I haven't got a clue about but that you probably do. Should I bother to mention TikTok? I feel like it might not be around too long and will only serve to date this book, as ephemeral in the social mind as Pizza Rat. (RIP, Pizza Rat.)

But that actually means something: the fact that you know about online communities that I don't. If you know about them without my telling you, that probably means you're a natural there. You go because you enjoy being there. If so, that's a *perfect* place to hang out as the resident author — not one always pushing the sale, but one people know is an author, and they're just waiting until their current book is done to look you up.

Let People Around You Know You're An Author

On the heels of that last thought (hanging out on social media as someone people know is an author), I'll add that the same thing works in real life, too.

My daughter is a club volleyball player, and high-level club teams are always traveling. My wife and I spend a lot of time in other cities and states, attending tournaments and interacting with other parents. Every year we get a new team with at least some people who are new to us, adding to the stock of folks we've known forever. Then, when club season ends, we begin the high school season. There's very little of the year that we're *not* traveling all over the place, seeing the same groups again and again.

I love my volleyball friends, and we're all pretty social. What's more, I've also met parents from other teams because we're always in the same places. (I know you listen to the *Volleyball Dads* podcast constantly, right? Well, that's the reason I was on it: because year after year, I kept running into the host.)

At first, I kept quiet in those groups about being an author. Talking about it felt self-indulgent, maybe arrogant. But because we spend so much time with these people, authoring always eventually comes up.

People who already know me — but who previously had no idea what I did for a living — are always intrigued when they realize I write books. Even the non-readers are intrigued. We authors don't think it because this is our everyday, but we're actually pretty fascinating to most people. Most never meet an author, and what we do is like magic to them.

I never "sell" to my volleyball friends. I *never* try to get them to buy books. We're in too close quarters for that kind of bullshit. Still, some of them always end up seeking me out and buying anyway.

Rachel turned out to be a serious collector, with signed first editions of Stephen King books in her home vault. She backed two of my Kickstarter campaigns.

Blake is one of the hungriest readers I've ever met, and only reads paperbacks. He bought a shitload of books from my direct store, then went down to Book People and bought their last copy of *Fat Vampire* so the store would have to place a new order.

Chris ordered *Unicorn Western* from my website in the middle of a happy hour. Not to be outdone, Tom, sitting next to him, then bought *The Target*. (I brought it to him the next day at a tournament.) Chris won out in the end, though. He brought his wife and daughter to my booth at a live event and bought three more books.

One of my daughter's coaches, on learning I'd dedicated *Winter Break* to one of her players, bought it from Amazon on the spot.

I'm always a tad uncomfortable selling books to my friends. I feel like I should just give them my books for free. Every single time I try, though, I get rebuked — almost in a "Stop insulting me by resisting" sort of way. They inevitably say, "I want to support you." And they mean it.

All three other hosts of my *One Drink Book Club* podcast — Mike, Bill, and Emma — have backed my Kickstarters, and not because I asked them to. Again: *a tad uncomfortable*. Bill's wife Paula is a big-time reader. Not only did she blow through the *Fat Vampire* books on audio; she also successfully pitched *Pretty Killer* to the local book club. Which actually brings me to another point: *A lot of these people know people.* Not just friends, but connections.

One of Paula's friends — an organizer at a popular live event — offered me a free vendor table just because Paula knows and likes me.

Kim, a volleyball Mom, introduced me to the Austin Junior League so I could sell in their big Christmas show.

Jake, who I met at my very first farmer's market, turned out to run a much better and bigger local market. Guess who always gets a corner booth now, because he knows the owner?

I pitched none of these people. I asked none of them to buy my books. I asked none of them to tell people about me. And yet, tiny local legends keep spreading about me. I meet new people and they say, "Oh, you're the author!" And they have questions for me, too.

Don't farm your friend group for customers, but *do* — in a humble way — let them know what you do. Some will be fascinated, and you just never know who knows someone who knows someone who knows someone else.

Local Media

If you're bold, you might also try reaching out to local media when you're involved in something newsworthy. Press releases are still alive and well, even in the age of the internet.

I'm still kicking myself for not contacting local TV, newspapers, and radio when *Fat Vampire* became the *Reginald the Vampire* TV show on SyFy. "Local Author Sells TV Show" makes a great headline. But, if you try your hand at this, you'll find that even "Local Author Releases New Book" is sometimes headline enough. Or if you're *very* clever, you might even find a way to pitch yourself as newsworthy without a landmark event at all: a headline that's more or less "Local Author Exists."

It's tempting to think that nobody in media will care about you, but if you try a few times, you'll find that eventually someone probably will. It's hard keeping newspapers and TV and radio shows stocked with content, especially now. Human interest stories like yours might be exactly what some poor, under-a-deadline reporter needs to fill their docket.

Hell, I was in the newspaper twice before I even went full-time. Once, it was because I'd won a writer's website award. Another time, it was simple human interest: my variation on "Local Author Exists." Both were significant coverage. I didn't just get a few column-inches. I got a whole damn spread, and all I did was roll the dice with a press release.

I'll say it again: *Simply because you're an author, you're automatically more interesting (and hence more newsworthy) than you think.* Appearing in media (I have a radio show under my belt, too) is a great way to get people to look you up and maybe become readers — in a truly slow-boil, "Artisan" sort of way.

If All Else Fails, Get Weird

Both of my parents are painters. My mom is also a super sharp entrepreneur, and the person I learned this way of life from. (They both also made me unemployable. After seeing their examples and hearing them talk about what they did my whole life, how the hell was I going to be able to do a normal job? Thanks, Mom and Dad.)

My mom approaches selling her art like a game that she doesn't particularly care if she wins. That doesn't mean she's not serious, because she is. It's just that everything is laid back and experimental. She has fun with it, in other words. She's hosted Zoom tours of her home studio, has an active email newsletter that's always fun and personable to read (especially when she spends a month or so in Portugal), and once she even put a painting up on eBay. I forget what it sold for, but it wasn't much. It also wasn't the point. The point was, she tried something different, just to see.

She *got weird,* in other words. Although if you know my mother, that's not a very far journey.

I can't know what "weird" might mean for you, so you'll need to think and find out for yourself. Maybe it's putting a book on eBay for the hell of it like my mom did. Maybe it's writing in public as a gimmick. I know a coach named Matthew Stillman who used to sit in a New York plaza and sell advice for whatever people wanted to pay. (My favorite story was when a gang leader asked him how not to get murdered — not out of fear, but for business reasons.) If you're weird, you could do something like that. Become known as the crazy writer who's always in the public square with a laptop, surrounded by pigeons.

The sky is the limit when it comes to Artisan Authors finding new ways to attract readers. You can get as creative with — and have as much fun with — your acquisition strategies as you do with the writing itself.

If you can imagine it, you can try it. Why not? Might be a kick to see what happens.

I'll close this cavalcade of options with a reminder to bring it all home: *Nobody is tapping any of these reader bases in these ways. NOBODY.*

Not one other volleyball parent I've met is an author, and nobody is trying to tap them as readers in the ways I described earlier. That includes me. Remember, I never ever pitch my friends. Despite my reluctance, some became readers anyway.

Most of the readers you gain in the ways I've described aren't even aware they're in the market. How much competition do you have if your best potential readers decide they like you without even visiting a store — without any prior intent to buy at all?

And best of all, how much do these methods cost? Most are free, and some even pay you. How hard do you need to advertise to get buyers where you can reach them? Nothing at all, because wherever you found them, they were already there.

Do you see now why I call this "Creating fans out of nowhere"? It's because one moment, your prospects weren't even looking for books ... but five minutes later, they're one of your fans — one who may even have met and liked you before the sale, fast-tracking them to True Fandom.

It's magic, I tell you.

Turning Readers Into Fans, and Fans into True Fans

There's a quote by entrepreneur Derek Sivers that you should understand before we start trying to turn the *readers* you've gathered into *fans*, especially if they came through Buckets #1 and 2. It's a vital concept for any Artisan Author — almost as important as Kevin Kelly's "1000 True Fans."

Sivers said:

> *"Pull in those people who love [your unique style]. Proudly alienate those who don't."*

What this means is that the process of "sifting and sorting" I've mentioned works in two directions. There's the direction you expect (pulling new readers closer, hopefully turning them into fans), but just as important is the repellant direction. You aren't just walking into an undifferentiated group of readers, showing them who you truly are and what you most authentically do, and inviting the readers who resonate with it to follow you on more adventures. Nope. You're *also* sort of telling the people who don't vibe with you to fuck off.

It sounds harsh, but it's necessary. You don't need to be mean to the readers who don't fit your style (and you shouldn't — karma and all), but you *should* alienate them. And, keeping Derek Sivers in mind, you should do it proudly.

The Artisan Author

If you're not sure how to "alienate the wrong people" or if you're uneasy about doing it, I can strip things down and make it super simple. Here's all you need to do:

Be authentically, unabashedly, completely yourself. Let your work be authentically, unabashedly, completely what it is when it's in its purest form. Then act, speak, and interact with your readers as if everyone's onboard with all of it as you move forward.

That's it. Your single-minded dedication to your most authentic self and work will handle the "alienation" part for you. The wrong readers will feel excluded by your *"of course* this is how it is" attitude and will either fall into the background or leave completely. They certainly won't expect you to change to suit them, and they'll know they're out of line if they complain that you should write differently, or do things differently.

When Derek Sivers said what he said, he was talking about music. In music, the edge is a bit harder than I'd bring to fiction, but you can still borrow the attitude. If you're in a loud, metal-grinding band with lots of shouting, saying that pop music is crap will alienate the pop crowd ... but it'll also endear you to the loud, metal-grinding crowd, who also don't like pop. They'll see how proudly you stand up and alienate "the wrong people for you," and it'll make them love you that much more.

I don't think you need to be that harsh. I do think you need to strut around with your unique brand of freak flag flying, loud and proud about it. Don't just be who you are; trumpet it. If you write stories about witches who disembowel each other for fun (just came up with that genre on the fly. Do you dig it?), your website should be chock full of disemboweling witches. It should be on your business card. You should wear a shirt at reader events that says something about entrails.

(Okay, that's kind of gross. If you write witch-disemboweling books, you've just successfully alienated me from afar. Congratulations! Now that your witch-disemboweling fans see me running away, they'll run right toward you.)

Absurd examples aside, I imagine you get the point:

Don't just follow your own path. *Declare that path loudly to the world.*

Don't just be unique. *Scream to the world about how unique you are.*

Don't just welcome your unique people. *Instead, put a figurative sign at the door that will piss off the folks who* aren't *your people.* Your ideal crowd will see that sign, same as the non-ideal crowd. They'll know that you're proudly alienating people who don't share their sensibilities and interests. Seeing it — knowing that you're standing guard at the gates of your own little world — will make them love you even more. They'll know that you stand with them, and that the place you've made with your stories and sensibilities is a safe one for people who think the way they do.

If you're wondering how exactly you should go about this, you're thinking too hard. It's extremely simple: *Just speak your truth. Just be you. Just write what's real and authentic to you.*

For most authors, I'd argue this is still best done through an old-fashioned email list. I send something to my reader list most Saturdays, but it's not the same old *blah-blah* that most authors send. Most author newsletters are irregular and dry as dirt: project updates and the occasional sale announcement. My emails are weekly and conversational. I've written about how I treat stories as real and unchangeable once they're published, how Google Maps wouldn't let me map where my characters needed to go (with hilarious results), and how I think I saw Steve Zahn at the Hole in the Wall bar in Austin.

I imagine some people think I'm too all-over-the-place. Some probably don't want to get an email every week, or to read about maybe-Steve-Zahn. Many others think my books aren't focused enough, that I make too many inside jokes, and that I swear too often. I imagine all of those folks feel pretty alienated indeed.

But my ideal people? *They* see that I never back down from being myself and speaking my truth. *They* see that no matter how much criticism I get and no matter how many people think I suck, I keep standing my ground.

And they love me for it.

We've spent this entire chapter talking about ways to find readers. We can let them find us through organic discovery, we can pay to get them through advertising, or we can fish in the reader ponds nobody else visits and seemingly create them out of nowhere. No matter *how* you get your readers, though, you're going to attract some who are perfect for your voice, style, and personality, and you're also going to attract some who aren't right at all. You'll get a mixed bag from any reader acquisition effort, and your job once it's done is to unmix that bag.

When you do, remember Derek Sivers. Stand tall, be you, and proudly alienate everyone who's got a problem with it.

Don't try to please everyone. Don't try to keep people from unsubscribing from your list, or be sad or hurt when they do. If a reader complains about something that's core to your style, kindly but firmly tell them that you aren't going to change. If the interaction happens somewhere public like your site or social media, let the world see you do it. *You are you.* Readers can take what you offer or leave it — no harm, no foul.

If you run a BookBub Featured Deal and attract thousands of new people into your orbit (on your email list, listening to your podcast, watching your YouTube channel, or simply browsing your catalog and considering your books), the best way to sift and sort those thousands is to just keep on keeping on. Just keep being you. Some of those 99-cent-or-free buyers from BookBub will turn up their noses at your $7 new release — and if they do, let them. If they complain, don't you dare reconsider your pricing.

New people who came in at 99 cents don't get the right to steer your ship. Your ship was sailing before they climbed aboard, crewed by dedicated fans who already know and love you. Changing or bowing to please newcomers is an insult to the fans who've been helping you sail this ship of yours. New people have two options: accept, or reject. "Change the ship" isn't on the menu. They can climb all the way aboard with what you're doing, or they can jump off into the sea, waiting for cheaper boats to pass.

You can think of any new reader who enters your sphere as being on probation. Everyone who joins my email list, regardless of how they got there (discovery, advertising, etc), goes through an introductory, "probationary" sequence of emails separate from the main list. The intro sequence explains who I am and what I write. That sequence is also chock-full of my personality, right down to the ridiculous photo I have from college of myself looking like a slob between two stoic Secret Service agents. At the end of the sequence, right before they enter my main list, I've added this to the bottom of the final email:

> **P.S: If the style, tone, or frequency of these emails isn't your jam, you might want to just scroll down to the bottom and unsubscribe from this list NOW, before the next message arrives.** *I won't be offended! I only want people on this list who truly want to be here with me.*

And I mean it. It's no fun to be yourself when there's a bunch of assholes at the back of the room disapproving of you. I want to be in a room where everyone laughs at my jokes and thinks I'm brilliant. I'm selfish that way, and you should be, too.

Some of the ways you find readers (like meeting people in person) will be very pure: full of high-potential candidates to become True Fans later on. Other ways, like mass advertising, will be far less pure: stuffed with a big percentage of low-fi chuckle-heads who won't fit your vibe at all. No matter what, you'll get a mix. No matter what, there will be some gems and some losers.

So you need to keep doing your thing, proudly and confidently. Do your thing as if everyone should agree it's awesome. Do your thing with the assumption that everyone loves it. Some will, and they'll stick around. Others won't, and they'll leave. That's what you want.

By the time you're done sifting and sorting, your group of readers will be at least nominally aligned with your specific brand of artisanship. All you need to do after that is to keep talking to them. Keep being the *you* they already know and love.

Listen to your readers. Answer their emails. Be interested in them, which might mean honoring their requests or even conducting polls. Engage them in clever ways — I told you I wrote a vote-along-the-way story with readers in my email list.

Treat them like gold. Or even better, do something that authors have mostly stopped doing in the name of commerce: *Treat them like the individual, special, and unique human beings they actually are.*

I told you there's nothing astonishing about being an Artisan Author. There are no ninja tricks here, no great revelations. It comes down to making good and authentic art in your own unique way, finding people who love it, and selling your work to them in the way sensible businesses do business.

Fair pricing — to you and to the customer.

Quality work.

Available everywhere.

Be yourself. Be human. Be cool.

And for the love of God, be nice to the people who support you. They're the reason we're fortunate enough to do what we do.

Part Four
Details, Details, Details

CHAPTER 9

WHAT IF?

No matter how much I say that being an Artisan Author is intuitive and simple — and that the core task of becoming one is actually *unlearning* the non-intuitive, complicated bullshit that's taken over our once-noble profession — you're still going to have questions about the complexity that honestly isn't there.

This section of the book is my attempt to anticipate and answer those niggling questions. Along the way, I'll also try to convince you that yes, *it really is simple*. It's only that cultural baggage we've been given that's getting in the way.

Let's begin with the most likely "What if ... ?" question I can imagine readers of this book asking:

WHAT IF I ALREADY HAVE A RAPID RELEASE CAREER?

If you're asking this one, let's ask a separate question first that you may not have asked in all this excitement: *Are you sure you truly want to jump ship and embrace the idea of being an Artisan Author?*

Think carefully before answering. Even this far into the book, I should remind you that as much as *I* love the Artisan approach (as perfect as it is for *me*, in my situation) it's not for everyone. Go back and read the "Double Down Or Run Away Screaming" section at the front of this book before you do anything rash, like dropping your Rapid Release gig like a hot potato. I've been burned before, so I'm extremely wary about offering false hope. I want to make sure everyone who reads this book understands that there are no Easy Buttons. You probably won't become a millionaire as an Artisan Author. You might not earn a full-time living. You might put yourself out there and completely fail. I *hate* false promises. Let's be clear that I'm offering none of them.

This all goes double if you're already a Rapid Release author, and a lot more than double if you're a *successful* Rapid Release author. I don't want any missed mortgage payments on my conscience. If you're making bank in Rapid Release right now but hate the grind, you're about to take a big pay cut by jumping ship as an Artisan. Have no illusions that you'll quickly replace those phat page-read payments. If it happens at all, it won't happen fast.

Artisan Authors aren't Artisan Authors for the money. *Can* you make money as an Artisan Author? Oh yes. Can you make a *lot* of money? It absolutely happens. Do I not-so-secretly believe that the entire Rapid Release economy will eventually collapse because it's built like a Ponzi scheme instead of on sensible business principles that have stood the test of time for centuries? Oh, yes; I *very much* believe that. For that reason, do I also think Artisan Authoring might be the best alternative to that fate, and may be the only viable self-publishing model remaining in the near future? Yeah. I believe that, too.

Despite those things, it's still true that Artisan Authors aren't in this for the money. Money is secondary, not primary, and the main reason we're Artisan Authors is because we can't *not* be Artisan Authors. That means this approach isn't for all types of writers in all situations, with all personalities and styles. In fact, it's abjectly *wrong* for a lot of authors. But for people like us, it's honestly the only way. We've considered the alternatives. If people like us are to be authors at all, it's the Artisan way or no way.

Things have gotten too crazy out there to do anything else. I'd quit before going into that fray.

If you're one of us — if you've been an Artisan Author trapped in Rapid Release because you thought you had to, or because you thought it was the only way — then yes, I can answer your question about how to make a change. Just make sure you're sure, and don't burn any bridges on my account.

If you're killing it in Rapid Release right now, your transition to Artisan Authoring will be a hard one. It will punch your income in the teeth, assuming you slow your Rapid roll to write Artisan books instead. Alternatively, if you try to keep one foot in each world (if you maintain your RR pace *and* write Artisan books on the side), the bad news is that the burnout you're already feeling will get worse before it gets better. But you *can* do it, if you're one of us and know you *have* to do it. It will just require picking your poison.

I suggest making the leap only if Rapid Release is causing you so much distress that any potential loss of income (or any temporary increase in workload) is *less* distressing by comparison. This is basically what happened when I quit grad school to become a Barnes & Noble Cafe barista. Was giving up hard, humiliating, and a big kick in my career's groin? Yep. But was it also *much much better* than continuing to have panic attacks, certain I was setting my sails for a horrible future? Absolutely.

If that's you, you're going to have to slowly stop doing one thing and start doing the other. You could also keep up the Rapid Release thing but begin Artisan'ing as well: Selling paperbacks in a more one-on-one way, for instance, because even if you're in Kindle Unlimited, it's only ebooks that have to be exclusive.

Or, if your discomfort is big enough, maybe you'll just go cold turkey and accept that you're nuking one career to build another. The good news is that you won't be starting from scratch. When I jumped whole-hog into the Artisan Author thing in 2024, I wasn't leaving Rapid Release; I was leaving a slowly declining non-Rapid-Release online strategy, but it felt like starting over just the same. It wasn't, though, because I had assets. I had almost 150 books already written. All I needed to do to begin was to clean them up — make them as pretty and artisanal as possible. I needed to start talking to my audience in new ways, but at least I *had* an audience. If you're already publishing, you'll be able to do the same.

If you're *not* making big money right now in the Rapid Release ecosystem, however, the transition will be far easier. Because you don't have a lot of momentum and income already in place, you have very little to lose. You can just stop doing that and start doing this. And if you're brand new and have only been considering and learning about the Rapid Release way of doing things? Well, that's easy. Just stop considering that and start considering being an Artisan instead.

This question most comes into play with the authors who are somewhere in the middle — those who have been working "the other paradigm," but middlingly so. Maybe you've got a few books in KU and they're doing okay — not great, but okay. Or maybe you've got a few more books written and a Rapid Release plan in place for them.

If that's the case, I'd suggest you simply begin shifting your mindset and workflow to a more Artisan bent. There's no rush. You could play out your time in KU; you could even keep releasing books into it. But, on the side, start writing something to release wide. Start talking to people in "Bucket #3" sorts of ways. Let people know you're an author. Begin speaking about your stories and your career with new pride — because although you may have felt like a machine before, you're an artist now. Sink into it. Start to believe. Read this book again, or listen to the audiobook on repeat with my mellifluous voice in your ears. Reprogramming your brain while tapering away from your old author life will, in itself, go a long way.

You can leave your existing books in KU if you want, but I'm not sure it'll do you any good once you stop producing new stuff every month. The engine will probably sputter to a stop, after which all those books will become useless. Alternatively, if you still have a few books in reserve, you might choose to release them into KU ... but use them as an inroad to your forthcoming Artisan life. KU readers won't convert to Artisan readers in high numbers, but you'll get a few. My friend Bill is an avid Kindle Unlimited reader, but he's also got a collection of old books that he loves. Hybrid readers absolutely exist, so changing the calls-to-action in your KU books — in an attempt to get them on a soon-to-be-Artisan email list, or to direct them to a new, non-KU book — isn't a terrible way to smooth the transition.

In the end, if you want to kick Rapid Release to the curb and become an Artisan Author, there's no way to do it other than to do it.

The answer to this question, if you've noticed, is no more intricate or complicated than the Artisan philosophy as a whole: *Don't want to do X and want to do Y instead? Okay. Quit X. Do Y. Task complete.*

If you're supposed to be an Artisan Author, you'll know it in your gut after reading this far. You'll know what you need to do.

The only hurdle is summoning the stones to do it.

What if I Only Have One Book?

Despite how bothered I am by the extremity of Rapid Release, it remains true that with all other things being equal, you'll make more sales and have more readers if you have more books to sell them. Sean, Dave, and I opened *Write. Publish. Repeat* by exploring the math of it all, and the same math still applies.

Makes sense, right? As an Artisan Author, I actually think having not just multiple *books* but also multiple *genres* can be beneficial. It certainly has been for me. Some people I find just aren't into sci-fi. No worries: I've got two thrillers those folks always go for.

If you only have one book, things will be relatively slow and difficult as an Artisan Author. But here's the good news, if you can see it as good news: *As a Rapid Release author with only one book, things would be infinitely worse.*

You can't play the old paradigm's game with one book. It simply doesn't work. If you have a single novel and just put it up on online bookstores — or, worse, if you put it in KU — that book won't stand a chance unless you get extraordinarily lucky. Even if you made it free as part of a promotion, it might build your email list but wouldn't help your sales. The algorithms are so strict now that a short-term free-book spike won't convert to more than a few paid sales afterward if any, and obviously the folks who got it free won't buy it again. And after the algorithm was done with your book once launch was over? Well, chances are it would vanish into Amazon's depths and never be seen again.

As an Artisan Author, on the other hand, sales will simply be slower than they would if you had more books. That's all. Your book won't die post-launch like it would in the Rapid Release world; it'll just become the first book in your catalog. You won't lose ground as the book ages, like you might in the old world. And if you want to gain more ground? Easy. Just write another book. Expand slowly and systematically, like authors of old.

Keep in mind that Artisan Authordom is based on human connection and personality. Those things don't care about momentum or quantity like an algorithm does.

Let's pretend you decide to try the live-selling thing with your single book. You go to some book fair or get a table for $30 at a small farmer's market. People will walk by you. They will see you. They will see your single book, and a few of those people will stop to talk to you about it. I've never seen 100% of traffic at any event that *has* traffic walk right on by.

If you smile and say hello, and if you get over your introversion to engage the people who stop, a few of those people will buy. If you do those things rather than sitting down and scrolling on your phone the whole time, I practically guarantee you'll make a few sales. That's probably true even if your book cover and description sucks, because people are cooler to artists than you might think and some will simply want to support you. But if you actually create a good cover and a good pitch? Hell yeah.

In person, my best seller is *Pretty Killer*, in part because it has an amazing cover. If I *only* took *Pretty Killer* to an event, you bet your ass I'd sell some. If it was a big event, I'd sell a bunch ... with just the one book at my table.

You'll only ever sell one book to anyone working this way, and you won't get repeat customers unless you publish more books, but that's okay. This is how it works. When you operate as an Artisan Author — and especially if you do a few of the Bucket #3 items I listed — you *will* make sales of your single book assuming you don't have terrible books and a terrible personality. It won't be a lot of sales ... but it'll give you some confidence. It'll give you something to build on.

And it'll be a lot better than your chances in the Rapid Release world. For authors with only one book, I'd suggest going the Artisan way or not even bothering.

What If I Write Slow?

The ability to write at your own speed is one of the biggest benefits to being an Artisan Author. Lest we forget, the "rapid" in Rapid Release is one of the biggest reasons we got out of Dodge in the first place.

If you write slow as an Artisan Author, you'll produce fewer books in a given period of time than someone who writes fast. That's it. That's all it means. In the other model, it would mean crippling the algorithms that drive most of your sales, and it would mean that your first book's momentum would die before you got the second one out, effectively torpedoing both books. For us, though, none of that matters.

All the same things apply for slow writers as the one-book authors in the last section, really. We don't care about algorithms — at least not that much. Discovery is the Artisan Author's least important reader acquisition bucket. Who cares what the algorithms want? Real people, in the real world, are far less demanding.

Want to hear something mindblowing? Some of the people I sold books to two weeks ago *haven't even finished them yet!*

Don't find it mindblowing that some people take more than two weeks to finish a book? Neither do I, but the algorithms do. Rapid Release *has* to be rapid because the algorithms reflect reader behavior, and KU readers (which is where more Rapid Release authors play than anywhere else) tend to be voracious. In Rapid Release, you'd better have a new book ready quickly because those KU readers will burn through your book like it wasn't even there. Artisan readers, on the other hand, don't read that way nearly as often. So why would an Artisan Author feel compelled to produce a book every month? Most of their readers wouldn't be ready to read it yet anyway.

If you're slow, then welcome home. This is where you belong. You, like the one-book author, wouldn't stand a chance in the KU snake pit. As an Artisan Author, though, you'll do just fine. I've spent the last year rebuilding my business, and as a result I haven't released anything new. It doesn't matter because my readers are either brand new to me or just working their way through my catalog. I show up over and over again with the exact same books — nothing new at all — and *it simply doesn't matter.* A new book would just be one more title on my table, no different from any of the others.

Stop worrying about speed. In the Artisan world, it doesn't matter.

What if I Write Fast?

Didn't I just say not to worry about speed? "Fast" is a speed. You people just don't listen.

Seriously, though, there's a temptation to equate speed with Rapid Release, and it's completely understandable. If we're trying to avoid that world, then might not *going too fast* be a mistake for an Artisan Author?

The answer is no. I'll repeat myself: *Speed doesn't really matter.*

In the common paradigm, a book's launch is everything. The first month or so after publication is that book's glory days, after which it typically drops back to baseline ... or possibly into obscurity. For us, though, "launch" just means that a new book has become available, nothing more. After launch, that book will *remain* available. You *can* choose to make a splash when you launch a new book as an Artisan Author, but you don't need to. I don't. I just show up the next week with one more book on my table.

Rapid Release is a roller coaster. You boom, bust, then boom again. It's like an engine with a weeks-long stroke cycle, where the spark plug of another new release needs to fire again and again to keep the engine from stalling. We don't work that way. Artisan Authors build an inventory, and people buy from that inventory. Inventories don't need to constantly boom and bust. They can "just sort of be there," for people to buy whenever they want to.

Think about it: Does your grocery store entice you to come back by releasing new ham every week? Or do you instead trust that ham will always be there when you decide you want some?

The other concern about "too fast" comes from a false assumption that speed equates to low quality. As a naturally fast writer who actually writes *better* when I go fast, I've been fighting that particular prejudice my entire working life. Artisan Authors insist on high quality; for Rapid Release authors it's nice to have but not primary. You're an Artisan Author if you insist on high quality. Period. It doesn't matter how often you publish, as long as you put care into each book, and keep art and creativity in the driver's seat.

What If People Can't Afford My Books?

Oh come on. We live in a world of $12 movies, $100 cell phone bills, and $9 quad mocha Frappuccinos. Even when you sell paperbacks, chances are you won't have many — or any — priced above $25. Unless you're exclusively live-selling special edition hardbacks in an area with extreme poverty, I seriously doubt you'll completely fail solely on the basis of unaffordability and nothing else. If people sincerely want your books, it won't be "I can't afford it" that stops many of them.

Now, that's not to say you won't run into readers who say they can't afford your books. It happens. Some are on fixed incomes and struggling to get by, and an irritating number of them are people just trying to play on your sympathies to get free stuff. The latter, I don't care about at all. The legitimate former, I empathize with. I've had senior citizen readers on pensions who have to stop buying books — and believe me, I feel for them.

There's a simple solution, though. *Tell those readers that your books are available in the library.*

Maybe their local library won't have physical copies, but making your ebooks available through the library system is easy. All you need to do is to publish to Overdrive and other library services, which are standard outlets through aggregators like Draft2Digital. Your readers may need to request your books from the local library, but trust me; they'll be able to get them even if they can't afford to pay.

What If I'm Not Tech Savvy, or Just Can't Learn It All?

Okay, this question is super legit. I've learned more in the past two years of rebuilding my business as an Artisan than I learned in the entire rest of my life, just because I had to.

I learned how to post my books on platforms they'd never been on before. How to format book covers, or re-format them to fit guidelines I never knew existed. I played with ISBNs for the first time, learned audiobook production, how to build a Shopify site, and how to use the new version of Wordpress. I learned credit card processing, how to do point of sale transactions, how conventions and markets and book fairs work, how to handle inventory, all about outdoor canopies and the best ways to weight them down (cinder blocks, BTW), that fitted tablecloths are better than draped tablecloths, Amazon ads, Facebook ads, how to price books for various venues, the best places to order books, working with cover designers ... and OMG, I'm just getting started.

If the amount of learning involved in Artisan Authoring is giving you hives — tech learning or any other kind — I totally get you. There are certainly things to learn in the Rapid Release world, but that world is easy by comparison. You just upload to one place, and then you're off to the races. Artisan life, by contrast, has many more moving pieces.

Here are my suggestions for dealing with it:

Go Slow

Remember, you're an Artisan Author now. Speed is no longer required. You're now the kind of author who takes your time to do things right. If some new venture intimidates you, learn it slowly. Don't insist that you learn it in a day, a weekend, or even a month. You have all the time in the world.

Tackle One Thing at a Time

You don't need to do everything at once. If you want to try a direct store first, ignore all the other Artisan sales venues and only focus on that. Consider expanding into something new only after you're comfortable with the last project.

Think "Minimum Viable"

Speaking of direct stores (which, by the way, I *wouldn't* recommend tackling first because they come with a monthly cost and won't work without ads or other traffic-creation efforts), Joanna Penn recorded a great episode of her *Creative Penn* podcast called "The Minimum Viable Store" about her own efforts to learn that particular piece of the puzzle. The idea was that because there was so much to learn and because Jo has a big catalog, the notion of tackling everything perfectly was overwhelming. So, she took a "minimum viable" approach, which she details in the episode. She didn't worry about getting it all right; she just got the minimum up and running. There are always ways to begin a venture small, then grow and optimize as you go ... which, by the way, was exactly how I handled the live events part of my business, and exactly how I'm *still* triaging parts of my business now.

Hire Help

From the neighborhood college kid in need of a summer job to freelancers on UpWork, there are all sorts of people you can hire to handle the parts of your business that you don't want to — or feel unable to — handle yourself. You'll pay for the privilege, so budget accordingly and don't dig yourself into a deep hole with the hopes that huge sales will pull you out of it, because chances are they won't do so quickly. But help *is* there, and you can use as much or as little of it as you need and want.

What If I'm An Introvert?

Introverts wanting to operate as Artisan Authors have two basic choices: They can choose the less-extroverted options for Artisan businesses that we talked about earlier and focus on those, or they can accept that a lot of the appeal for Artisan readers is getting to know the author, and find ways to power through their fear of extroversion.

The latter is the more effective choice, but it's easy for me to say "get over it" as a natural ambivert who leans toward extroversion. I know many introverts, and I know how draining (or terrifying) it can be for those people to be out in public, even if "in public" happens through a computer. A lot of introverts don't want their voice to be heard or their face to be seen, let alone networking or attending a convention.

I understand all of that, but a fear of "being out there" will remain the biggest roadblock to maximizing your Artisan potential unless you find ways to work through or around it.

My suggestion, as with the learning we just discussed, is to go slow and take things one step at a time. You can start your Artisan efforts online, or *remain* entirely online. Being public on Zoom is less scary than being public in real life.

If you decide to venture into in-person environments as an introvert, do so slowly. You can attend writer's conferences for a while (not bookselling events) and just try to spend a bit more time out of your hotel room every day. If you decide to try a book event, split a table with another author so that you can come and go while they stay at the table, assuming that's okay with them.

Or, here's another thing I learned from Todd Fahnestock's book *Failing to Fly*, which I mentioned earlier. Todd was having trouble "being a salesman" at his first events. It was just too big, annoying, and out-there. What changed things for him — and made him the master of the con circuit that he's become — was realizing that he didn't need to *sell*. He just needed to tell stories. When people came over, he learned to simply re-immerse himself in his own story worlds — worlds he knew and loved. Then, he simply told a short version of the story. It stopped being about huckstering and became more like storytime.

You *can* be an Artisan Author as a staunch and bunkered-down introvert, but it's going to be a whole lot harder if you want to make money at it. The things that makes you different from (and more appealing than) other authors — the ones your ideal readers see as faceless and anonymous — is that you're *not* faceless;

you're *not* anonymous. In a depersonalized world, Artisan readers appreciate us in part because we're personable. Because everything now is digital and ephemeral, Artisan readers often want people they can see and books they can touch. You're robbing yourself of so much if you don't find a way.

Stepping out of introversion into some degree of Artisan extroversion *can* be done. You just have to be brave and step out of your comfort zone — and again, I'd recommend you do it one step at a time. But here's the cool part: Once you take a few steps, you may find that you actually enjoy the breed of "comfortable extroversion" you settle on. It becomes your new comfort zone in a way, and it'll then be up to you whether you want to stretch further.

Take your time and find a way. I believe in you.

What if I Embarrass Myself?

Ha. This will happen. But after my talk about being brave — and with all you have to gain as an Artisan Author — you're not seriously going to let something as insignificant as embarrassment get in your way, are you?

Part of being ideal for some readers is being non-ideal for others. That's just how things work. Seth Godin said, "You will be judged, or you will be ignored." He meant that if you want your work to be seen and potentially loved, you need to put it out into the world ... but a side effect of putting work into the world is that some people (not *your* people) will criticize it. The only way to avoid embarrassment and criticism is to make yourself and your work invisible, but that also removes all possibility that anyone will be able to love it.

You can be judged, or you can be ignored. If those are the only options — be visible and risk criticism, or avoid criticism but be irrelevant — I know which one I'm choosing. Why make art if you won't let anyone see it? The creation of any art is, in part, an act of authentic self-exposure. If you're not willing to open up enough to risk judgment, you're frankly not much of an artist at all.

Or culture has coddled us into believing we all deserve to be universally loved, at all times and in all ways. In a cosmic sense, maybe we do. In reality, however, we seldom get what we feel we deserve from the cosmos. Opening yourself up to be adored also opens you up to be disliked. You don't get to pick one but not the other.

Success doesn't come without risk, no matter what some courses' money-back guarantees might promise. But are you going to let it stop you? The truth is, at one point in your career you will probably embarrass yourself. If you don't, you're not trying very hard to make it.

So be bold.

Haters gonna hate; that's what they do. At least if you're brave, the readers who love you will appreciate and revere your bravery.

Haters are *never* brave.

They're not worth your time, and definitely not worth changing yourself to please.

What If I Fail?

You might. Sorry. I can't sugar-coat that. But how is that any different from anything else worth doing?

Failure is inevitable. Even the people who succeed fail over and over again before they do. Tony Robbins describes a successful entrepreneur (and have no illusions, self-published authors are entrepreneurs) as "a person who manages to earn enough money to make up for all their failures." I've also heard entrepreneurs described as people who've succeeded at least one more time than they've failed.

As I write this, I'm about to turn fifty. I've reached the place where there's more life behind me than ahead of me, and realizing it has made me intolerant of the pollyanna bullshit our world spreads around like truth. Don't get me wrong; I'm a power-user optimist. I believe there's hope in everything, and that even the most dire situations will turn out okay. But optimism is different from delusion ... and you and me, we've been fed a lot of delusional horseshit by a lot of people in this world.

No business is guaranteed. *Never ever ever.*

The world does not owe you anything.

Great work isn't automatically rewarded. If you've ever complained that crap is succeeding while your great work languishes — and I know I have — knock it off. Saying "this is unfair" changes nothing. It took me most of my life to truly get that one.

You have to work *hard* to succeed. You hear me? *HARD*. It's so much harder than people think. In my transition to full-on Artisan Author, I worked harder — and continue to work harder — than I've ever worked in my life. The good news is, it's joyous work. I love it. If you're anything like me, you'll love it, too.

I'm throwing the bad news about success in your face because nobody else does. Look around the self-publishing world and you'll see nothing but success stories. Everyone's a six figure author or can tell you how to become one. Everyone's got a new technique that will blow up your sales. Everyone on YouTube is smiling and telling you all about the good times. Read between the lines, though, and you'll see it's not the whole story.

So if you're asking, "What if I fail," I'm not going to pat you on the head and kiss your boo-boo. I'm not going to tell you you'll do fine. Because *nobody* has easy answers. *Nobody* does well all the time. When you see success in the world, you're only seeing the glorious now — or, often, someone's false-faced attempt to *project* a glorious now.

I failed to get through grad school. Had panic attacks, thought I was dying.

I invested in real estate right before the market bust. Lost my shirt. Went bankrupt.

My copywriting business collapsed.

More than once, I've been informed without notice that the paycheck I usually counted on wouldn't be coming anymore.

I've borrowed money. Lots of money. Plenty of it, I haven't yet paid back.

I've felt I was worthless. An abject and total failure. That I should quit. That I'd led my family on a fool's errand. I've made so, *so* many dumb choices.

Embarrassed myself. Looked like an ass. Banked on so many failed ventures. I've gotten my hopes up on a sure thing more times than I can count. How many worked out? I don't know; what's your definition of "worked out"? Some of those ventures got me to the next thing — the next noose to slip around my neck and hope this time it wouldn't hang me. Is it *working out* if all it did was lead me from the current failure to a new one?

Almost nobody talks about their failures. I'm doing it to make one point: that *you will fail sometimes.* More often than you succeed, you will fail.

But then you'll get back up, undaunted, and you'll try again.

It's trite, but it's true: *All you need to do is to stand up one more time than you're knocked down.* That's it. That's all there is to success. Success isn't about avoiding life's punches. It's about taking them, dusting yourself off, and trying again while everyone else calls you a fool.

Things are great for me right now. I've never been happier. But the road to it was long and very hard. So I say to you: *You might fail.* Even if you don't, you're more likely than not to fall short of your goal. But what else are you going to do? Give up on your dream?

Of course not.

Because eventually something's going to work ... and because dreams are worth fighting for.

Chapter 10

Tips and Tricks

Now that we've talked about the core of being an Artisan Author and covered the many "What Ifs?" you've been silently asking, I'd like to close this book with a bonus round.

In this final chapter, I'll share some of my best tips and tricks. They're not the kind of Ninja Tricks you're used to hearing, though. They're not hacks that I'll promise will solve everything or make money rain from the sky. They're not even really tactical: specific, mechanical things you'd do to amp up your results or sales. Instead, they're honest, sensible tips that actually work.

There's nothing whiz-bang here, and yet if I were you, I'd listen to every one of them. Unlike the prior suggested actions in this book, what's in this chapter *isn't* "it depends" and is instead — in my mind, at least — universal. Everything that follows has made a big difference for me at one time or another. Everything that follows will, I think, make a big difference for you, too — and also allow you to rest easier, have more fun, and adapt optimally to becoming an Artisan Author.

Speaking of "resting easier," we might as well start with an obvious one:

DON'T PANIC

Other than always carrying a towel, DON'T PANIC is perhaps the most useful advice in the universe, and the best advice I can give you about becoming an Artisan Author. It's also the most nebulous and the hardest to implement, because emotions are like artists: They say whatever they want.

We've covered a lot in this book. I wouldn't blame you for being overwhelmed. At the very least, your head is over-full. At most, you're overwhelmed by all the new things to do and consider, all the new modes of thought, and all the stuff you potentially need to learn. *Maybe just publishing ebooks exclusively into Kindle Unlimited isn't so bad after all*, you might be tempted to think. *Even if it doesn't do anything for me, at least I know I can handle it.*

You don't want that. You wouldn't have reached the end of this book if you did.

When I first started talking about being an Artisan Author at the Author Nation conference in November of 2024, people practically rejoiced in the aisles. For the rest of the week, people kept coming up to me and telling me how badly they'd needed to hear what I'd said: that the high-stress meat grinder of Rapid Release was not, in fact, the only way left to be an author — and thank God for that.

Right now, you might be feeling the relief and sense of freedom those people felt: freedom of time, freedom of self-expression, and freedom from rules laid down by platforms you don't control. Emotionally, you might be all in. If anything, it's the to-do's and minutia that are dragging you down.

If that's the case, I'll say again: DON'T PANIC.

There's a lot of detail in this book, but you don't need to understand or implement it all right now. You don't, in fact, need to implement it all *ever*. My goal was to give you options, not a set of instructions. That means you can — and should — pick and choose only the ideas that work for you. Every author is different and every situation is different. That's why I'd never give you a map, because there is no valid map. You're charting your own path now. I've given you tools that might help, but if they *don't* help at any given time during your journey (and "overwhelming the hell out of you" counts as "not helping right now"), simply set them aside and return to the core of what it is to be an Artisan author:

Make good books, then sell them to ideal readers at fair prices.

That's it. That's all there is to being an Artisan Author; thank you and good night. Everything I've given you in this book boils down to 1) making good books, 2) finding readers who appreciate those books, and 3) selling them at fair prices for all parties involved.

The lists in this book are by no means comprehensive. They can't be, because this book was written for creative people, and creative people come up with all sorts of cool things on their own. I can't possibly imagine every single thing that might end up working for you. As long as something allows you to write the books you want and find readers willing to pay fair value for them — and as long as you enjoy your creative lifestyle along the way — then it's correct.

Just keep coming back to that simple idea over and over and over again if you start to freak out. We're not in this to be millionaires — not primarily, anyway. *We're in this to write good books for good readers.* You can do that in *some* way to start with, can't you? And after you do, you're willing to take small steps and grow from there, aren't you?

See? No problem.

Just don't forget to bring that towel.

Answer Your Email

I mentioned this tip before, but I'd like to increase its font size to a billion, add a bunch of exclamation points, and circle it with sparkly pens. If you're overwhelmed and panicking about all the stuff this book has put in your mind, this tip is the most easily-actionable one I've got. Anyone can do it starting right now.

If you aren't sure where to start being an Artisan Author, start here. *Start with answering readers when they send you email.*

Every time I share this bit of wisdom, I feel ashamed for authors as a community. Remember how shocked I said readers are when I reply, and how I can only conclude from it that most authors don't?

What a bunch of assholes. Remember that?

I want to grab those non-responding, too-good-for-everything authors by the lapels and shake them. These are *readers* emailing you! These are people who read your book and liked it enough to send you a message, afraid they might be annoying you because they think you're a big shot ... and what do you do? You act like a big shot and ignore them.

Come on. You can answer emails. Every author can — and in my opinion should — do that much.

Until you become Stephen King and your inbox explodes from all the messages you're getting, you can answer your own emails — or at the *very* least, get someone to answer them for you. Readers should never be ignored. These are the people who make your creative life possible. These are people you're trying to nurture into True Fans, who will literally *set you free* from financial bondage (and possibly a day job you hate, if that shoe fits) if you accumulate enough of them. But instead of treating them like the golden angels they are, you ghost them like a bad date. What's wrong with you?

If you want to become an Artisan Author, do this: The next time a reader emails you, email them back. Don't just dash off a reply, either. Take some time. If they sent you a few paragraphs and shared a personal story, give them more than a "Thanks! Bye!" in your response. Instead, pretend this is a friend who's emailed you and respond in the way you'd answer a friend, because that's what fans sort of are: not your best buds, but on the spectrum of friendship.

They like you. That's why they emailed. So *let* them like you. Do you want True Fans or not?

Make Connection (Not Just Sales) Your Goal

If you try any of the quasi-extrovert things I covered in this book, my best advice is not to focus on selling your books. Instead, focus on making connections. Focus on having good conversations. Pretend you're out there to meet interesting people, which is fun in and of itself. Sales, if they happen, will be a bonus.

This little mental hack takes the pressure off, and taking the pressure off might just make you enjoy yourself more (or hate what you're doing less). Ironically, it also might make you a better salesperson. Customers can smell discomfort and desperation. It's the salespeople who sort of don't care if they make a sale who end up doing best.

"Just connect with readers; don't worry about selling" has been a useful mantra for me when crowds are slow at live events, so I don't get frustrated and wish I'd stayed home on the couch. I've met the most interesting people this way.

I met a guy who said he used to have a corporate job, but one day threw it all away, changed his name, and now looks like a hippie and hasn't worn shoes in ten years. I didn't care if he bought anything. I didn't think he would — and judging by his appearance, I didn't think he *could*. He bought *Fat Vampire*.

I met a guy who told me about a friend of his who's in prison, and how he's got a stack of correspondence with said friend that he thinks might make a good book one day. He asked me for advice, as an author. I told him to find a story in all that happened. Nobody wants to read straight correspondence. There's a *story* in there somewhere, and it was his job to find it. The conversation went on for over ten minutes. I assumed it was just a chat. Then, he bought *The Target*.

But again: I didn't care if either of those people bought. I'm not suggesting this as a sales trick; I'm suggesting it as a mindset hack. If you're going to put yourself out there, you owe it to yourself to find the best ways to enjoy it.

Connecting with people — especially if they like books, even if they don't want a book right now — can be really cool if you open your mind and let it be cool. It'll turn a dragging day into a great one ... but only if you allow it.

Nobody Is On Your Timeline

When you're excited about your new book, you want your readers to read it right now. When you put anything on sale in any way, you hope people will buy it. This is natural. It's normal. We all do it, present company included.

But it's also natural and normal for even avid readers to *not* want a new book right now. It's natural and normal for them to hear about a book, then remember it months later — or to forget about it and be reminded months later, when they're in more of a buying mood.

You as an author have your own timeline, and it goes like this: *You're going to put a book on sale today, sell X number of copies in a week, increase the price on this day, then send people through a certain specific email sequence to pique their interest in the next book.* But readers, being full-fledged human beings with minds of their own rather than mere targets for your book marketing, *also* have agendas and timelines. They aren't robots who sit around doing nothing until your new book is finished. They've got meals to make and soccer games to go to and relatives who are sick and arguments with their spouse. They go on Candy Crush kicks and neglect reading for a while, or they *do* read, but not your book right now. Readers are polygamous, you know. They didn't swear an oath to read *only you*, and they don't drop all other books the second yours arrives on the scene.

That's obvious, but authors never treat it as obvious — especially in the Rapid Release world. In that world, authors tend to think their Rapid Releasing is serving readers who must always be

Rapid Consuming. And although there are readers who churn that fast, it's not everyone. Modern self-publishing authors have been trained that there's no time like RIGHT NOW ... and so like toddlers, they want everything RIGHT NOW.

Life doesn't work that way. Especially not for the high-quality, Artisan-style readers we want in our corner. Our readers are discerning, and we should thank our lucky stars for it. It means they're loyal. It means that if you and your books hook them, you've passed their discerning filter and should be flattered. They don't just like your books; they think they're special. That's a good thing, y'know.

All of this is to say that Artisan Authors should think long-term. Don't think "sale today." Instead, think "connection made." The seeds you're planting right now might take *years* to germinate. I've had people on my mailing list for two or three years before they finally pull the trigger and buy something. Before then, they'd just been sitting there watching, reading my emails, being interested in what I was doing. By being patient, I showed them that I wasn't some desperate author treating them like a wallet with a heartbeat. I was a pro, and they only want to read the work of pros.

I suggest you chill out if you get edgy, and learn to do the same.

Finance 101

I thought about skipping this section. There's a lot in this book and I don't want it to be a doorstopper, but ultimately I decided I should at least give a few base-level financial insights simply because I've heard so many ridiculous financial stories in the self-publishing wild.

Some of you might be financial wizards. In aggregate, though, we authors are not a superlatively fiscal bunch.

Here's the least you should know about finances as an Artisan Author:

Track Net Income, Not Just Gross Income

"Gross" refers to the total amount of money you bring in. So for example, let's say you attend a Comic Con and collect $2000 in sales. In this example, your gross income for the event is $2000.

But did you *really* make $2000? No; you had to buy the books to sell. Maybe they cost you $500. Then, you had the table fee: The con charged $500 for the booth. $150 of what you collected was sales tax (not yours to keep), and you also had to spend two nights in a hotel to attend the con — six hours from home — in the first place. That's another $250, if you're lucky and it's not a lot more.

So you didn't actually make $2000 at that con. You really made $600: $2000 gross minus $500 for the books, $500 for the table fee, $150 for taxes, and $250 for the hotel. Oh, but you had to pay for gas, right? Meals are slippery; you can argue you'd've needed to pay for meals even if you'd stayed home. In terms of direct money paid to sell these books for gas and extra food, let's say you spent another $100. Let's not forget that the credit card processors take their cut, too — say another $50. Subtracting this last $150 from our earlier $600 total leaves you with about $450 profit, also known as "net income."

(My wife, an accountant, is probably rolling her eyes right now. I've probably gotten some technicality or terminology wrong, but the core ideas are correct.)

Here's where writers get in trouble all the time: *They confuse gross with net.* They tell people they made $2000 at the con when in fact they only made $450. Or worse: They tell people they made $2000 when in fact they *lost* $550 because there were additional expenses, like flights and rental cars, that we didn't consider above.

As you run your business, be sure to keep an eye on income *and* expenses — on net, not just gross. You want to know the amount you're truly *taking home,* versus just what you *took in.*

Ego Has No Place in Accounting

This one is truly absurd, but mentioning it is necessary.

I once heard a story about a seven-figure author who wondered why, with all of their sales, they never seemed to have any money. Analysis revealed that they'd confused gross and net (see above) and had in fact been spending almost as much as they earned.

A friend clued them in, letting them know that although they were bringing in just over seven figures, they were *spending* in the extremely high six figures to earn that income. But there was good news! The friend — an accountant — told them that if they made some changes and cut some expenses, they could actually earn more net income than they already were. *They could spend less and earn less, but keep so much more of that money for themselves!*

But the author didn't take the advice.

Instead, they kept doing what they were doing. They kept spending almost as much as they were earning, netting much less income than they would have if they'd cut their gross, cut their expenses, and greatly increased their profits.

Why? Because if they made the changes their friend recommended, they'd no longer be able to call themselves a "seven-figure author." They would instead be a lowly *six*-figure author.

They let their ego — their need to be perceived as more successful than they actually were — eclipse good sense. They chose to *actually* earn much less so they could *appear* to be earning more.

Don't do this. It's dumb.

Invest (Sensibly) in Yourself

You're running a business, and businesses come with expenses. The expression goes, "You have to spend money to make money," and within certain limits, it's true.

If you want the benefits of advertising, you have to pay for advertising. If you want to sell paperbacks, you have to buy paperbacks. If you want to sell at conventions, you have to pay to be at conventions — not to mention all the other stuff you'll need for those conventions, like signs and banners and racks. If you want books that attract people with their stunning covers, you have to pay a good designer to make stunning covers, and good designers aren't cheap.

"Spending money to make money," though, walks an exceedingly fine line, and you'll have to find that line for yourself. I can't and won't give you specific financial advice, but I'll encourage you to juggle two contradictory truths as best you can:

The first is to invest in yourself. I have no problem plunking down a few thousand dollars for paperbacks at this point because I know I can sell them, but it's an investment: I have to pay first, then hope to reap later. Some of those investments come as educated guesses. I can't be sure I'll sell well at an event I'm considering this November that requires a $2500 table fee, but I believe from past experience that I can. More importantly, I know that if I don't take the leap, I'll obviously sell *nothing* at that event. It's a give and take: When are investments in yourself wise, and when are they foolhardy?

Which leads to:

The second is to not be ridiculous about it. If you're brand new to authoring, a $2000 book cover might be a terrible idea. I've been through the mill; I know when a $2000 cover is worth it — when I'll easily earn back much more than that because the cover is my #1 conversion element. You won't know at first, so tread carefully. I don't want you missing rent because you took some guy named Johnny B. Truant's advice.

Just keep it in mind. Take small risks, then see how they pay off. Over time, you'll learn what's wise and what's not, and thereafter you may be inspired to take bigger gambles on yourself. Just be smart about it. And listen to the people around you, especially if any of those people are joint on your checking account. Just like

I don't want you missing rent, I don't want you getting divorced, either.

The point is to be the right amount of bold. For the longest time, I wouldn't spend any money on my business — even on ads that I knew would pay off, like BookBub Featured Deals back in the day, which always rained money from the sky.

You need to be brave as an Artisan Author. Just don't be *too* brave, okay?

Have a Side Hustle

If your goal is to go full time into writing, sometimes the worst thing that can happen is to almost achieve it. Or to achieve it for a little while, but then discover that full-time isn't sustainable. I've seen this happen. Early on, I *had* it happen. Authors have a few good months, decide they can quit their job, and then do so.

But then the next month, their sales are lower.

And the next month, they're lower still.

The cycle can go on for a long time — and if you're determined to never return to your old job, the boom and bust cycle can be an psychological killer. You spend every moment freaking out about each sale. About whether or not you'll earn the nut you need to survive.

For a whole lot of want-to-be-full-time authors, taking some sort of a side hustle job can be a godsend — financially, yes, but the biggest benefits are in your mindset. Desperation to earn enough money will make you foolish. Decisions made out desperation are often terrible ones. When you're desperate, you stop considering *what's best overall* and instead start obsessing on *what will make you money right now*.

If you have a day job that you'd like to quit, I encourage you to quell your author's enthusiasm and keep it longer than you want to. If you've made the leap to full time and are struggling, I'd encourage you to go out and find some sort of part-time job. It's not a defeat. It's a safety net. And as much as people like to say "leap and the net will appear," it's kind of crappy advice in the real world. Few people have the fortitude to make sane and sensible business decisions when they're wondering where their family's next meal will come from.

Being neurotic and nervous about the money you need to earn from your writing business is a great way to make sure you hate every minute of it. Do that, and writing quickly becomes about profit rather than creativity and joy, and that's not what we as Artisan Authors want. So, for your own sanity, consider not relying on your writing for vital income until you're completely and totally sure it can easily sustain you — or, like many authors, just never go full time at all, and make your writing the purely joyous diversion it is, with no pressure attached.

Karma Is Real

I've definitely been a shortsighted asshole in my life. I've definitely thought only about myself. But in recent years, I've done my best to knock most of that off. I've started paying very deliberate attention to other people and what they might be thinking — what might matter to them that doesn't automatically matter to me.

After doing that for a while, I started to realize something very interesting: The best things in my career came, in some way, because I'd once-upon-a-time been cool with someone else. They came because at one point, I'd helped someone with no expectation of personal gain, or because I was kind when I didn't need to be. Or because I chilled out and didn't push, whereas in the past I'd always pushed for what I wanted.

I was only invited to the set of *Reginald the Vampire*, invited to be an extra on the show (I'm "uncredited guy in Slushy Shack window wearing a black fleece" for a solid five seconds in the first episode), asked to moderate their San Diego Comic Con panel, and given the green light to host a companion podcast for the show because I wasn't pushy or precious about how they adapted my books.

And that's just the TV show. I have example after example of other good things that came from not being a pushy jerk, and just trusting that what comes around goes around. The list, once I thought about it, was endless.

I believe that karma is real. I believe that what you put out is what you get back, and that how you treat others is how you're treated. But even without that, I know that people like to work with people they like, whereas they don't like to work with assholes.

These days, I try to help anyone I can. Most of the time, I don't want anything in return, and I try to let people know that. I ask "How can I help?" not just because I'm trying to be a good person, but because frankly, it's turned out again and again to be good business. Eventually, word gets around that I'm cool. That's always turned into good things.

So as you go about your Artisan Authoring, don't be a dick. Sooner or later, the fact that you were cool with someone will come back to you — not that that's the reason you did it in the first place, right?

Stop Comparing Yourself to Others

Just knock this off. Comparisionitis is a killer.

We've all had it happen: We achieve something and are super happy about it, but then we talk to someone else and they mention that they did double what we did. Suddenly, instead of being amazing, our achievement looks like crap. It feels less-than, as if we're a big ol' loser.

There's no reason for — and no benefit in — comparing your results in life and business to anyone else's results. For one, it's not apples to apples. Everyone is different, so how exactly are anyone else's results relevant to you, given that they have different goals and priorities?

Here's a personal example: I live in a pretty rich area of Austin. It's annoying, because although I'm not poor, I'm definitely not rich. The neighborhood kids all go to Belize on Spring Break, and each winter, whole families nearby fly to their second homes in Vail. My kids never have anything to do when it happens because their friends are off being Rockefellers, and we're home feeling like we might as well be eating gruel.

Sometimes I'll think, "Why not me?", but then I remember that I work at home and don't go into an office. I tell stories for a living; I don't deal with bosses and boring reports. I don't work evenings or weekends. I spend tons and tons of time with my family, whereas the people in those families are always flying off to other cities to run their empires.

You can't compare me to them. We're not chasing the same things. And neither should you. If your successes meet *your* standards, they're good enough.

Period.

Have a Left-Brained Check and Balance

Self-published authors are half artist, half solopreneur. That makes us doubly insufferable as far as delusion goes.

My poor wife. For decades, I've dragged her from one crazy, creative and high-minded adventure to another. I'm always optimistic. In my mind, everything always works out, and anyone who thinks it won't is just a shortsighted killjoy.

I've had two distinct phases of my career: the phase wherein I believed all of the above and the phase wherein I realized I might not know everything about everything after all. Turns out I'm not infallible. After enough hard knocks caused by my head-in-the-sky stupidity, I finally got the message. I finally started listening to Robin.

Once I got over myself and realized that *maaaybe* I didn't know the future and *maaaybe* she was more intelligent than I'd been giving her credit for, it occurred to me that the two of us could be a great team. We were only two people so we couldn't form the whole of Voltron, but at least we could form his mighty right leg and torso.

When that penny finally dropped, I stopped fighting Robin's assertions that "maybe this will bankrupt us again" and started wondering how we could synergize our very different viewpoints. I'm the blue-sky creator; she's the left-brained numbers person. She thinks in details; I argue that details get in the way of all the cool stuff. So instead of butting heads, we united them. Instead of me saying "yes" and Robin saying "no," we started saying "yes, if." I learned to take everything to her and say, "I'm thinking about doing this crazy thing. What can I do to make it less crazy?"

When I did my first Kickstarter campaign in years, I asked Robin what could go wrong. I asked her to tell me all the ways we stood to lose money if we didn't prepare properly ahead of time. I lovingly called her my CPO, for Chief Pessimism Officer. It wasn't a killjoy sort of pessimism. It wasn't a "no" sort of pessimism, but instead the "no, unless" or "yes, if" variety.

You're a creator, but your optimism about that creativity can be a weakness if you let it. I've found that directly involving someone who thinks very differently from me in my work has been wonderful. Robin doesn't poo-poo my ideas, but she does refine them. She helps me brainstorm. She helps me fill inevitable gaps, like "What am I not thinking of," or "What am I missing?"

In addition to protecting me from myself, it's also led to a more harmonious household. We crazy creatives can really benefit by being pulled back to Earth now and again.

Learn to Remember Names and Faces

I love this tip. It's something I've taught myself over time, and that I think anyone who does any sort of selling or networking should (and can) learn to do at least a little. I take a lot of pride in my name-and-face memory. I think of it as a superpower. So many great things have happened because I've been able to remember something about one-off encounters that most people never would.

One year, Sean and I attended the Austin Film Festival and saw a panel that included a scriptwriter named Jono Matt. Jono was just enough of a renegade to feel like our people. We wanted to talk to him afterward, but too many people mobbed the stage so we gave up. Then, one year later, we were back at AFF and sitting in the bar. Jono walked by, so I called out: *"Jono Matt!"* His name had come to me in a blink, from a year ago as seen briefly from the back of a big room, because I'd trained my brain to hold onto that sort of thing.

That drive-by encounter became a friendship and a project that was damn near green-lit for TV ... all because I remembered a guy we'd only seen once.

A few nights ago as I write this, Robin and I were at a Bob Schneider concert. There was a guy sitting near us who looked familiar. Later I walked up to him, gave him a name, and asked if it was his. He said, "Do I know you?" I told him that I shook his hand two and a half years ago at a Christmas concert. Once.

We talked. He's super connected in the music business. Who knows? We may end up working together one day.

It's mystical, man. But I'm telling you — if you can learn to remember names and faces, it'll be the best networking tool you've ever known.

It's something I'm naturally good at, but I didn't used to hold onto names like I do now. I can do it now because I've more or less trained for it by taking notes and paying very close attention. I'm always the first to learn the names of all the parents on my daughter's new volleyball teams, but it doesn't happen by accident. It happens because after I meet someone new and learn their name, I write it down. I use the Notes app on my phone. I'll start a new note, like "Volleyball parents 2025," and then I'll write something like: *Tim. Tall with poofy brown hair. Daughter is Charity, outside hitter.*

Then I'll study. I'll go through my list while we're at the

court, running through the roster in my head and naming first the girls and their positions, then the parents.

It reminds me of something that happened at The Smarter Artist Summit, an author conference Sean and Dave and I used to host. At one of those Summits, word got around that an attending author named Ben Hale had met and memorized the names of everyone at the event. So in the closing address, we invited Ben onstage. He asked everyone in the audience to stand up ... and then he named them, one by one.

The next year, the conference was larger. I think we had around 250 in attendance, maybe more. This time, we knew Ben's ability. So again at the end, we asked him to name everyone.

And he did. Every single person.

We were so astonished that we couldn't resist asking for his trick right there on stage. But Ben said there was no trick. "The way to get good at learning names and faces," he said, "is to remember that every person matters."

That stuck with me. I've used it for my own name-remembering ability. *Every person matters.* Think about that for a second.

Why do we forget names as soon as we learn them? Come on; I know you've done it. We forget because we don't make a serious effort *not* to forget. We hear, "I'm Jen" and it just goes in one ear and out the other. We've decided that the information (who this person is and what her name is) is irrelevant, so why would we bother to remember it? That's why, the next time we see Jen, we just say, "Hi there."

But what if it didn't have to be that way? Let me consult my "WWBHD" bracelet, to see what Ben Hale would do.

Why, he'd *pay attention* to Jen, of course. Instead of considering her name and face as irrelevant, he'd remind himself that it — and she — matters.

There are three types of memory. There's long-term memory, short-term memory, and sensory memory. Sensory memory is what it sounds like: Your senses observe something, like the fact that there's a lamp in the corner of a room, but then they usually move on and observe something else. Only certain sensory observations make their way into short-term memory, and only some of what enters our short-term memory ends up in our long-term memory. Long-term memory takes some effort to encode. You have to keep entering information and retrieving it, entering it and retrieving it, before it really sticks. But when it sticks, *man* does some of it stick. To this day, I can still tell you the hierarchy of species classification and Avogadro's number from high school ... and, more vitally, every word of "Ice Ice Baby." Those things come in handy whenever I need to count molecules or remember which Florida street Vanilla Ice cruises (A1A — Beachfront Avenue!)

Information moves from short-term to long-term memory through encoding, which usually means rehearsal and repetition. That's what I do when, after taking notes about the parents on the volleyball teams, I test myself on them again and again. But do you know what's required to move information from sensory memory into short-term memory so it has a chance of being encoded in the first place?

Attention.

In order to move from observing something to remembering it even a little, you have to pay attention to it. You have to acknowledge it as worth remembering.

That lamp you noticed in the corner of the room? You'll forget it if it's just a lamp, but you'll remember it if someone told you that a lamp in that particular room sometimes randomly catches on fire. If someone told you *that*, the lamp would leap from your sensory memory to your short-term memory the second you saw it because you'd be paying attention to it. Suddenly, that boring old lamp it *matters*: It's the thing that might burn the building down around you.

When we meet people, their name and face enters our sensory memory the same as a random lamp might. What most people do, though, is to not actually pay attention. Their brain has already decided that the name and face don't really matter, so why bother moving them into short-term memory?

Okay, but what if Jen — the woman you met above, before I started talking about Vanilla Ice — *actually matters?*

What if, instead of being irrelevant like a non-flaming lamp, Jen *was* relevant and meaningful to the world? What if she *does* matter? What if she's a mom with two kids, works for the city water department, and watches true crime shows when she's stressed out? What if Jen is a real person instead of just someone we walk past as if she's ancillary to our oh-so-important lives?

I'm convinced that Ben's tip is the reason I'm so good with names and faces today. I don't remember everyone, but I do damn well.

Today, after someone buys one of my books in a particularly memorable exchange, I try to remember to focus if they tell me their name. I try to not let it go in one ear and out the other. I try to *actually listen*, in other words — enough that if I see them again, I can greet them like a friend.

I don't do it all the time. It's probably less than ten percent, because to truly make a name stick I need to write it down, and in a live-sales environment I don't always have time. Life is busy and I'm still human. But sometimes I'll make a note, I'll remember, and then that person will return. And *oh my God*, you can't imagine how impactful it is when a guy comes up to my booth at some random market and I'm able to say, "Luis! How are you? Did you enjoy *Unicorn Western?*"

Don't you think that making an effort to learn at least a few of your regular customers' names (and faces, if you see their faces) will do wonders for fan bonding? If one of our biggest Artisan Author tasks is fan engagement, don't you think this is a skill worth working to learn ... so you can prove to your readers that they matter to you?

Be Worth Bringing to the Party

Social connections are a form of currency. There's value for people in knowing certain *other* people. If a person knows a lot of interesting and fun people, they can use their connection to those interesting folks as leverage to gain social standing. The interesting people they know, in other words, make *them* seem interesting by association — but only if they share those fun and interesting friends by introducing them around.

You *want* to be introduced around. You *want* to be known as a cool author who writes good books. You want people liking you so that maybe one day, they'll decide to read what you write. You want advocates who will tell their friends about you and your work, and those friends will tell their friends.

Networking is so much easier when people are dying to tell their friends about you. It's so much easier to score invites to potentially-influential parties when people are dying to invite you, just so they can say with pride: "Ahem. Yes, *I* was the one who invited the author."

So how do you make yourself a valuable introduction? How do you make yourself worth bringing to the party?

Simple. Mostly, you just have to get over yourself and let you be you. You're *already* pretty intriguing simply because you're an author. If you can just find a way to stop being self-conscious and be confident instead, half the work of "being worth the invite" is already done.

Authors are inherently interesting people. If you can lose your introversion enough to simply be yourself in a group, you'll learn how true that is. If you're invited to an event and are the only author there, and if people know it, eventually they'll start asking questions. Your answers, though they may feel mundane to you, will fascinate others.

Nobody gets to do what they love for a living.

Nobody gets to make stuff up and get other people to read it.

You're a unicorn, dear author ... and if you can find confidence enough to embrace it, you'll find yourself the talk of the town.

But remember, this isn't about you. When I say "be worth bringing to the party," the "worth it" part is for the person who brought you. This tip isn't truly about being good around a dinner table; it's about understanding that *the person who invited you to that table benefits greatly if you turn out to be a good guest.* It's not about your social cachet. It's about theirs.

They tell people about you.

They benefit, if you make yourself worth meeting.

And then *you* benefit, because the Artisan Author game is about people ... and you just met a bunch of new people who might like what you do. And the best part? Although you should say thank you for any introduction or invite you get, you really won't need to. If you're worth bringing to the party, it's the introduction-maker who should be thanking you.

The more people you talk to as an Artisan Author, the more potential readers you'll find — and the more potential opportunities you'll walk right into by knowing people who know people who know people. The more fun and engaging you are, the more people will start to wonder what your fiction is like. I said before that I don't try to sell books to friends, and I also don't sell to friends of friends. But guess how many friends of friends have bought my books anyway? Guess how many friends of friends will brag to *their* friends about you: *OMG, they know an author!*

Most authors are so humble, they're almost prideful about how humble they are. It's kind of annoying, really — and a waste of good Artisan Author potential.

Stand up. Be proud. If you can make yourself worth bringing to parties, more people will invite you to parties — as a celebrity guest of honor in a way. You'll become the author in their midst, whom everyone wants to know more about, including their published works.

You Are [Johnny B. Fucking Truant]

I've saved the best and most obnoxious tip for last. If you thought the last tip felt arrogant, just wait for this one.

But first: Is it *arrogant* to know your own worth? Is it really?

Arrogance and pride are two ends of the same spectrum. If you're irritatingly self-important, then okay; you suck. But if you're simply proud of yourself and your accomplishments, you're proud, not arrogant. You *should* be proud of yourself. You've taken steps so many people want to take, but never had the guts.

As a whole, authors are a shy and self-conscious bunch. We don't like drawing attention to ourselves, which is ironic because we very much want attention on our work. Being humble is good, but too much humility hurts us. Our work needs attention ... and as Artisan Authors who are selling ourselves as much as our work, *we* need attention, too.

That's why my final piece of advice is to tell yourself now and again with a puffed-out chest that *you are you, dammit.*

It looks like this for me: *I am Johnny B. Fucking Truant.*

And *you, my friend, are fucking you.*

I'm not a typical author. I'm not shy, and can be confident to the point of annoyance sometimes. I think it was more true in the past that it is now. When my constant writing partner Sean Platt met me for the first time, he and the person he was with declared me afterward to be "an arrogant motherfucker." But hey, in my defense, I was barely 30 back then. I *was* a motherfucker.

Over the last handful of years, life has humbled me a bit. I lost a lot of that cocksure manner. It was even something Sean noticed, and lamented. He said that I used to write with such bold flair. I was elbowing people out of my way with my words. That's how sure I was of myself, and it made for scintillating prose. Humbled, my writing was a lot less interesting. We just never had that same spark later on that Platt and Truant had at the start.

After a few years of droll humility, something hit me. I realized I'd gone too far in the opposite direction. I was no longer pushing hard enough. Ironically, I was no longer *arrogant* enough. I was afraid of saying the wrong thing and being cancelled. I didn't want to offend anyone, so I'd started watching my mouth. It made me nicer, but it also robbed my work of its fire.

Your work has fire, too. You just have to let it out.

Once I realized what I'd done and how bland my writing had become, I puffed myself up and tried to remember the person I'd been. I tried to embody "Johnny 1.0" — the guy who'd written a mega-viral essay called "The Universe Doesn't Give a Flying Fuck About You" with all the brass nuts in the world — all over again.

Around the time I had that realization, I was contemplating going out into the world to sell books by hand for the first time. I wanted to pitch myself and my books people who didn't know me. How was Timid Me to do those things? So I ripped a double-thick piece of blue painter's tape from a roll in our junk drawer, wrote on it with a Sharpie, and stuck it on the bottom of my computer monitor.

It says, *"I am Johnny B. Fucking Truant."* And if you feel too timid to do what you think you were meant to do with this life of yours, you could do worse than do the same with your own fucking name.

You, my friend, are not some sad writer hoping to be discovered by fate or coincidence. Nope; you're the kind of person who makes things happen. You're the kind of person who isn't afraid to put themselves on display, because dammit, the world should be fortunate to have you.

You, my friend, are *[first name] fucking [last name]*. You're an artist worth reading, and you damn well know it.

Be it.

Own it.

So now, get out there and do it.

Artist, Go Forth

I'd like to give you one final reminder as we close this show down.

And it's this: *Being an Artisan Author is not a thing.* Don't make it a thing. Don't make it THE THING that every author going forward believes they should seize on as their next big Easy Button for success.

I'm going to be honest with you: I'm scared as hell to publish this book. I'm afraid that it'll take off, that millions of authors will embrace it, and then before you know it, we'll see Reddit threads full of authors deciding that "Artisan Authoring" is the next success hack.

What are the best strategies for being authentically myself? they'll ask.

I hear I'm supposed to take my time in order to succeed as an Artisan Author, they'll ask, *but how much time is ideal?*

Check out this new software, they'll say. *It converts readers into True Fans in half the usual time!*

It pisses me off, how everyone's after a tactic. How everyone wants clear and clean directions, and how everyone wants a map. It's like we've all lost the ability to think and be human. Instead, we need instructions. Are we not creators? Is it not in our very definitions to make our own choices, and draw our own conclusions?

Don't ask me for universal answers, because there are none. Don't hold me up as an example — or, God forbid, some bullshit guru. I'm not an expert. I'm just a guy with some ideas. I follow my own compass, just like you should follow yours.

You're an artist. So please. Stand up and be one.

There are a lot of authors right now singing the blues. *We had a utopia for a while,* a lot of them seem to feel, *and for a while the act of writing was glorious. It had its day in the sun, but it didn't last long. We rose and we fell, just like Rome. Now, the dream is over. Now, the sun has set on the glory days of the once-great self-published author.*

Royalties are falling.

AI is taking over.

It's impossible to be found. Impossible to be seen. Impossible, in this sea of noise, to attract any attention.

And so, to so many authors, it seems we face a bleak future. We can only keep bowing at the shrine of Amazon and its KU machine, cranking out books until we drop dead on our keyboards. And those are the lucky ones. Most will never make it that far, because content farms and artificial intelligence will soon rule the day.

I disagree.

For the bold authors, like us, times have never been brighter.

People still want books. People still love to read. And those people — the very best of them — are tired of the same rat race we're trying to escape. They don't want the shlock being churned out any more than we want to churn it. They want real books by real people. They want to know their creators. In an alienated, over-corporatized world, they want the connection we've so sorely been lacking.

You, dear Artisan Author, can give it to them.

They're hungry for it. Not for the system of it — the "how can I work this scheme that much quicker" of it — but for the genuine humanity that only we can create, and that can only be created one person at a time.

We won't move faster.

We won't churn harder.

We won't work the system, because there's no system to work.

There is only you and the reader.

So go forth, Artist.

There's never been a better time.

Get Inspired as F**k

If you're an author and weren't "proudly alienated" by this book, you should totally subscribe to my Substack for more of my well-meaning bullshit.

Or don't. Whatever. I'm an artist and I'll do what I want.

Get your unicorns on at JohnnyBTruant.Substack.com

Also by Johnny B. Truant

Winter Break
Pattern Black
Pretty Killer
Cursed
The Bialy Pimps
Namaste
The Target
La Fleur de Blanc
Axis of Aaron
Devil May Care
Screenplay
The Island
Burnout
Sick and Wired

UNICORN WESTERN:

Unicorn Western
The Wanderers
A Fistful of Magic
Shimmer to Yuma
The Man Who Shot Alan Whitney
The Spectacular Seven
Open Meadows
The Unforgotten

The Magic Bunch

Unicorn Genesis

FAT VAMPIRE:

Fat Vampire

Fat Vampire 2: Tastes Like Chicken

Fat Vampire 3: All You Can Eat

Fat Vampire 4: Harder Better Fatter Stronger

Fat Vampire 5: Fatpocalypse

Fat Vampire 6: Survival of the Fattest

The Vampire Maurice

Anarchy and Blood

Vampires in the White City

Fangs and Fame

Game of Fangs

INVASION:

Invasion

Contact

Colonization

Annihilation

Judgment

Extinction

Resurrection

Save the City

Save the Girl

Save the World

Longshot

THE INEVITABLE:

Robot Proletariat

The Infinite Loop

The Hard Reset

Cascade Failure

Reboot

En3my

DEAD CITY:

Dead City

Dead Nation

Dead Planet

Dead Zero

Empty Nest

THE DREAM ENGINE:

The Dream Engine

The Nightmare Factory

The Ruby Room

The Pandora Core

The Engine Convergence

The Tinkerer's Mainspring

GORE POINT:

Gore Point

City of Fire

Plague of Demons

Mine Zero

Moloch

Suicide Flats

THE BEAM:

The Beam: Season One

The Beam: Season Two

The Beam: Season Three

The Beam Season Four

The Beam Season Five

Future Proof

Plugged

The Future of Sex

THE TOMORROW GENE:

The Tomorrow Gene

The Eden Experiment

The Tomorrow Clone

Null Identity

COMEDIES:

Everyone Gets Divorced

Greens

Fiends

Decoy Wallet

NONFICTION:

The Artisan Author

Write. Publish. Repeat.

The Story Solution

Fiction Unboxed

The One With All the Writing Advice

The Fiction Formula

Iterate & Optimize